PLUGGED & ABANDONED

A Semi-Professional Memoir

Steve Moore

My Epic Failure to Achieve Self-Actualization after 40 Years of Reservoir Engineering in the Oil and Gas Industry.

Plugged & Abandoned

Published by Blue Quest LLC

Cover Art by Indi Martin - Tortoise & Hare Creations
Indimartin.com

Print ISBN-13: 978-1-7360243-2-4
Ebook ISBN-13: 978-1-7360243-3-1

The historical incidents described in this book are real; they are also subject to the normal fuzziness and limitations of the author's mind and memories after 40 years of sitting in a box studying tens of thousands of oil and gas production graphs.

Dialogue is not intended to represent conversations verbatim; they are recreations designed and compressed to capture the essence of what was said at the time and the emotions experienced by the author.

With few exceptions, actual names of people and companies have been omitted or fictionalized to maintain anonymity.

To Mom,

who taught me the value of books and reading

and to Dad,

who taught me what to do with the rest of my time

THIS PAGE

UNINTENTIONALLY

LEFT BLANK

INTRODUCTION

31 Flavors of Career Guidance

My first reservoir engineering experience occurred when Phillip knocked the spigot off the Moa-Moa punch dispenser.

It was a hot July night in 1975, my high-school sophomore year, and I had a summer job in a small Baskin Robbins ice cream shop in east Tulsa. Phillip and I were handling the after-movie crowd, scooping orders from deep freezers containing exactly 31 varieties of ice cream and sherbets. We were in the zone that night, quickly dodging around each other, throwing up freezer lids and diving head first into the frosty air for a single dip of Baseball Nut, or a double scoop of Jamoca Almond Fudge. Sugar cone or regular cone? In a cup? Sure, you got it.

Phillip turned to the back counter and grabbed a double-scoop cup from the stack. As he rotated back toward the freezer the scoop in his hand banged into the Moa-Moa punch dispenser, knocking the spigot off and down to the floor.

Instantly opening the choke to the maximum setting (64/64ths) exposed the Moa-Moa reservoir to atmospheric pressure and Absolute Open Flow conditions, resulting in a glorious gusher with the unmistakable fragrance of tropical fruit. Without a blowout preventer the red-orange liquid splashed onto the floor in steady-state single-phase flow. (Note: Moa-Moa punch is a low-viscosity fluid and the effects of gravity drainage yield excellent production rates.)

Phillip was oblivious and went into the freezer for a scoop of Pralines and Cream. I saw what happened, along with a dozen now-delighted customers, and sprang into action to contain the spill and mitigate surface damages. To control the flow I grabbed a three-scoop cup and held it below the nozzle. Flowing at an estimated rate of 73 barrels per day the cup filled up in 0.8 seconds and overflowed onto my hand. I yelled at Phillip, put the cup on the counter and grabbed another. Phillip finally figured out what happened and rushed over to help. For the next 45 seconds we treated our audience to a free performance of our interpretation of the classic *I Love Lucy* scene where Lucy and Ethel cope with a runaway conveyor belt in a chocolate candy factory.

The Moa-Moa reservoir quickly depleted with an Estimated Ultimate Recovery of 99% of the OPIP (Original Punch in Place). The one percent residual saturation covered the bottom of the tank below the outlet. We had about a dozen cups of punch scattered around the back counter, and a reportable sticky spill all around the location. The customers gave us a nice round of applause.

Mopping up the mess later, I made a Serious Life Decision: I would not pursue a career in retail frozen-dessert sales. I had no idea, however, that the fluid properties and flow behavior I observed that night would be an integral part of my work and career for the next four decades.

Dear ___: If you're reading this, my career is already dead.

I'm going to skip the typical memoir self-introduction for now, as there's a very good chance you already know me. While I hope everyone on the planet buys multiple copies of *Plugged & Abandoned,* realistically it's hard to imagine anyone other than a relative, friend, or former colleague being interested in autobiographical stories written by a reservoir engineer.

Why did I write this book? The "unexamined life," blah blah blah. Oh, I've examined. If Socrates was right and the unexamined life is not worth living, then I should live to be 328 years old.

As I write this in early 2022, there are several indications that my petroleum engineering career is over. My contract work ended a couple of days after Christmas. The number of oil and gas companies with offices in Tulsa is rapidly approaching zero, and my wife and I have no desire to relocate. Finding a full-time engineering gig at my age also feels like a challenge. And there's this: my industrial-strength lack of enthusiasm for returning to the Dark Arts of Production Forecasting, Reserves, and Property Valuation.

It sure *feels* like I am now a "retired" reservoir engineer. However, there was no cake, so I'm not 100% certain.

When crashing oil prices and a nasty virus combined forces to cause the Great Time Out of 2020, I was home every day, unemployed. Or, as someone so elegantly described on LinkedIn, I was "aggressively engaged in self-directed personal enrichment." For me, that meant writing. I got busy, finished a science fiction novel I started a decade earlier, and self-published *A Fortune of Reversal* in November. I also spent countless hours of introspection while strolling, sitting, and sipping adult beverages. I had an infinite number of internal conversations with myself and completed a deep dive into a lengthy list of Questionable Life Decisions.

I chose the wrong profession. This will be clear from the anecdotes and essays that follow, but please note: this book is not about regret. I believe I made decent decisions with the data, experience, and limited amount of wisdom I had at the time. Still, a bunch of decisions turned out to be wrong, and occasionally stupid. It wasn't a total debacle, but more of a series of micro-failures to synchronize my work and career with my true personality, interests, and skills. It is obvious to me now that I would have enjoyed and perhaps thrived in another line of work more compatible with who I turned out to be—or perhaps already was.

I like to write. My forty years in Oil and Gas were filled with humor, comedy, and satire. Almost immediately, I started jotting down notes and recording details of preposterous situations and memorable moments of corporate life. Later, in the 1990s, I'd write quick summaries of bizarre behaviors and crazy-funny attempts at communication by coworkers and managers and email them to my personal account. I archived hundreds of these anecdotes, thinking I might use them in a book someday. (One of my better decisions.)

My primary goal for *Plugged & Abandoned* is to entertain, by sharing many of the laughs and absurdities I experienced and by poking fun at myself for mismanaging my own career. As the verbose subtitle suggests, I also wanted to explore and understand my failure to achieve self-actualization during four decades of work.

I believe this semi-professional memoir will close out my time as a petroleum engineer and serve as a launching point for my second act as a writer.

Thank you for taking the time to read my book.

Steve
August 2022

About This Book

The **About This Book** section includes a short description of the contents of each part of the book.

Born Young is my engineer/writer Origin Story from childhood through college. Note the foreshadowing of the existential and philosophical challenges that lie ahead for our hero.

California includes my relocation to Bakersfield and the first 4.63 years of my career.

The Muddle includes seemingly endless nonsequential anecdotes, humorous adventures, and insightful commentary from 40 years of nonsense—sorry—from My Life as a Reservoir Engineer. *The stuff you committed to read when you started this book. No backing out now!*

My Failure to Achieve Self-Actualization is just what it sounds like. Note the existential and philosophical challenges experienced by our hero that were so aptly foreshadowed earlier. *This section will make you feel better about yourself.*

The **Epilogue** includes a couple of speculative scenes from The Future. The **Appendices** include a complete list of Moore's Laws and other goodies. (No peeking - finish reading the book first.)

Acknowledgments: the section you'll most likely skip, unless you think your name might be included among the people I'll thank for their support and friendship.

Author's Notes and Cave Outs*

The F-Word:

With one obvious exception, I have refrained from the mundane cheap-humor practice of substituting variations of "fracture" for the F-word. You're welcome.

Also, please note that I did not use cutesy oil and gas terms like Prospecting, Spudding In, etc. to label portions of my career or the parts of this book. Other than the title, of course, which was just too good not to use.

Meet the Team:

The anecdotes and stories that follow are presented for humorous entertainment, and to describe my experiences and reactions. They are absolutely not intended to criticize or embarrass anyone specifically. Accordingly, with few exceptions I have not identified the people involved by name or the company for which I worked at the time.

I have worked with or reported to many men and women during my time in the industry. When necessary, I have used "Pat" as a convenient gender-neutral generic name for coworkers or managers, with a tip of my unusually clean hard hat to the terrific writers of *Saturday Night Live* and Julia Sweeney for her famous character. (Pat's preferred pronouns in this book are *he, him,* and *boss.*) When a second name was occasionally required for clarity, I used the neutral name "Alex."

Of course, there could be people reading this book who were actually present during the original incident and will recall the situation and specific individuals involved. *Remember, most of us are professionals.* I trust everyone to remain discrete. Please contact me if you have a different recollection of events, especially if you recall any humorous details I may have omitted.

On the Cover:

R/P is the ratio of Reserves to Production, a common metric used by petroleum reservoir engineers to assess and compare volumes of hydrocarbons and their relative production lives.

If Reserves = 10 million bbls of oil, and Production = 1 million bbls of oil per year, then R/P = 10 years. The higher the R/P value, the longer the expected producing life. An R/P value approaching zero indicates reserves are nearly depleted and/or the productive life is almost over.

I originally planned to use R / P = 0; the resemblance to the familiar R.I.P. seemed perfect. My friend and colleague Trent Mitchell astutely pointed out that if both reserves and production are zero, then 0 / 0 is mathematically undefined. I chased this topic down an InterWeb rabbit hole and found two principles to consider: A number divided by itself always equals 1, or any number divided by zero equals 0.

My engineering brain agreed with the mathematical purity of "undefined." My comic/writer's brain REALLY liked the idea that Zero Reserves divided by Zero Production = Zero. Done. Finito. Career over. Cue Monty Python's Dead Parrot Sketch.

I replaced the equals sign with the tilde symbol, which represents mathematical equivalence: **R / P ~ 0**.

Now that I'm no longer a practicing engineer, that's close enough.

* *Cave Outs* will be explained later.

BORN YOUNG

I was born at a very young age, first child of Barbara and Harry. I've been told my parents really wanted to have a child, so you can imagine their surprise when the doctor announced, "Congratulations! It's an engineer!"

A decade later in 1969, I was one of a handful of new kids in fifth grade at Robert E. Peary elementary school in east Tulsa. Instinctively knowing my place, I took an open seat at the back of the room and activated my Cloak of Invisibility. I quickly discovered I couldn't make out anything the teacher wrote on the blackboard at the front of the room.

I was sharp enough to realize this was a Really Big Problem, and reluctantly raised my hand and told Mrs. Brown I couldn't read the board. She instructed a kid on the front row to trade seats with me, which automatically disabled my COI. I squeezed by the boy in the aisle, red-faced from making a spectacle of myself for needing spec—sorry, not going to do it—for not being able to see from the back of the room. I felt sick and hated being the center of attention.

Alerted to my defect by the school staff, Mom sprang into action and took me to an optometrist. In 1969, the only glasses option for vision-challenged ten-year-olds was a frame style known as Durable Yet Hideous Black Plastic. I didn't make the connection at the time, but my goofy new glasses and short haircut resembled the now-classic look of NASA engineers and flight controllers seen on television during the Gemini and Apollo space missions (and impressively replicated years later in the outstanding engineer's movie, *Apollo 13*.)

Despite—or perhaps because of—my sporty new goggles, I turned out to be a half-decent fifth grade student. I believe a huge factor in my academic success was my love of books and reading.

"Please pass the milk and *The Amazing Spiderman*"

I read constantly as a kid. During breakfast or lunch, I'd prop up a Hardy Boys book with the napkin holder, or strategically place a comic book or *Mad* magazine where it wouldn't get splashed but close enough to read while munching. In rare nothing-to-read emergencies, I would study every word on the back of a cereal box, even if I wasn't having cereal. My favorites boxes were Life and Captain Crunch (with Crunch Berries, of course). One of my favorite quips as an adult (but so far not popular with anyone else) is "Life is a bowl of cereal, best enjoyed before it gets soggy."

Mom took me and my brother and sister to the library every couple of weeks, and I returned home each time with a tall stack of books. Mom and Dad financed my purchase of dozens of paperbacks from the Scholastic Book Service flyers my teachers handed out monthly. I loved stories about quirky kids and child geniuses (natch!). A few of my favorite series:

Brains Benton	(Charles Spain Verral)
Henry Reed	(Keith Robertson)
Encyclopedia Brown	(Donald Sobel)
The Great Brain	(John D. Fitzgerald)
Rupert	(Evelyn M. Parkinson)
Alfred Hitchcock and the Three Investigators	(Robert Arthur, Jr. and others)

Two books really had an impact: *The Mad Scientists' Club* and *The New Adventures of the Mad Scientists' Club* by Bertrand R. Brinley. A bunch of wise-cracking kids with a super-smart leader (who wore black-frame glasses!) cause science-based trouble for the local townsfolk and hilarity ensued in each adventure. I read these books at least a dozen times each. I purchased 50th Anniversary hardback editions in 2011 and read them again with great delight. Books are excellent time machines.

"Live on KOFN Radio: the Joplin Spelling Bee!"

All of my early reading paid off with A's in spelling. I won the 3rd grade bee and represented my school in the city-wide contest, broadcast live one Saturday morning on a Joplin radio station.

The format allowed for a do-over if you spelled a word wrong. I survived a couple of rounds, then got tripped up by the ridiculously simple word "often." I stepped to the microphone confidently.

"O f…e n."

"Steven are you sure that's correct?" the moderator asked. "Would you like to try again?"

I thought for a quick second and couldn't come up with anything. I leaned toward the microphone and tried to sound confident again.

"O f…E n?" This time I put extra emphasis on the letter E, thinking somehow that would correct my mistake. It did not. I was eliminated. Saying something wrong with confidence or carefully placed emphasis did not result in a positive outcome.

Years later, however, in my professional life I observed the opposite was frequently true. Nonsense and BS communicated with absolute confidence by colleagues and managers *often* seemed to work quite well, with senior executives nodding their agreement. Instead of being eliminated from the career contest, many people who spoke incorrectly but with a bold tone and style were promoted right up the ladder.

Huh. Moore on this later.

Doesn't everyone remember their first Science Fiction book?

One of the earliest books I remember owning was a gift from Mom when I was eight or nine. It was a Tom Corbett Space Cadet Adventure written for juveniles: *Stand By For Mars!* by Carey Rockwell, first published in 1952.

For years I remembered a particularly enthralling scene in which Tom and two other cadets had to cross the Martian desert with air supplies running dangerously low. Air supplies in science fiction stories are almost always "dwindling" or "quickly becoming exhausted" or "running dangerously low." One rarely reads about air supplies that are "safely adequate" or "running fantastically high."

In 2018 I found a hardback copy of *SBFM* and read it again, transporting myself back to childhood. Here is the review I posted on Goodreads:

This book had a huge influence on me. A gift from my mother when I was 8 or 9, it is the earliest book I can remember reading - 50 years ago! - and I became a life-long fan of science fiction. I don't know what happened to it, most of the books I enjoyed in my youth were "lost," hopefully passed on to others to enjoy.

Over the last several years when I thought of this book I could clearly see the image of Tom in his bubble helmet on the cover. The only part of the story that I could recall (SPOILER ALERT!) was the three cadets struggling to cross the brutally hot Martian desert as their food and water ran out. In particular, I remembered an illustration showing the largest cadet carrying one of the others who had passed out. I looked for the book in used bookstores over the years and finally ordered a first edition (1952) from Abebooks.com. After it arrived I found the illustration on page 205, exactly as I remembered.

I am grateful to "Carey Rockwell" (pseudonym for one or more unknown authors) and Mom for introducing me to science fiction through this book. (5 Stars)

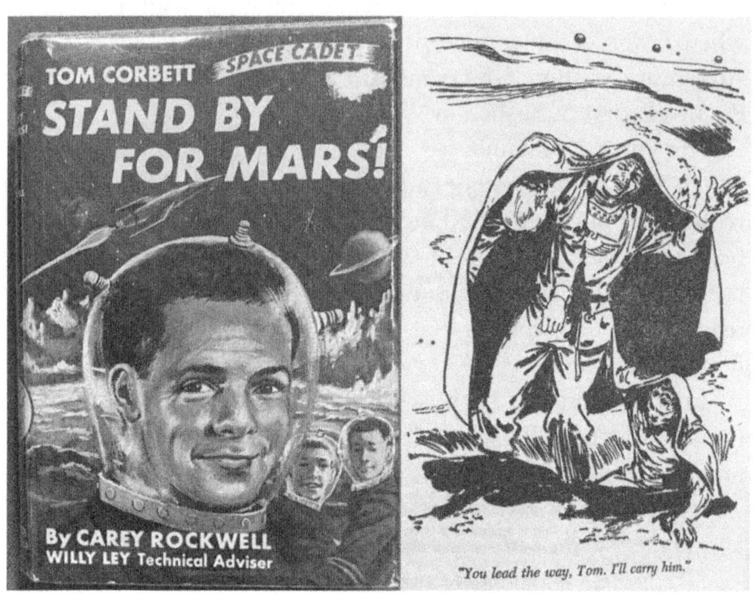

Memories can be tricky. My adult mind recalled air supplies as critical to Tom and the boys in the Martian desert, but when I read the book again a couple of years ago I discovered the cadets' chief concern was running out of food and water. Air wasn't a problem; they weren't even wearing helmets!

After reading *SBFM* as a kid, I was forever hooked on Sci Fi. I read *A Wrinkle in Time* (Madeleine L'Engle), *The Phantom Tollbooth* (Norton Juster), and novels by Jules Verne, H.G. Wells, and Edgar Rice Burroughs.

"Yes, Tarzan *is* hanging around my attic. Why do you ask?"

While reading *Boy's Life* magazine one summer afternoon in 1971, I saw an advertisement and leaped from my chair. The ad was for a rare book catalog, and asked, "Is Tarzan hanging around your attic?" If so, "you could be $75 richer."

I had already explored boxes of old books that belonged to Dad when he was a kid. I had read several, including three very old Tarzan books written by Edgar Rice Burroughs. I raced to the closet, tore through the boxes, and found it: a first-edition *Tarzan of the Apes*, published in 1914. I ran to tell my parents that we were rich and remember being disappointed that they didn't seem all that excited. Eventually I realized that someday the books would likely become mine, and if I was patient I'd get rich later.

I was right. The books did come my way years later, but a couple of boxes had been discarded with water damage. I searched the remaining two boxes and found *The Beasts of Tarzan* (1st edition, 1916, 3rd in the series), but *Tarzan of the Apes* was missing.

I still have Dad's books, now stored in waterproof totes. In 2015 I remembered Tarzan and the advertisement and located a searchable *Boy's Life* archive (thank you Google). I easily found the ad, just as I remembered.

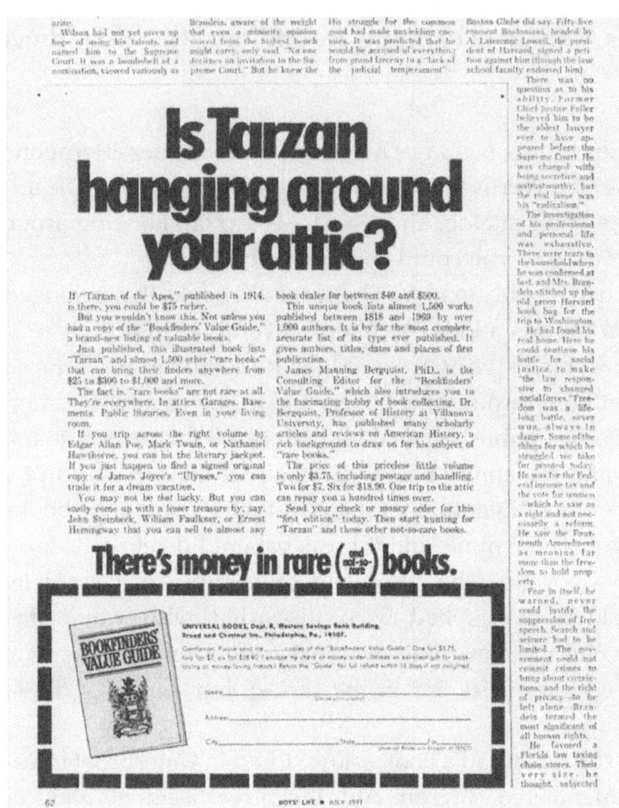

"Scoot back from the TV, it's bad for your eyes!"

I heard that a lot growing up. Given what we know today about screen time, I guess my parents were even smarter than they thought they were.

Pop culture via television had a formative influence on me in the late 60s and early 70s. Considering there were only three networks at the time, I'm impressed with the number of programs that were technologically creative or straight-up science fiction. Dad and I would settle in the living room with big bowls of salted popcorn popped from an actual popcorn popper (drizzled with real melted butter) and enjoy our favorite shows: *Star Trek, The Man from U.N.C.L.E., Batman, Lost in Space, The Avengers, The Twilight Zone, Mission Impossible, The Wild Wild West,* and edited-for-television James Bond movies.

I loved television comedy too: *Laugh-In, I Love Lucy, The Smothers Brothers, Get Smart* (Don Adams was a comedy genius), *Hogan's Heroes,* and *The Dick Van Dyke Show.*

And later: *Monty Python's Flying Circus, Cheers, Barney Miller, MASH,* and many others. Eventually, I came to realize that the humor I enjoyed so much was created by largely unknown *writers,* working behind the scenes.

I was heavily influenced by watching teams work together, as in World War II movies like *Where Eagles Dare* and *The Dirty Dozen,* and disaster movies such as *The Poseidon Adventure* and *The Towering Inferno.* I was enamored with the television show *Emergency!* and how well paramedics Gage and DeSoto worked with fire fighters, police and Rampart Hospital staff to rescue and treat accident victims.

Moon Landing

I was ten years old during the first moon landing in July 1969. I have a clear memory of watching the grainy black-and-white television pictures with my family in the house we rented in Tulsa just a few weeks after moving from Joplin, Missouri. I think I was just old enough to sense the enormous effort by thousands of people that paid off with a successful landing and returning the astronauts safely to Earth (more *teamwork*). Thanks to NASA and the Apollo missions, Tom Corbett, Captain Kirk, and many others, I was a fan of space exploration before and after that fantastic Giant Leap.

My Wonder Bread Years

A kid unknowingly destined for a future in engineering was bound to nerd out over comic books. My favorite superheroes were Spiderman, The Fantastic Four, and Batman. I liked Green Lantern too but for some reason was not that impressed with Superman. I really enjoyed team-ups like the Justice League, and Spiderman working with the Fantastic Four. There was something about characters working together on a shared goal while tossing snarky comments back and forth that really appealed to me.

Something Wonderful My Way Came

I read every Ray Bradbury book I could get my hands on. My favorites were *The Martian Chronicles, Something Wicked This Way Comes,* and of course *Fahrenheit 451*. I was fortunate to meet Mr. Bradbury at a book signing in 1994 when he was in Tulsa to accept the Peggy V. Helmerich Distinguished Author Award. It was a special moment when I told this fantastic writer how much I enjoyed reading his novels growing up. He signed my hardcover copy of *Fahrenheit 451,* and I consider it the crown jewel in my collection of autographed books.

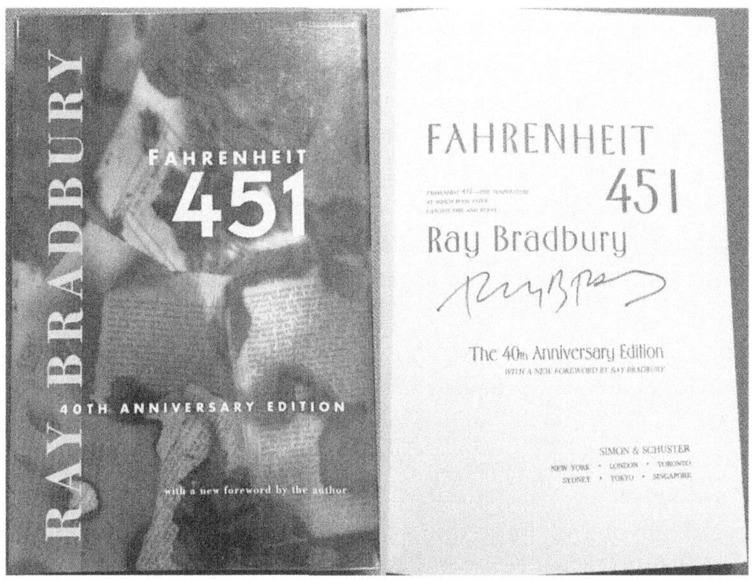

1977: A Waste of Time Oddity

Starting around age twelve, I devoured as many books as possible from the "Big Three" science fiction authors: Robert A. Heinlein, Arthur C. Clarke, and Isaac Asimov. At one point my collection included every single book Heinlein had written. I dove into Asimov's *Foundation* series, the Robot novels, and many of his non-fiction science books. I soon realized Asimov was much too prolific for anyone to read his entire bibliography in a lifetime—he has written more than 500 books! I also read many of Edgar Allan Poe's stories in two of Dad's books he bought for college English courses. Poe's macabre stories led me to read most of Stephen King's novels years later.

2001: A Space Odyssey by Arthur C. Clarke was also a favorite. I can't remember if I read the book before or soon after seeing the movie with Dad at the Continental Theater. The Continental was one of the last, great single-screen theaters to remain open before the proliferation of small-screen multiplex cinemas all over town. I liked the book, reading it at least three times over the next few years. The ending of *2001* has sometimes been described as confusing, but I don't recall having any problems with it.

As high school seniors in 1977, my friend Jim Zodrow and I complained to Mrs. Dobie, our English teacher, about the lack of science fiction in the reading program. We wore her down and she said fine, you two go ahead and work up a reading unit for an SF novel. Picture us grinning with glee and rubbing our palms together as we selected *2001: A Space Odyssey*. We figured the mind-blowing ending would bewilder many of our classmates and possibly Mrs. Dobie, too.

During the next few classes Zodrow and I worked in the library, preparing a study guide and final exam. The class read the book over the next couple of weeks. They hated it. It was a waste of time, dull, and stupid. What were they supposed to learn from this? What was the point of the bizarre space-baby thing at the end?

Mrs. Dobie seemed to enjoy the students' reaction to our book selection. For Zodrow and me, it was a pragmatic lesson in "how not to make friends."

A Foolish Act of Monumental Stupidity

Sometime around my freshman year in high school I needed cash, lost my mind, and sold all of my sci-fi paperbacks, comic books, and *Mad* magazines in a garage sale. As I write this, I can hear many of you gasping in horror as you read that sentence.

It was a colossal mistake. A tremendous, brainless act I have regretted a thousand times. I'm also a little bit mad at Mom for "letting" me sell my books. She could have pretended they were sold, gave me the cash, then produced them years later in the ultimate You Should Have Listened To Your Mother moment.

As of early 2022, I have re-collected 36 of Robert Heinlein's novels, mostly from used bookstores scattered across the country. If fourth-dimensional technology develops sufficiently during my lifetime, I intend to travel back in time and convince myself to keep forever all of my books and comics. If young dumb Steve doesn't agree, the Writer from the Future will deliver a mighty butt-kicking. It could be fatal, paradox be damned.

Bill Ram and the Space Creature's Journal

My second-earliest attempt at creative writing occurred when I was about twelve years old in sixth-grade English class. The teacher stood at the front of the class holding a book and reading aloud a short science fiction story, one of the rare occasions when this genre popped up during twelve years of public education.

My memories are fuzzy but here is the gist of the story: as a group of astronauts in space suits explored a new planet, they come across an alien city in decay. There is no evidence of any living inhabitants. Moving through the ruins, the group is surprised to find a structure still standing. They enter and discover an interior chamber sealed with an airlock. Through a glass portal they see a bizarre creature sitting motionless at a strangely shaped desk.

After discussing the situation, the astronauts decide to force their way into the chamber. When they break the seal on the airlock there is a puff of atmosphere and the creature instantly disintegrates. The leader of the group moves to the desk and finds a notebook with a great many pages filled with words, apparently written by the pile of dust in which he is standing. He flips to the beginning of the notebook and starts to read…

The teacher closed the book and announced that our writing assignment was for each of us to use our imagination, pretend that we were the creature and write down the story that the astronaut found in the journal.

I had questions. They only found one ancient resident in the entire city? How did the airlock stay sealed for apparently centuries while the rest of the city deteriorated? Why did the astronauts break in to a sealed chamber containing a perfectly-preserved specimen of intelligent life on another planet? Were the astronauts morons? What were the odds that the creature's manuscript was written in English?

The teacher said, "Okay, that's enough. Everyone get to work."

This essay would probably be much more interesting if you could now read my version of the space creature's journal, but I have no record and no memory of what I wrote. I remember the story and how the teacher set up the writing prompt, and always thought it was a great way to engage the students and encourage creative thinking and storytelling.

I don't know what grade I received for the assignment. As a writer today I'd like to think I aced it, that I wrote a well-crafted, entertaining post for the Ancient One's blog and received an A+ for my effort.

I do, however, possess an original document from what I believe to be my earliest attempt at creative writing. My mother saved it in my "school papers" for several decades before suddenly deciding she no longer had any use for it. She stuck it in an old wooden frame and gave it to me as a Christmas present several years ago.

Apparently, this third-grade assignment was to write a short story using double-letter "o" words, which are underlined in the document (see the image below). Here is a transcript, complete with spelling and punctuation errors as originally composed by the author. (Apparently traumatized from my live radio failure, I was no longer a gud spellur.)

Boy Scout At Camp

Oct. 5, 1967

Once there was a boy scout named Bill Ram, he was going on a campping tripp. His mother said Goodby as he got on the bus.

When he got there he new the first thing to do, cut fire wood, as he was doing this he cut his foot.

So he decided to cook his food. He was looking at some birds when he burned his food, he looked around. He saw a Gun, he picked it up and fired it, it back fired and put out his tooth, finally it was night time. His face was full of bugs, the moon kept him awake. finally it was time to leave. When he got off the bus he was glad to be home.

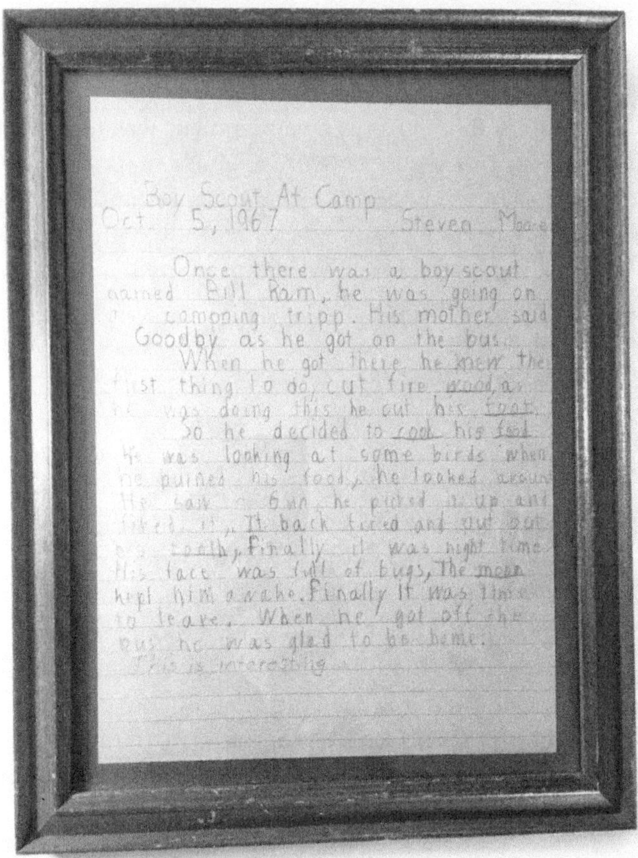

Boy Scout At Camp
Oct. 5, 1967 Steven Moore

Once there was a boy scout
named Bill Ram, he was going on
a camping tripp. His mother said
Goodby as he got on the bus.
When he got there he knew the
first thing to do, cut fire wood, as
he was doing this he cut his foot.
So he decided to cook his food
He was looking at some birds when
he burned his food, he looked around
He saw a Gun, he picked it up and
fired it, It back fired and cut out
a tooth, Finally it was night time
His face was full of bugs, The moon
kept him awake. Finally it was time
to leave. When he got off the
bus he was glad to be home.
This is interesting

The teacher corrected my errors in red ink and wrote at the bottom of the page, "This is interesting."

This gripping wilderness saga of the heroic struggles of young Bill Ram clearly indicates the paranoid darkness in the mind of the eight-year-old author. Perhaps this story served as a cautionary tale, a warning for my parents to keep an eye on their troubled oldest child.

We can extrapolate the literary style and content of the Bill Ram adventure and theorize about the nature and tone of the missing "What the Creature Wrote" story by the same author four years later. Clearly, the journal would have chronicled a horrific, civilization-ending apocalypse that destroyed the city, decimated the population, and made the creature-writer very uncomfortable.

One final thought: As I read again my childhood story of Bill Ram's dismal camping experience, I realized it was the origin of what later became a central and dominant theme in my adult life philosophy:

Moore's Law of Pessimistic Optimism:
"I don't know if the glass is half full or half empty, but when someone knocks it over, I'm the guy who will have to clean it up."

"Psst! Can I borrow your eraser?"

There are only two things I can remember about my 6th grade math class: the name of our teacher and the lesson she taught us on the last day of school.

Mrs. DeShazo announced a pop quiz. We all moaned and groaned. She walked up and down the aisles, methodically placing the test face-down on our desks. "Be sure to read the instructions first and when you finish, turn it in and you can leave. Ready? Begin."

At the top of the page: "Read all questions carefully before beginning." Our anxiety turned to glee as we realized it wasn't really a test, but a last-day-of-school goof:

WRITE YOUR NAME: ______________________

WHAT LETTER COMES AFTER "E" IN THE ALPHABET: ___

WHAT DOES 2 + 2 = ? ___

SPELL "CAT" ___ ___ ___

We rushed to scribble our answers, finish the test, and start our summer vacation. There were 20 questions on the page. One item I distinctly remember, about halfway down:

STAND UP AND SAY YOUR NAME OUT LOUD

Eventually everyone in the class stood and said their name, then sat back down and continued working. A minute or so later I noticed kids were furiously erasing their answers. I reached the bottom of the page and read the last item:

DO NOT MARK ON THIS PAGE. DO NOT ANSWER ANY QUESTIONS. TURN IN THE QUIZ AND HAVE A GREAT SUMMER!

Mrs. DeShazo was standing by the classroom door, grinning as she watched her students learn a valuable lesson about following directions. We all failed the quiz that day, but I think about that final day of math class ofen—sorry. *Often.*

I type the same way I swim: like a fish out of water.

In high school, I was a straight-A student except for two Bs I received in 9th grade. My father strongly recommended that I take typing, telling me it would be a valuable skill I would use the rest of my life. (Thanks Dad, you were right.) Our grades were based on speed tests, and I could never type accurately and fast enough on those clunky manual typewriters to earn anything higher than a B.

My other B in high school was for gym class. Back in 1974, 9th grade was taught in the junior high school, but grades were included on your high school transcripts. It was my bad luck that our school gymnasium included an indoor swimming pool.

For a few weeks each semester, gym class was held in the pool doing aquatic activities like relay races and water volleyball. This was both problematic and traumatic for me: I swam like a fish out of water. I could get to the other side of the pool and back, but looked like a perch flopping around the bottom of a boat. Plus, the chlorine made me sneeze, so I used a nose clip strapped around my head. (Yeah, it was every bit as embarrassing as you are imagining.)

Always picked last for relay teams, I swam so poorly that Coach McLain gave me and one other hapless kid remedial swimming lessons after school (an activity he probably would not be allowed to do today). The lessons didn't help much, and my swimming performance knocked my gym grade down to a B.

My Life Soundtrack: The Early Years

Everyone has a soundtrack playing in the background of their life. If—I mean *when*—this memoir is made into a movie, I know exactly which songs should be played to enhance every scene. I'm sure a huge number of people who went to high school and college in the late 1970s and early 1980s have a similar list, but these are the musical artists and bands who helped me get through life, in no particular order:

Emerson Lake and Palmer, Boston, Yes, Electric Light Orchestra, Ted Nugent, Rush, Styx, Chicago, Steely Dan, Aerosmith, The Guess Who, The Who, Elton John (especially *Yellow Brick Road* and "Funeral for a Friend / Love Lies Bleeding") Fleetwood Mac, The Doobie Brothers, Bachman-Turner Overdrive, The Alan Parsons Project, David Gilmour, Trans-Siberian Orchestra, 3rd Force, Pete Bardens

The answer is: Kansas (first 7 albums)

"What is the music former reservoir engineer Steve Moore would most like to hear through headphones if he fell into a long-term coma?"

If I had a nickel for every dollar I earned that summer, I'd have a few hundred nickels.

To earn spending money during junior high summers, I mowed a half-dozen lawns in the neighborhood each week. My first "real" job was slinging ice-cream at the aforementioned Baskin Robbins shop not far from my home. During my brief time at BR I learned a couple of serious life lessons and gained my first insights into the minds of the aliens collectively known as "Management."

My starting pay rate was $1.10 per hour. This was in 1975, when the minimum wage was $2.10 per hour. The manager explained that BR did not have to pay the minimum rate, citing some obscure quirk of state law regarding interstate commerce. I realized later he was probably just spouting BS to justify substandard wages to high school kids.

The manager, Mr. Jezik—he pronounced it *Yay-zik,* although the staff came up with some creative variations—told me not to worry. While my "training wage" was only $1.10 per hour, after two weeks my pay rate would go up. I nodded and got to work.

Somehow, I survived Baskin's boot camp and the rigorous training regimen: "Each scoop of ice cream must be no larger than three ounces. Practice your technique and weigh your scoops on the scale until you can create a perfect sphere of frozen dairy product close to—but not over—three ounces."

At the end of my first two weeks I received my first paycheck. I worked 80 hours and earned $88 (before taxes, which thankfully were small at my pay scale). I was disappointed but carried on with the knowledge my next check would be bigger. I didn't know what my new pay rate was, I'd been too intimidated to ask. I guessed it might be another fifty cents an hour, a significant bump but still below the minimum as the Boss led me to expect. I continued smiling and scooping.

Two weeks later I stared at my second paycheck: another 80 hours worked, $92 gross. Four extra dollars. After completing my training program, my (insert dramatic finger-quotes here) "raise" was a nickel. I was now earning $1.15 per hour. Mowing lawns paid far better than shoveling ice cream at Bastard Robbers.

I realize now that pay-raise experience was consistent with a Life Lesson learned many years later: negotiate the highest starting base pay you can. Raises can't be relied on to improve your financial situation. This was true for my entire engineering career. Annual performance raises typically were 2 to 3%, and rarely covered the incremental costs from inflation. Bonuses could be nice but were never certain, and almost always tied to corporate metrics and not just individual performance. The largest increases in salary occurred when promoted or accepting an offer to work for another company.

I was irritated at my ice cream colleagues who had not warned me to expect the tiny post-training increase. They agreed it sucked, and that Yaze-Dick was a bad guy, then taught me their payback strategy: make a mistake. If you screwed up a customer order, like putting extra hot fudge on a sundae when they had requested strawberry topping, you cheerfully apologized and made a new sundae. You put the "mistake" in the freezer and ate it later on your break or took it home after your shift. After getting my second paycheck, I admit the percentage increase in my "errors" was much greater than my percentage pay raise.

By then a month had passed, too late to find another summer job. I decided to stick it out until school started in September.

Ah, the best laid plans.

Two Scoops

A few weeks after the Moa-Moa punch disaster, Phillip got me again one night. We weren't very busy when a college-age couple strolled into the shop. The girl was hot, wearing a transparent yellow top and no bra. I don't remember anything at all about the guy.

It was my first time to encounter a girl in a see-through shirt, and it was extremely distracting. But I was a frozen-desert professional and did my best not to stare as I took their order. I opened the freezer door and went in for the first scoop. I took my time swirling, trying to check her out through the glass without obviously lifting my head. It wasn't quite as provocative as the car wash scene in *Cool Hand Luke*; that would have been too much for me to handle. Still, she was standing just inches away in soft focus through the frosty glass.

I plopped the scoop onto a sugar cone and handed it to the girl. I turned to grab a cup for the guy's order, mentally copying the image I had just collected to my brain's Long Term Storage area. Thus distracted, I failed to notice that Phillip had closed the freezer lid as he passed behind me. I turned back to the freezer, stole another look at the girl, and plunged my arm down. The scoop banged noisily into the freezer lid, spraining my wrist. I yelled and dropped the scoop, more noise as it clattered on the floor. The girl and her date busted out laughing while my face turned the color of Flavor 29, Bing Cherry.

I grabbed a clean scoop and managed to get the guy's ice cream with my sore hand. They both left the store giggling. I made a fool of myself and nearly tanked my Baskin Robbins career with a season-ending injury.

Worth it.

"You can't quit me, I'm fired!"

It was a slow afternoon near the end of July. I was working the counter and Boss was off to one side, working on a custom ice-cream cake. During a break when no customers were in the store, Mr. Jezik got a little chatty.

"Hey, Steve. What do you think of me?"

Uh-oh. "What?"

"What do you think of me as a boss?" His dark eyes, comically magnified by his thick glasses, bore into my soul.

I turned away and started cleaning the milk shake mixer for the second time in twenty minutes. "Fine. No problem." *C'mon, drop it, old man. Just ice your cake.*

"Okay, so what do the other employees think of me?" YD stared at me, holding a squeeze tube of icing in one hand, a cake trowel in the other.

"I don't know."

"Do they like me? Say bad things about me? What?"

"I haven't heard anything like that," I lied. None of us liked the guy, and this conversation was validating our feelings.

"Tell me what they say about me." He crossed his arms in a not-at-all-intimidating stance, still holding the cake tools in his shamrock-green hands. I thought quick and decided to bail.

"Nothing, no one says anything. Gotta go to the bathroom." I walked past him to the back of the shop and shut the bathroom door. I washed up slowly, hating the idea of going out front again. *He wants me to rat on my fellow scoopers? Is this what managers do?* I returned to the counter and the boss was back to work on the cake. Nothing more was said.

Two afternoons later I was off work but dropped by BR to see what shifts I was working the following week. The new schedule was pinned to the bulletin board in the back. My name was missing.

Kathleen was working the counter, intently cleaning the freezer doors. She never looked up. YD was working on yet another cake at the other end of the shop.

"Excuse me, Mr. Jezik. I didn't see any shifts for me to work next week?"

He set his spatula down and wiped his hands with his dirty apron in classic television noir style. "Steve, I had to leave your name off the schedule. We can't have that kind of trouble here."

"Trouble? What trouble?"

"You have a personality problem and don't fit in here. Wash your uniform shirts and bring them by tomorrow and you can pick up your final paycheck." He walked off to the back.

After two and half months, I had been fired from my first job. My dream of shoveling ice cream for $1.15 an hour had been crushed. I went home, pissed off and frustrated. I found out later that a number of guys and girls had been hired and fired by Jezik, who was a paranoid S.O.B. Apparently, he asked every employee what everyone thought of him, and those who survived apparently told him what he wanted to hear.

I've heard it said that when a door closes on one low-paying job, another door opens at another low-paying opportunity. Within a couple of months I landed a part-time job as a stock boy at TG&Y, which was a much nicer experience and lasted all through college.

My short time with Bastard Robbers taught me valuable insights into manager-employee relationships, the pros and cons of people-pleasing, and surviving a termination. I also learned to be on the lookout for people with personality disorders.

The Mad Science Teacher's Club

In preparation for a potential engineering career, I took every science class I could in high school. Chemistry was great fun, thanks to our teacher, Mr. Ward. He gave everyone a nickname the first week of school; I was "Mooron" and embraced it proudly. (I'm sure this would not be considered a correct teaching practice today.) All of Weird Ward's students participated in the Fellowship of Heathen Chemists. The FHC club mostly goofed around, ate Hydrox cookies, and mustered for the occasional food drive. For some strange reason my FHC T-shirt still hangs in my closet, even though it no longer fits.

The only thing I remember from Biology class is the teacher. She was short, grumpy, and years ahead of her time in dyeing her hair an unnatural shade of red. Years later I would think of her while watching Gimly dismember Orcs in *The Lord of the Rings*.

Physiology was a terrific class taught by Mr. Matheson, an excellent teacher who liked using the phrase "still yet" but pronounced it as one two-syllable word: *sti-yet*. I can still recall much of what we learned about the various systems of the human body. We also partnered up and dissected fetal pigs. I don't know if dissections are still done in high school classes today, but in my opinion you have not been fully educated until you can correctly identify whether the tiny purple organ skewered with a numbered toothpick flag is the little piggy's spleen or pancreas.

Physics class was a bunch of crazy cats unsuccessfully herded by Mr. Hall, a nice, goofy old guy. One day during the holiday season (we called it Christmas back then) the physics class spontaneously combusted musically and started singing *The Twelve Days of Christmas.* We kept at it, spending the last ten minutes of class each day practicing, and eventually wormed our way into performing for the entire school in the Christmas program. Right before we were to take the stage we broke into the Music Department closet and donned choir robes. Our unique interpretation of the song went over well with the audience. (I bet you didn't know Ian Anderson of Jethro Tull led a gang of ten other pipers.)

Engineering a career solution

I was leaning toward engineering in college. I had read hundreds of science fiction novels and enjoyed SF television shows and movies. I followed the accomplishments of NASA and the space program. In school I liked my science classes and could handle the math. I assumed I would enroll at Oklahoma State along with most of my friends, but I did not know which flavor of engineering to choose.

Dad crunched the numbers and told me I could either go to OSU and live on campus, or go to the University of Tulsa if I lived at home. I have a vague memory of someone from TU making a presentation at our high school on a career in Petroleum Engineering. It might have been a member of the Society of Petroleum Engineers student chapter. I'm pretty sure this was the first time I learned there was a career called "Petroleum Engineering." No one in my family was associated with oil and gas. Except for a family friend who was a pilot for Getty (formerly Skelly) Oil, I didn't know anyone who worked in the industry.

In late 1976, a family friend who was a mechanical engineer wrote a terrific recommendation letter for me, addressed to the Dean of Engineering at TU. I accepted an invitation to tour the engineering facilities on North Lewis, a couple of miles from the main campus. Formerly offices and labs for Humble Oil (which later became Exxon), North Campus included the technical library, science and engineering classes, and labs. I was leaning toward mechanical or electrical engineering and met several faculty members.

A few days later I received a second invitation from John Day, Petroleum Engineering Chairman. I met with faculty and students and visited TU's impressive drilling research facility, which included an actual working drilling rig.

The chairman explained that oil and gas companies provided funds for a number of scholarships. My grades were good, and I would receive a scholarship if I enrolled as a petroleum engineer. I had already decided to go to TU and knew the first two years of classes were basically the same for all engineering programs. I could declare a PE major and receive the scholarship. If I decided to change to another major later, I'd lose the PE scholarship but the freshman and sophomore classes would still apply to my new degree. I accepted Chairman Day's offer and took my first steps on the path to a career in Petroleum Engineering.

The Oil and Gas Industry had successfully recruited me with my first financial incentive. It was not anything close to a free ride, but definitely helped with the expensive tuition. I was advised that my scholarship had been funded by Tenneco, a company I had never heard of. I wrote a thank you letter to Tenneco and a short time later received a package from the company: A gold Cross pen and pencil set customized with the Tenneco logo.

13th Grade

I could have selected Oklahoma State and lived on campus in Stillwater like many of my high school friends, or live at home to save money and go to TU. I chose TU for engineering. Big mistake.

Not choosing TU, but living at home. For the fall semester of my freshman year in 1977, I made the daily commute from home to campus to be in class by 8am. It was so much like my high school routine that I joked I was in 13th grade. My college friends talked about campus life, dorm parties, and various stay-up-all-night shenanigans. My only story was describing the challenge of returning home after 10pm and opening the noisy front screen door without waking Mom. I was missing the campus life experience and was miserable.

By the end of the semester, I was ready to transfer to OSU to get away and live on campus. Dad suggested I use my savings and move into a TU dorm for the spring semester. Twin Towers dorm had an opening, and I had no idea who my roommate would be, but I jumped at the opportunity and moved to TU in January of 1978.

Roommates, suitemates, what's the difference?

Twin Towers dorm at TU was set up as suites, with three rooms (two people each) sharing a small living room area and a two-sink bathroom. Over the next three years I roomed with a bunch of quirky American and international students who will unknowingly inspire terrific characters in my future novels.

Ratnajit Barua was from Bangladesh. He introduced himself as "Barua." Later he told us why he wanted us to use only his last name. "You Americans shorten everything to abbreviations and nicknames, and I do not want to be called Rat." Shrewd fellow.

Mario was from El Salvador. He taught me an important safety tip: never get in a rum-drinking contest with a guy from El Salvador. He would sit on the couch reading *Playboy* and tell everyone he was "masturbating my mind."

John, a super-nice, hard-core Baptist from Shawnee, Oklahoma, never touched a *Playboy* or alcohol. John drove a weird, peach-colored two-tone Mercury Cougar, large enough for small aircraft to land on. We called it the Pimpmobile to his chagrin.

Fred, another nice guy from Shawnee, was not opposed to reading *Playboy* or teasing John about it.

Alex was from my high school in Tulsa and my roommate for a couple of semesters. He talked and farted in his sleep a lot, or at least pretended to be asleep. One night after blowing out a big one he yelled, "it's pouring down rain outside!" It wasn't. A second or two later he muttered, "Course, I could be wrong."

Javier was an engineering student from Honduras. He was known as "the piss whisperer" for the strange, soft sounds he made to encourage his own urination.

Bill was a psychology grad student from Hawaii. He smoked a lot of hash and was extremely fond of quoting a specific Led Zeppelin lyric with an evil grin (something about preferring back doors when making an entrance).

Rick was a pre-med student—or maybe pre-law, what's the difference? (If you don't recognize this reference, I feel sorry for you.) Rick was from Arkansas and had a hot cheerleader girlfriend who was later crowned TU Homecoming Queen.

Tawfig, an engineering student from Iran. There were more than a hundred Iranian students on campus during the hostage crisis in the late 70s, but TU was pretty tame back then and nothing ugly happened. The worst thing I saw was stupid chalk graffiti which was quickly removed from the sidewalks. Everyone yawned and carried on. John was Tawfig's roommate and noticed a sickening odor that got worse by the day. He found a large bag of dirt and weeds in Tawfig's desk drawer. He had brought it from Iran to stay connected to his homeland. We convinced him to get rid of the horrid thing and find another way to connect.

Earl was my roommate during my senior year at TU, a friend from high school and a petroleum engineering major. Earl was an easy-going guy with an amazing tolerance for the foolish behavior of the rest of us.

Finally, meet Ahcene, a crazy engineering student from Algeria. He was my first roommate when I moved into the dorm in January 1978.

Beyond the Green Thumbtack

A day or two after moving into Twin Towers I invited Earl up to see my room. A couple of years later we would be roommates, but at that time Earl was living at home and experiencing his own frustration commuting to school every day.

It was late afternoon when we entered the suite. Rick and Fred were on the couch playing backgammon. They looked up with unusual expressions and said hello. I unlocked my room door and pushed it open. It stopped half-way, bumping into something.

I peeked around the door and there was Ahcene the Algerian, naked and crammed into the corner. One hand inadequately covered his crotch, the other pressed a finger to his lips in the universal "keep quiet" sign, a strategy doomed to fail before implementation as Rick and Fred were already losing their shit in the front room. I glanced at Ahcene's bed and a body was covered head to toes with a sheet, quivering in silent laughter or embarrassment, there was no way to tell.

Earl pushed past me, took a seat on my bed and looked around. "Hey, this is great!" He spotted Ahcene in the corner, then noticed the body in bed just three feet away. He jumped to his feet, his face a brilliant OU-crimson. We left without another word, pulling the door shut. Rick and Fred were in convulsions on the couch, the backgammon game scattered on the floor.

Later, Ahcene and I agreed on an Early Warning System. When either of us wanted to use the room in private, we'd stick a green push-pin thumbtack into the door just above the knob, meaning "kindly delay your entry for at least an hour." Ahcene was quite gregarious and made frequent use of the EWS. I think I used it three times over the next three and a half years, and two of those were faked encounters in a pitiful attempt to enhance my engineering student persona.

(By the way: Is there anyone else besides me who hears the word "push pin" and immediately flashes on Neidermeyer in *Animal House,* spitting and shouting "A PLEDGE PIN!!" ?)

Later that semester, I made a grocery run and Ahcene asked me to pick up some inserts for his shoes. Returning, I passed by the dorm TV room and Achene was there talking to friends. He waved to me and I stupidly pulled a package of Odor Eaters from the bag and waved them in the air, mission accomplished. This was a HUGE MISTAKE. It never occurred to me that I embarrassed him in front of his friends. Ahcene never mentioned it. He just got even.

A few days later I got a phone call from a girl who told me she was in one of my classes and thought I was cute. She flirted with me but wouldn't tell me her name, or what class we shared. She called a few more times and we talked about meeting to get to know each other. I was jazzed for several days, scanning each of my classes and trying to figure out who might be the Mystery Girl.

Ahcene finally admitted it was a payback prank for the Odor Eaters thing, the girl was one of his many friends.

Well played, sir, brilliant! I might be wrong, but I'd bet serious money I am the only Petroleum Engineer on the planet punked by a disgruntled roommate after a flagrant display of smell-suppressing insoles. I had learned another valuable Life Lesson and made a solemn vow: Never again would I purchase foot-odor control products for an Algerian engineering student.

It's been tough at times, but I've honored that pledge for more than forty years.

Game of Squirrel Thrones

It was Pat's idea to install a toilet in a tree on the U. My friend and tennis teammate from high school, Pat maintained his crazy free spirit in college. He had spotted the toilet atop a junk pile in an empty lot and thought, "I must have it."

"Goes without saying," I agreed when he told me. Late Friday night we crowded into a friend's El Camino and made our way south to Jenks. The toilet rested cockeyed on a pile of trash, the porcelain surface shining dimly in the moonlight due to a thick layer of crud. We hoisted it into the bed and headed back to TU. Hopefully we did somebody a favor, removing a piece of junk from land that would later be the location of a Sonic Drive-In.

Pat's plan was to clean it up a bit and install it in the branches of a tree growing close to John Maybee Hall, the men's dormitory commonly known as The John. Late the next night, Pat showed up wearing dark coveralls and we lugged the toilet across the U in a clumsy imitation of John Belushi prowling around the campus of Faber College after dark.

Pat had come prepared, and we looped a chain around the bowl. I gave Pat a boost and he climbed up a few feet and got situated. He hauled up the toilet, installed it in a sturdy spot, then padlocked it to a thick branch. I brought along a Polaroid camera and snapped a couple of pics.

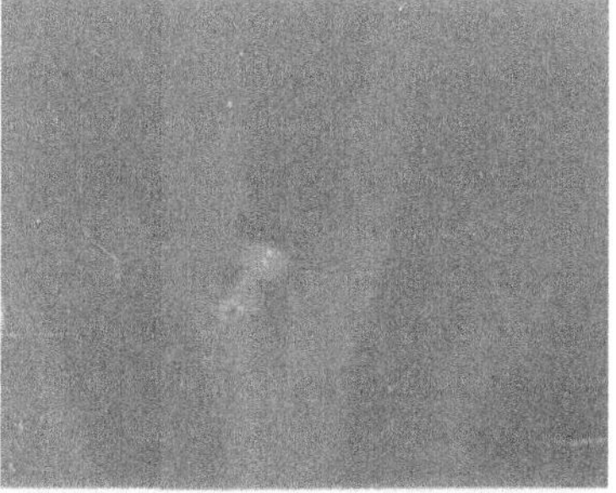

For me, this prank ranked up there with the time a bunch of us picked up a Volkswagen Beetle and moved it from the parking lot to the grass near Sharp Chapel. (Yes, beer was involved.) The license plate popped off during the relocation and someone left it leaning against the chapel door. I always wondered how the Bug owner reacted the next day when he or she discovered they had parked the car on the lawn.

A footnote: the toilet remained installed in the tree for more than a year. The chain and padlock prevented it from being easily dislodged, and apparently it was too much effort to drag over a ladder and bolt-cutters. Eventually, construction crews took possession of the Squirrel Throne by removing the entire tree when the U was redesigned to the current configuration for the construction of the new library.

"Let's keep the engineers as far away from the normal students as possible."

Studying engineering at any university typically imparts a unique, nerdy flavor to campus life. Locating the engineering classes and laboratories miles away from the main campus is a force multiplier for this phenomenon.

TU's North Campus was originally the site of Humble Oil and Refining Company. The facility had been converted to laboratories and classrooms creatively identified with names like Garage 1 and Garage 2. The university provided free shuttle bus transportation to and from the main campus. If you had enough time between classes, you could hop the shuttle back to the dorm for a quick lunch, then shuttle back to class. I distinctly remember sitting on the bus in the early afternoon, passing by the U. Girls were sunbathing in the grass and business majors tossed Frisbees while I was returning to North Campus for a 3-hour chemistry lab. It was depressing as hell.

Most of the time between North Campus classes was spent in the basement, studying with friends. The Canteen was windowless and dreary. Several vending machines lined one wall, and a very nice lady named Jo kept the machines stocked and made change. Lunch might be a mystery meat sandwich generously described as "chicken fried steak" and a Dr. Pepper. If you were feeling confident you might try a tuna sandwich.

It was not uncommon to see Dave Rader studying at the next table. Dave was the quarterback of the football team and a mechanical engineering student. I thought it was really cool to attend a university where the quarterback was an engineering major, unlike OSU and OU where the quarterbacks were, well, *not* engineering majors.

Adventures in Temperature Measurement and Natural Gas Processing

One day in physics lab a large thermometer slipped from my fingers and a ball of mercury rolled to rest among the glass shards. The lab instructor, Dr. Hawley the Ancient, immediately yelled for everyone to stand back and not touch the mercury. Then he looked at me without another word.

OK, it was my mess, and I knew how to clean it up. I found a couple of pieces of cardboard and pushed the mercury and pieces of glass into a pile so I could scoop them up. The ball of mercury took evasive action and rolled away.

As I bent over to corral it with the cardboard, the egg salad canteen sandwich I ate a few hours earlier served as a catalyst for a live demonstration of Boyle's Law. The increase in gas volume caused pressure to increase until the excess methane was expelled with a short but highly audible squeak.

The entire class burst into laughter. I was embarrassed but laughed too, it was pretty damn funny. I tried again to capture the little ball of mercury but kept cracking up. After a couple of minutes I finally maneuvered it against a wall, scooped it up in a paper cone, and disposed of it in the safety container Dr. Hawley had been patiently holding.

Other than writing up lab reports on lonely Friday nights, this is my only memory of physics lab.

Introduction to Failure 101

Freshman engineering students were required to take "Introduction to Engineering," a class in which glorious engineering achievements throughout history were celebrated alongside lectures on topics like safety factors and Monte Carlo simulation.

We were also assigned a mechanical project in which each student had to design an original machine or device according to exact specifications and performance criteria. My assignment was something like this: *"Construct a device weighing less than 1.0 pound, no more than 8 inches tall and 8 inches wide, suitable for transporting a hard-boiled egg six feet without electric power or batteries."* We were to present our designs in a live performance for the class in one week on a Monday morning.

Moore's Law of Getting Things Done:
Never put off procrastination.

I blew off the project until Sunday afternoon. With the deadline less than 24 hours away, I drove to the nearest TG&Y store to purchase raw materials for the prototype of my revolutionary new egg transporter. I remember this journey of procurement well, as I was pulled over for driving 40 in a 30mph zone on a sleepy street just a few blocks from campus. I was exceedingly compliant and polite to the officer while seething inside. *Really? 40 in a 30?* The cop explained they were "cracking down" on speeders because the Tulsa Roughnecks, the brand new NASL soccer franchise, were hosting their first home match later that afternoon in TU's Skelly Stadium. The fine was $40, and for the rest of my life every time I drove on that street I flashed back to my first and only speeding ticket. (I borrowed from my beer fund to pay the ticket and never paid myself back. I've been living with the guilt ever since.)

When I was a kid Mom would occasionally let me get one of those flimsy balsa wood airplane kits from the toy aisle in the grocery store. The cheapest were simple gliders, with "Some Assembly Required." Using stubby child fingers barely dexterous enough for nostril digging, you would carefully pry apart the wings and tail piece and somehow force them through non-existent slots in the fuselage without snapping them into splinters.

If you managed to get the plane assembled, you could then experience the miracle of flight. Once. The plane would immediately loop and smash into the side of the house, never to fly again. Or it would crash in a massive imaginary fireball on the driveway, the terrified screams of the passengers and crew echoing in your tiny, undeveloped brain...until you went inside to watch cartoons.

Maybe you were lucky and launched a perfect, majestic flight, the little plane soaring high over the evergreen trees until it lodged in the rain gutter. You had to wait until Dad got home to grumpily retrieve it after backing the Impala out of the garage to get to the extension ladder.

If it was close to payday Mom might let me get the Deluxe Model: same non-durable balsa materials with a plastic propeller and a cool extra-long rubber band you hooked to a half-staple on the bottom of the fuselage. It even had landing gear, tiny red plastic wheels mounted on the thinnest of wires, clearly designed to last for only a single flight.

At TG&Y I grabbed a handful of the Deluxe model airplane packages—those big rubber bands were critical components in the propulsion system I had in mind—and a half-dozen basic gliders for spare parts. I also grabbed a couple of rolls of scotch tape and a bottle of Elmer's glue. I drove back to the dorm at exactly 29 miles per hour.

The rest of the day I experimented with several designs, but two things were quickly evident: First, college-age fingers that could deftly open beer bottles had no advantage over nose-cleaning kid fingers when it came to the Required Assembly. And second, my project was going to fail. Miserably.

I'm not saying there wasn't alcohol involved with my next decision. I'm saying I don't remember, which is completely different. In any case, I realized I had to accept the reality of an impending Negative Outcome. I decided to steer into the skid and go for laughs instead of a passing grade.

Monday morning I slid into my seat clutching the paper bag shielding my invention from prying eyes. The class was held in a large auditorium-style multi-purpose room. There was also a piano up front, pushed off to the side. The instructor announced the presentations, and I was stunned when mine was the first name called.

I stepped to the front, pulled the Balsanator 5000 Elastic-Powered Egg Mover from the bag and placed it on top of the piano. It was the shittiest mess of tape, glue, plastic, and balsa wood anyone would ever see, a total abomination. It looked like a Father's Day gift made by a 5-year-old with one hand tied behind his back.

The instructor handed me an egg with a skeptical frown but said nothing and stepped back. The entire class seemed mesmerized as I carefully placed the egg in the soft pouch constructed from multiple layers of scotch tape and paper clips. I hoped the egg was indeed hard-boiled as promised.

I primed the propulsion system by winding the propeller until the rubber band constricted into a continuous series of tiny knots. Determined to live on the edge, I kept spinning the propeller until a second layer of knots formed. I set my Frankenplane on top of the piano at the back, aimed it toward the audience, and without ado removed my thumb from the propeller.

The Balsanator 5000 screamed across the piano, grabbed a couple of feet of air, then spiraled into the floor and disintegrated. It was not even close to an "Oh, the Humanity!" moment. The egg was indeed hard-boiled and rolled several feet before stopping against the shoe of a guy in the front row. Everyone laughed, even the instructor, as I retrieved the egg and recovered the remains of my project.

It was easily the worst academic effort of my life, and powerfully confirmed what I had suspected for some time: I suck at mechanical stuff and do-it-yourself projects. Still, I got a bunch of laughs that morning and a fair amount of "street cred" for fearlessly humiliating myself before the instructor and the entire class. It was an experience to which I probably should have paid greater attention.

Rhetoric and Writing and Recycling

Another signpost on my journey toward self-actualization: my affinity and enthusiasm for writing. All freshman students were required to take Rhetoric and Writing I and II; I tested out of the first but enjoyed writing for the second class.

Our assignments included a research paper, fully documented with footnotes. In what I considered to be a flash of brilliance, I decided to use a research paper I wrote a couple of years earlier for my high school junior English class. The subject was "The Search for Extraterrestrial Life," graded A by my teacher. (The subject was yet another clue that went unnoticed at the time.)

In the TU library I located the same sources I used for my high school paper to update the bibliography and footnotes. I retyped the manuscript with only minor edits and received another A by my college instructor. Recycling my high school project saved me many hours I used to study for my engineering classes.

Fried Physics

We were also assigned a "personal essay" to write on any topic. After receiving a magical kick in the butt from my Muse, I was inspired to document the crazy antics of my high school physics class. I grabbed a chunk of green and white continuous-feed paper from a Fortran project and a red Bic pen (a stupid choice, very hard to see when typing). I wrote the draft in one long session and filled 11 oversize pages. It was over 5,000 words, way too long. I typed it up anyway, titled it *Fried Physics* and submitted the manuscript.

The teacher described it as "entertaining" and she "enjoyed it very much," then told me the assignment was to write a true, personal essay, not a fictional story. I explained that everything I described happened during my senior year in high school. Earl was also in the physics class, so I introduced him to the R&W professor and he confirmed the stories were true. I received an A on the paper, and really enjoyed writing those humorous stories.

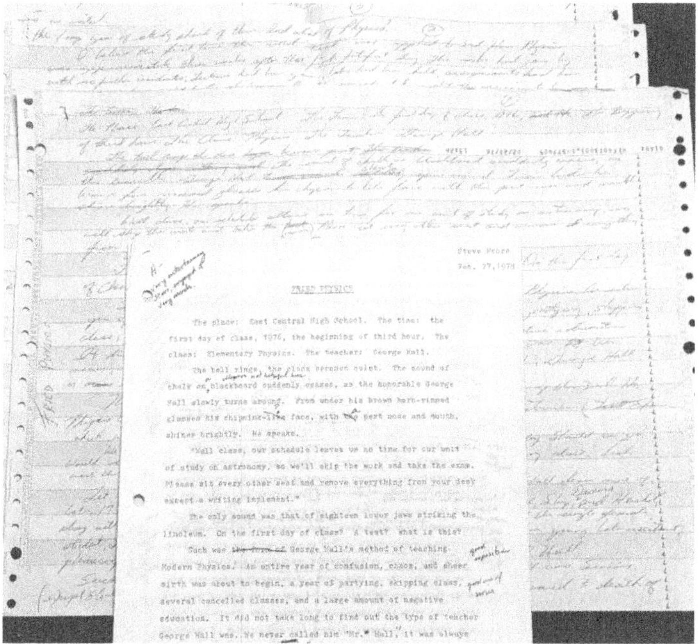

Steve [illegible]
Feb. 27, 197[illegible]

FRIED PHYSICS

The place: East Central High School. The time: the first day of class, 1976, the beginning of third hour. The class: Elementary Physics. The teacher: George Hall.

The bell rings, the class becomes quiet. The sound of chalk on blackboard suddenly ceases, as the Honorable George Hall slowly turns around. From under his brown horn-rimmed glasses his chipmunk-like face, with the pert nose and mouth, shines brightly. He speaks.

"Well class, our schedule leaves us no time for our unit of study on astronomy, so we'll skip the work and take the exam. Please sit every other seat and remove everything from your desk except a writing implement."

The only sound was that of eighteen lower jaws striking the linoleum. On the first day of class? A test? What is this?

Such was ~~the form of~~ George Hall's method of teaching Modern Physics. An entire year of confusion, chaos, and sheer mirth was about to begin, a year of partying, skipping class, several cancelled classes, and a large amount of negative education. It did not take long to find out the type of teacher George Hall was. We never called him "Mr." Hall, it was always

Fried Physics draft scribbled on green bar continuous computer paper and the final submittal version

The Power of BIO

My friend Trudi was in my high school class and we shared many classes at TU. At some point we started expressing our attitude toward the intense engineering work and adopted a reactionary philosophy: BIO (*bye-oh*). Blow it Off. I know, not all that creative, but it became our favorite meme at the time. (My friend Jim described us as pledges to Beta Iota Omicron - nice! Wish I'd thought of that.)

Embracing the spirit of BIO one day, instead of studying I dashed off a poem on the back cover of my college-ruled spiral physics notebook. It is reproduced below as originally written, with way too many commas and **a glaringly wrong word choice**, a variation of which would pop up later in my professional life.

(George Hall was my high-school Fried Physics teacher. Dr. Blais was my physics professor at T.U.)

Of Physics + Students.

George Hall would turn over in his grave, were he dead,
to see all of his physics student's grades in the red.
His chipmunk-like face would reveal such a frown,
and all of his students would really feel down.
Dr. Blais, although good, has no merciful soul.
He purposely flunked, all those students on his **role**.
Just who in the world, did Newton think he was,
Sitting around, thinking Calculus, and all of those laws.
Did we, the human race, ask him his opinion?
Why should we, T.U. students, visit Einstein's dominion?
I feel as though, there's some misunderstanding here
We should be elsewhere, slurping wine, and beer.
Oh the money's good, and is there anything else in life?
But an Engineer's education is full of internal strife,
and worry, anxiety, ulcers, and such,
Should anyone have to put up with this much?
A re-evaluation is needed soon, I think,
If grades were ships, we'd all start to sink.
But if nothing else, to escape misery and woe,
Screw up your courage, go out and BIO!

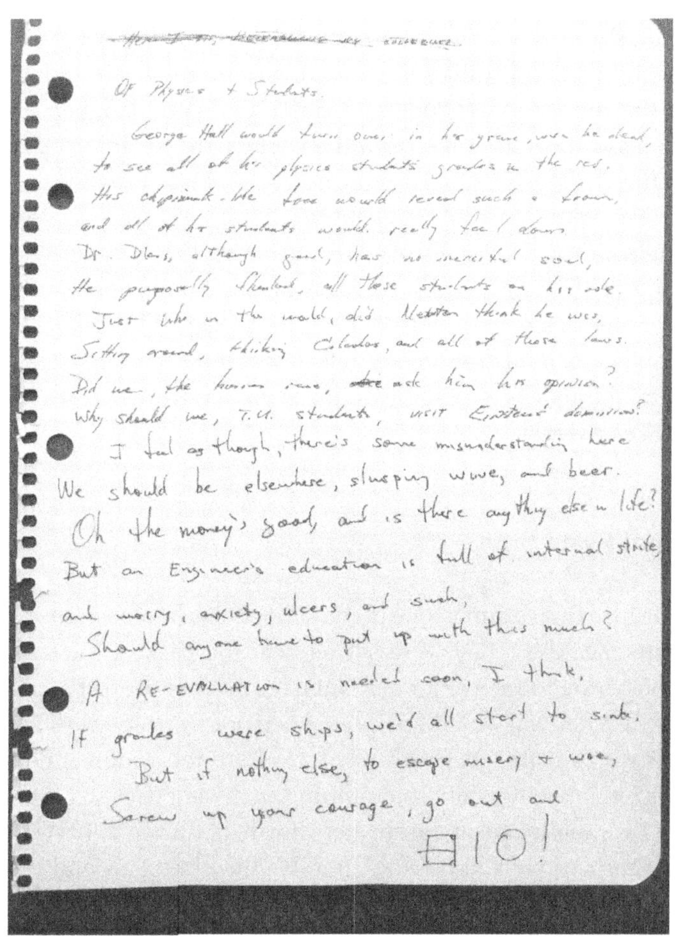

Of Physics + Students.

George Hall would turn over in his grave, were he dead,
to see all of his physics students grades in the red.
His chagrined face would reveal such a frown,
and all of his students would really feel down.
Dr. Dlers, although good, has no merciful soul,
He purposely flunked, all those students on his role.
Just who in the world, did Newton think he was,
Sitting around, thinking Calculus, and all of those laws.
Did we, the human race, ask him his opinion?
Why should we, T.U. students, visit Einstein's dominion?
I feel as though, there's some misunderstanding here
We should be elsewhere, slurping wine, and beer.
Oh the money's good, and is there anything else in life?
But an Engineer's education is full of internal strife,
and worry, anxiety, ulcers, and such,
Should anyone have to put up with this much?
A RE-EVALUATION is needed soon, I think,
If grades were ships, we'd all start to sink.
But if nothing else, to escape misery + woe,
Screw up your courage, go out and
[illegible]10!

Reservoir Engineering Class was a Real Snoozer

I fell asleep in Reservoir Engineering class one day. Something woke me up and all the guys sitting nearby were looking at me with shit-eating grins. I assumed I had been snoring. After a second or two I shifted to straighten up in my chair and jumped at the sound of a thunderous crash. Everyone laughed and the professor peered at me from the chalkboard for interrupting his lecture.

The guys had constructed a Leaning Tower of Reservoir Engineering, a tall stack of textbooks precariously balanced on the edge of the empty desk in front of me. Someone—I've always suspected Pat—had tied my shoe to the leg of the chair. When I moved my foot, the books fell. I was totally embarrassed but tremendously impressed with the group effort.

Teamwork!

Final Exam Stress

During a final exam in one of the Garage classrooms, four students were cheating. They were sitting near the back of the room and whispering to each other in a language none of the rest of us knew. The teacher was oblivious, even when one of us loudly said "shut up!" to alert the professor. He looked up for a moment, but did not get out of his chair, said nothing, and went back to his reading.

Eventually one of the cheaters finished, turned in his test to the teacher and walked out the door. He then hung around the open window at the back of the room and continued to whisper to the other three.

We were all pissed, but Pat was incensed. He went to the dean of engineering and complained about the cheating and the lack of monitoring by the professor. The Dean told Pat that without "proof" or the professor's input there was nothing he could do. This was an early lesson both in politics and in the Life's Not Fair category: Figures of authority often did nothing when informed of violations of ethics or rules.

Pat was involved in another final exam situation the following semester in Thermodynamics. After a week of intense Dead Week studying we were about to take our first final on Monday morning. As we settled into our chairs we noticed Pat looked red-faced and distraught, he had obviously been crying. We asked what was going on and he broke up, sobbing, and said his father had passed away suddenly early that morning. We were stunned and concerned for him, why was he here and not with his family? He said after all the studying that he wanted to go ahead and take the test.

The professor entered and passed out the exam. We started working but none of us could concentrate knowing what Pat was going through. Pat finished quicker than the rest of us, turned in his test and left without a word. After the test I took it upon myself to inform the professor what was going on. I was concerned that Pat might have done poorly and might be given a chance to retake it later.

I ran into the Thermo professor a few days later, and he thanked me for letting him know about Pat's situation. He said Pat had actually done well on the test. The rest of us, not so much. Pat had impressively handled a horribly stressful event, and his friends learned much from his example.

"Engineers in training, sir!"

Several professors encouraged us to take the Fundamentals of Engineering examination (also called the EIT: Engineer-in-Training). They suggested we take the eight-hour test as juniors without preparation for the experience, then take the test "for real" a year later as seniors.

I discussed strategy with a couple of friends. The test format was multiple choice, and there was no penalty for wrong answers. Since we were only taking the test for practice, we decided to work any problem we thought we could handle, but if it was beyond our experience or education, we would guess the answer and see what happens. One of us would always guess B, another C, and so on. My plan was to use C.

Shortly before 8am Saturday we settled into our seats in Garage 1 at North Campus. It was an open reference-book test, everyone had a calculator and a stack of textbooks. The sharpest students brought chargers for their calculators and arrived early to sit by an outlet. The exam covered a wide variety of engineering topics. I plowed right in and worked to solve as many problems as I could.

Four hours later the morning session ended. We bought sandwiches from the canteen vending machines, then sat on our cars in the parking lot for a half-hour before the afternoon session started at 1pm.

After only forty-five minutes, I'd had enough. I was auditing the test for grins, so I zipped down the answer sheet filling in C circles with my number two pencil. I turned in my exam, gathered my books and drove back to the dorm thinking of an ice-cold beer. I told myself I'd make a better effort next year.

Several months later I got my EIT results. I remember the moment very clearly: I was the only one home and I heard the mailman stuffing the box mounted outside below the kitchen window. Standing on the porch, I opened the envelope. The minimum passing score was 70, and my score was 71. I sat down on the step and laughed for several minutes. I had skipped most of the afternoon test session, but my "C" strategy had paid off. I learned later that my A, B and D friends were not as fortunate.

I didn't realize I had angered the Mighty Gods of Certification. Eight years later I would be punished, not once but multiple times.

Summer of 1978: Gerry Rafferty Songs and Sausage Biscuits

A family friend contacted me near the end of my freshman year in 1978 and offered me a summer job. I'd be assisting with the construction and testing of a new kind of pump in a joint research project run by TU and a local engineering firm.

The pump was being fabricated in a machine shop in North Tulsa. I worked for Kenny, a talented, slow-talking mechanic. He was both amused and slightly irritated at being assigned an assistant who had no relevant experience. Between smoke breaks, Kenny machined parts to exact specifications and fastened them together, frequently tossing a bad part and starting over. There wasn't much for me to do. My most important task each day was making the lunch run for everyone in the shop. I used my college education and math skills to organize a dozen different orders from various restaurants, map out an efficient driving route, and calculate each person's total and amount of change owed. The guys in the shop got quite a kick out of sending the college kid out for burgers and tacos every day.

Otherwise, I mostly sat on a stool, watched Kenny work, and listened to Top 40 music on the radio. Gerry Rafferty was having a great year; I'm positive I heard *Baker Street* and *Right Down the Line* a thousand times each that summer. I also frequently snacked on surprisingly tasty sausage biscuits from the break room vending machine.

One day I rode with Kenny in his truck to pick up some materials needed for the project. On the way back Kenny cut through a neighborhood and parked in the empty lot of a dive bar with a CLOSED sign in the window. He banged on the door and a woman let us in. She locked the door and Kenny immediately pulled her close, put his hand on her chest and kissed her. She didn't seem to mind and groped him right back. I stood nearby and pretended to admire the dingy ambiance of the place.

When they unclenched, Kenny introduced me to Ellen. She handed each of us a long neck beer and Kenny challenged me to a game of pool. It was 11am, we were both on the clock, and I had no idea what to do. A few shots into the game, Kenny told me to keep playing and followed Ellen into a back room. It was soon obvious that Kenny was fully engaged in another pump project. I won the game of eight ball by running the table—that's what I told Kenny, anyway—and practiced until the friendly couple returned. For the next two hours we played pool and drank beer, with Kenny frequently skipping his turn to make out with Ellen right in front of me. They both seemed to enjoy my discomfort.

A few weeks later the prototype was complete, and we transported the pump to a mechanical engineering lab at TU for testing. The design didn't work as planned and the project was suspended. My summer was only half over and I had nothing to do. Eventually I was assigned to work with an electrical engineering professor, and I spent several weeks cleaning labs, inventorying equipment, and hauling junk to the dump. It was a bummer of a summer, but I earned enough money to pay for my dorm room during my sophomore year.

Summer of 1979: Roustabout
Hominy, Oklahoma

For my sophomore summer I accepted an offer from Union Oil of California to work as a roustabout in the Osage Hominy oil field, 70 miles north and west of Tulsa. My pay rate was around $15 per hour, with time and a half pay for overtime, and double time and a half pay for holidays (Memorial Day and July 4th). It was a significant improvement from my pay four years earlier at Bastard Robbers.

A company rep told me their summer hire the previous year had rented an upstairs room in a house owned by a retired couple who lived in the town of Hominy. Mr. Wilcoxson was in a wheelchair after a stroke, and Mrs. Wilcoxson was Aunt Bee straight out of Mayberry. The upstairs apartment had a complete kitchen and half-bath and was accessed by stairs just inside the back door of the house. I could use the shower downstairs behind the kitchen.

I could have commuted from Tulsa to Hominy, but it would have required two and half hours of driving each day with long, hot hours of work sandwiched in the middle. For a couple of hundred bucks a month it was easier to stay in Hominy and travel home on weekends. It was the right choice, but it made for a long, lonely summer. There was a tastee-freeze style drive-in, a gas station with snacks, and a small grocery store. I ate a lot of sandwiches, canned chicken lo-mein and frozen TV dinners. There was nothing to do in town. One evening I spotted a cute girl in a corvette parked at the drive-in. I kept an eye out for her the rest of the summer, but she must have been passing through town. Another night I decided to make the 50-mile round trip to Pawhuska just to get a pizza from the Hut.

One day after work, as I entered the house through the back door, I heard Mr. Wilcoxson calling out. His wife was away on an errand, and he had managed to get out of his wheelchair and onto the toilet. He asked for help to get off the pot and back in his chair.

Of course I agreed but felt nervous and awkward. It was my first experience assisting someone in a highly personal situation. I helped him stand and have a vivid memory of him saying, very slowly, "a little higher" as I pulled his underwear up for him. I remember thinking at the time what a perfectly normal request: facing long hours sitting in his chair, Mr. Wilcoxson wanted to make sure his underwear was comfortable. Working together we got him seated in the wheelchair, and he thanked me as I rolled him back to his favorite spot in the living room to watch television.

Roustabout Work

With apologies for the tired cliché of using a dictionary definition, Merriam-Webster (2022) describes ***roustabout*** as:

> 1: deckhand or longshoreman
> 2: an ***unskilled*** or semi-skilled laborer, especially in an oil field or refinery
> 3: ***a circus worker*** who erects and dismantles tents, cares for the grounds, and ***handles animals and equipment***
> 4: ***a person with no permanent home or regular occupation*** also: ***one who stirs up trouble***

During the summer of 1979 I was living the roustabout life: I stayed in a temporary home working a temporary job in an oil field carnival. I had no skills and did odd jobs like lubricating pumping units and mowing the grass around the office while trying not to chop up any snakes. Meanwhile, the veteran performers had some laughs watching the college rube bumble around.

I caught a ride to work at 5:30 each morning from an operator named Dick. We stopped at a gas station to get a half-dozen bags of ice, then drove 15 minutes to the field office. Along the way we passed by the new medium-security prison. I remember a highway sign warning that hitchhikers could be inmates.

More dangerous than an escaped felon was the daily risk of asphyxiation and exposure to toxic gas. Dick was quite skilled in the *fine art* of venting methane. He derived some creepy pleasure from my horrified reactions, and never rolled his window down to ensure the nasty vapors floated my direction. When we arrived at the field office I tumbled out of the truck, gasping for fresh air. We filled the water coolers mounted on the crew trucks with ice, then went inside for the morning meeting.

Dennis was the ringmaster, a grumpy, grizzled foreman who sent the crews out each morning with their assignments. He also decided which operator would be lucky enough to have me as his helper for the day.

John, the pumper, was flabbergasted one afternoon when I admitted I had never learned to drive a vehicle with a standard transmission. He immediately skidded to a stop and insisted I get behind the wheel. He taught me how to clutch and shift, and by the end of the day I had a valuable skill I would use the rest of my life. I had one close call a few weeks later, when John asked me to move the truck to make room for some equipment. The truck was parked on a steep slope, and I had not mastered how to engage the clutch and accelerator quick enough to avoid rolling backwards first for several feet, nearly flattening a couple of the hands.

Sometimes I'd ride with Danny, who was a bit closer to my age. He was super friendly and invited me to his home one night to shoot pool and have dinner with his family. One morning we made a quick side-trip to check on a half-dozen marijuana plants growing near one of the more isolated well locations. I found an old sign for an abandoned well on the ground not far from the weed patch, and Danny told me to keep it as a souvenir of my summer.

All My Children

Whoever I was riding with, we always tried to get back to the office by noon for an hour lunch break. There was an old beat-up television in the break room that could only receive one channel, and the entire gang of tough field hands (even Dennis) had become addicted to the daytime soap *All My Children*. Danny was particularly smitten with the fiendish Erica Kane. For many years whenever I came across a reference to Susan Lucci, I flashed back to that blistering summer in the oil field and watching *AMC* every day while munching peanut butter sandwiches and Fritos.

The Kid Stays Safe and In the Picture

Most of the time I rode with Jim, a former schoolteacher. Years earlier, Danny had been one of his students. Jim quit teaching to work in the oil field for better pay and benefits. He was still an excellent instructor, and I learned a great deal from him. We drove to various leases and facilities to change out seals in water plant pumps, grease giant Mark II pumping units, and haul joints of tubing from well locations to the yard.

One thing everyone took seriously was keeping me safe: no one wanted to be responsible for the college kid losing a "calculator finger" or two. (There would be a monster stack of incident reports to fill out.) Besides the occasional sunburn, the worst thing that happened to me was getting a big whiff of noxious gas from the underside of an old water tank we tipped over to haul off. I tossed my lunch and had to take the afternoon off.

Jim drove a big winch truck, which had a steel cable wrapped around a spool with a serious looking hook attached to the end of the line. To haul tubing between locations, we looped the winch line around a joint of pipe and hoisted it onto the bed of the truck. We'd get a half dozen joints loaded, secure them with tie-downs, and drive to the target location. We reversed the process to offload and stack the pipe, then drove back to the well site for another load. It was tedious and repetitive, but you had to stay sharp to avoid crushed fingers or toes.

Frequent late-afternoon thunderstorms would pop up and it was common for lightning to knock out the power and wells would go down. Oil prices were up (1979 Energy Crisis), cash flow was king, so Jim and I drove around in the rain restarting pumping units. Jim taught me an Important Safety Tip which I've always remembered: brush the control box with the back of your hand first before restarting the unit. If the box was live when you clutched the handle, the electricity would cause your muscles to clench, preventing you from letting go and risking electrocution.

"Get Jurassic back in the truck!"

After restarting a pumping unit located in a small valley, we got stuck in the muddy road as it started to rain again. We had a radio in the truck but Jim didn't want to interrupt the rest of the crew until we tried to help ourselves first. He stayed at the truck to operate the winch, and I started up the hill dragging the hook and several yards of steel line. My target was a large tree about halfway up the slope. I sloshed through the mud in my heavy steel-toed boots, the winch line cutting into my shoulder. It was tough going and I slipped several times. Eventually I reached the tree and took a brief rest. I had a hell of a time getting the hook around the tree before finally snapping it onto the line.

I gave Jim a thumbs up, just like in the movies. He put the truck in neutral and started the winch. When the truck was free from the mud, I unhooked the line and Jim wound it back on the spool. He drove up the hill and I climbed into the cab.

"At least I wasn't attacked by a Dilophosaurus," I said.

No, I didn't say that. But if you thought the scene above sounded familiar, imagine my surprise 14 years later in 1993, sitting in a theater watching *Jurassic Park*. The devious Dennis Nedry (Wayne Knight) drives his jeep through the jungle in a rainstorm to deliver his precious Barbasol can of dino-embryos to the dock. He skids off the road and gets stuck. Nedry struggles to attach a winch cable to a tree to pull the jeep free, and suddenly

I'm back in Osage County reliving my version of the same scene. It was a strange, surreal experience. (If you search the Internet for "Dennis Nedry Death Jurassic Park" you can watch video clips of the scene.)

Eli the Welder and His Traveling Library

During most of the second half of my summer I helped Eli the Welder. He was a contract hand who had enough work to be in the field every day and had become a regular member of the crew. He was straight from Central Casting: crusty and cantankerous, like Quint from *Jaws*. He dressed in thick protective denim with a baseball cap flipped around backwards to accommodate his welding helmet. He had a bristly mustache that was possibly an aggressive extension of nose hair, and constantly adjusted his eyeglasses while working in the sweaty summer heat. His favorite phrase was "Aw, horse shit!" He combined and stretched the words so they sounded thick and slow: "Horssshhhit."

Things were different back in 1979. Eli maintained a well-stocked library of porn magazines stashed behind the seats in his truck. He called them his f___ books. There were several well-worn issues of *Female Body Part 1* and *Female Body Part 2*. The massive year-end *Holiday Spectacular XXXtravaganza Special Edition of Body Parts 1+2* was particularly popular with the crew.

Sometimes a project required working in a small metal shop near the field office. Each time we entered Eli would say hello to Ashley, the centerfold he'd pinned to a support post just inside the door. Most of the time we were in the field to isolate and repair flowline leaks. After supporting the line with a winch cable, Eli would cut out the bad spot with a torch. He'd fabricate a patch from a spare piece of pipe and weld it in place. Meanwhile, I'd check out a book from the library and sit on the ground in the shade of his truck. Eventually Eli would yank off his helmet, remove his glasses, and holler "Okay, Junior, your turn!" I'd use a wire brush to clean the welds while Eli poured water over his head to cool off. (In 2011, I would recall my time with Eli when a manager mentioned a creative use for a wire brush. Moore on that later.)

My last two weeks of summer were tough, helping return an old free-water knockout vessel to service. Idle for many years, it was in bad shape. Eli cut a man-sized hole in one end to let it air out for a couple of days, then we crawled inside to shovel the nasty muck from the bottom and scrub the walls. Over the next several days, Eli cut out a half-dozen bad spots from the walls, then welded huge, curved metal patches into place. He worked non-stop in 30-minute sessions, standing inside the hot tank wearing his gloves and helmet. I helped every way I could. It was brutal work in miserable conditions.

I gained tremendous experience that summer and learned a lot about the practical work required from competent field crews to implement projects conceived in corporate offices. I have a huge amount of respect for the drilling crews and field hands of the oil and gas industry. They literally work to keep everyone's lights on and wheels turning.

Summer of 1980: Engineering Assistant
Woodward, Oklahoma

Oil was still booming in 1980 and industry demand for Petroleum Engineers was strong. My roustabout gig in Hominy went well enough (no fatalities, only minor injuries and zero lawsuits) that I was offered another summer job by the same company as an engineering assistant in their Woodward field office in western Oklahoma. I was grateful for the opportunity and accepted the offer. Late in the spring semester I started working on the logistics of moving across the state and finding a place to live for three months.

During finals week I answered a knock on my dorm room door. I recognized Tim from campus. (Years later I realized Tim looked like a college fraternity version of Scott Farkus from *A Christmas Story*.)

Tim was a petroleum engineering major who had landed a summer job with a drilling company, also in Woodward. He asked if I was interested in rooming together to save money. It sounded like a no-brainer and I quickly agreed. It turned out it did require some brain work and I should have checked him out first.

My folks had set me up with everything I needed, including kitchen utensils, dishes, and linens. Along with clothes and stereo, my car was loaded. I had planned to meet Tim in Woodward, then look for a place to live. The day before leaving I got a surprise call from Tim. He "forgot" to tell me he didn't have a car. Not only did he need a ride to Woodward, he also had to move out of the frat house, which meant taking all of his junk with us. We repacked my car to the gills (FYI, the gills on a 1970 Oldsmobile Delta 88 are located just behind the rear wheels) and headed west. After a four-hour drive we checked into a cheap hotel, and the next day a very nice apartment manager let us rent a furnished two-bedroom unit with a month-to-month lease.

Forty-eight hours later I realized it was going to be a long, crappy summer.

Always Check for Water Before Diving into the Roommate Pool

Walking to the apartment from the parking lot after my second day of work, I was stopped by the office manager who had set us up with our rental. She told me Tim, who had not yet started his new job, had disturbed some of the other tenants by spending the afternoon sunbathing shirtless, drinking beer, and listening to loud rock music *while lying at the bottom of the empty swimming pool.*

The pool would not be cleaned and filled for use for another two weeks, and several of the neighbors were concerned about the strange young man who had set up camp in the deep end. She described Tim's behavior as "weird and off-putting." I told the manager I'd speak to Tim, and as I walked to the apartment an imaginary Nut Wagon screeched to a halt in my head and the Uh-Oh Squad rolled out.

The first line from a nursery rhyme kept repeating in my mind: *Tom Tom the Baker's Son.* I silently replaced Tom with Tim, and Baker with a word that started with A and ended with hole.

Now that's just embarrassing

I was working regular office hours, but Tim was a roughneck on a rig working shifts around the clock. He had a tough, dirty job and was also a slob. The EPA could have declared his bedroom a hazardous toxic waste site, so you can imagine how the bathroom looked.

About three weeks into the summer, Tim wanted to chat. He said he was disgusted when he took a shower and there were hairs stuck to the soap. He requested I clean them off before getting out of the shower.

I laughed so hard I fell to the floor. He was clueless and just stared at me. It took me a while to pull it together, then I told him I totally agreed with him about the disgusting soap bar. I took him to my room and showed him a plastic container on top of my dresser with a bar of soap inside.

"I never touch your soap in the shower, I use my own and store it here. The hairs are yours, pal." Tim looked like the family dog caught peeing on the rug. I told him I'd appreciate it if HE would clean the soap before stepping out of the shower. He didn't say anything, just walked back into the living room. The soap never came up again, until now.

Pro Tip: Never put the entire cow in the freezer.

A month or so into the summer, Tim became unemployed. I don't know what happened, but somehow he was FIRED from his SUMMER JOB after being RECRUITED as a TU PETROLEUM ENGINEERING STUDENT on campus by a DRILLING COMPANY. It's the only time I've ever heard of something like that happening.

Tim now had time on his hands but was stuck at the apartment without a car. At least there was water in the pool by then.

I came home from work one night and Tim proposed a trip to the grocery store. He showed me a newspaper ad for ground beef on sale: ten pounds for $1.29 or something. I don't remember the exact cost, but I do remember the amount. Here's why:

We drive to the store and sure enough, Tim finds a giant shrink-wrapped package, ten pounds of ground round. He said we could freeze it and have plenty for a long time. I agreed and told him to be sure and break it into smaller packages before freezing or it would be useless.

The following weekend my parents and sister visited from Tulsa for my birthday, and we decided to grill burgers at the RV park where they were camping. I went to the fridge and discovered a slab of frozen beef the size of the monolith in *2001: A Space Odyssey*. Tim had tossed it in the freezer without separating it first into smaller, usable chunks.

Dad got a hacksaw from the RV, and he and I took turns sawing off a corner small enough to thaw in a skillet. It was a good reminder that if you wanted something done right, you should do it yourself.

How to Train Your Roommate

Somehow, Tim managed to find another roughneck job with another company. He'd catch a ride with another hand and get home well after midnight. Thanks to Mom, we had a skillet, pots, dishes and silverware, everything needed to fry an egg or sauté Hamburger Helper. Tim would cook himself a meal at 2am, leave the dirty dishes anywhere and crash in bed. The next day I'd have to wash the dirty dishes before I could use them for my lunch or dinner.

To cut expenses further we invited my friend Randy to move in. He was also majoring in engineering at TU, and like Tim had a summer roughneck job on a rig drilling in the area. Randy also had to deal with Tim's dirty dishes before he could cook for himself.

I told Randy about the thing with the soap and we came up

with a plan. For the next couple of weeks Randy would be working a day shift on the rig, so we decided we would eat out for every single meal. Sonic, McDonald's, Pizza Hut, whatever. We wouldn't wash the dishes until Tim did so first. To our surprise it took nearly a week before Tim spoke up. It went something like this:

TIM: "Hey, guys? I noticed that neither of you have been cleaning up after you use the plates and skillets and stuff."

US: "HA HA HA HA HA HA." (Pause to suck in air) "HA HA HA HA HA HA."

TIM: "What?"

Eventually we were able to communicate effectively again, and informed Tim that the dirty dishes and skillet in the sink were those he left there himself after his dinner. From LAST TUESDAY. We told him we ate every meal out for days, waiting for him to figure it out and do his share of cleaning up.

He acted like he didn't believe us, but he did put in a slightly better effort after our stunt.

Gone, Like a Greyhound Down the Road

I tired of living with Tim, who somehow lost his second job too. It's possible the rig finished drilling a well and the work ran out. It's also possible he managed to get himself terminated twice in just a few weeks. In either case, Tim was now home 24/7. He watched my TV, listened to my stereo, and worshipped the sun every afternoon. He had switched careers mid-summer to full-time apartment-dwelling pool rat.

In early August, Tim started talking about finding a way back to Tulsa. He needed to be at school a couple of weeks before the semester to prepare for fraternity rush. I was excited at the prospect of living my last few weeks in Woodward without Tim and helped him come up with a plan: he could catch a bus to Tulsa and take as much of his stuff as he could carry. I'd bring the rest of his stuff when I moved back to TU a few weeks later.

The day finally came. The bus departed at 1pm, and I told my boss I'd be late coming back from lunch. I picked up Tim at the apartment and it was like a scene from a 70s sitcom. I tossed his gear in my car and hurried him along so he wouldn't miss the bus or change his mind. Like the lyrics in one of my favorite Kansas songs, I wanted him gone, like a greyhound down the road.

I dropped him off at the station and said good luck (wishing it to myself as well.) I pulled away, circled the block, and parked down the street with a view of the bus and people waiting to board. I had to verify with my own eyes that Tim got on that bus.

After the last passenger stepped on board, I kept my eyes on the door to make sure Tim didn't get off at the last second. The bus finally departed, and I followed it in my car for a couple of miles, doing a happy dance in my mind before finally returning to the office.

After work I picked up two 8-packs of Little Kings and a pizza. I celebrated being Timless all evening. Randy got home around ten to find me sprawled on the couch in fine form, a half-dozen empty green bottles on the coffee table. The Democratic Party National Convention was the only thing on television that night, broadcast live on all three networks. I had turned off the sound and was lip-syncing my own speech.

"Furthermore, if elected President, I guarantee individual bars of soap for all Americans and a ten-pound slab of beef in every freezer..."

Easy Day, Easy Money

The Union Oil of California office in Woodward was small and staffed with a petroleum engineer, a superintendent, two foremen and an administrative assistant. I worked at a small table against the wall in engineer Pat's office. Pat graduated from college just six years earlier, but like Eli the previous summer, insisted on calling me "junior." (I vowed at the time to never refer to an intern or young engineer as junior. So far, so good.)

It turned out I wasn't hired to do much of anything. It was basically a recruiting program for the Company: Pay me well to observe and learn and hopefully I would consider joining the Company a year later after graduating.

The first six weeks of summer I updated individual well production plots with oil, water, and gas volumes from field reports. I did this manually, using drafting pens and the straight edge of a triangle. Computer databases and decline curve analysis software were still years away. If you needed a group plot summarizing multiple wells, you created a ledger table, added the volumes using a calculator, and plotted the results. It was tedious and boring, but necessary for well surveillance and trend analysis.

A typical day in the office:

7 - 8am Arrive at office, drink coffee, talk in the break room.
8 - 9:15 Update production graphs at my table.
9:15 - 10:45 Engineer and I take company car to nearby cafe for breakfast. The place was always crowded, and every day without fail someone from a service company would pick up the tab.
10:45 - 12:45pm Return to office, work.
12:45 - 1:45 Break for lunch. Usually went to apartment, not hungry after late breakfast
1:45 - 5:30 Update production graphs at my table.

I was aware it was a boom time in the industry, but still thought this was a ridiculously easy way to earn a very nice paycheck. I had learned how to design a pumping unit and rod string in a class at TU, and the engineer showed me how it was done in the real world. It was mostly a cookbook process laid out on pre-printed forms with the Company logo at the top.

Occasionally I'd accompany one of the foremen to the field to observe a workover or installation of a compressor. One morning on the way to the field in a company truck, the foreman made a blind left turn around a semi-truck and another pickup truck hit us head on. No one was hurt. The truck driver worked for an oilfield service company and recognized the foreman. He started apologizing profusely even though it clearly wasn't his fault. I was gaining useful insight into the nature of relationships between oil and service companies.

Engineers in Company Cars Getting Stupid, Part 1: Western Oklahoma

Engineer Pat needed to meet with the field hands at a waterflood project in Farnsworth, Texas, and brought me along. The only memory I have of the trip is the two-hour drive to get there.

We stopped for gas, then Pat told me to drive the rest of the way to the field office. In 1980 the national speed limit was still 55 miles per hour, as it was when I learned to drive 5 years earlier. I settled into the driver's seat and we cruised along nicely for 20 minutes in very little traffic.

Pat tilted his seat back as if he was going to nap and said, "Okay, Junior. That was the last town before the state line. You can goose it up to 90 now."

I kept it on sixty and glanced at Pat.

"Seriously, jack it up. Won't be any highway patrol cars until we hit Texas."

I increased speed to 65, and Pat gave me a look that suggested he was about to repo my Man Card.

"C'mon, get going!"

The company vehicle was a new LTD Crown Vic, easily capable of smooth cruising at 90 miles an hour. But I wasn't. For my entire driving life my max speed was 65, maybe 70 a couple of times passing a truck on a highway. I slowly increased my speed to 75, then 80. The ride was smooth overall, but I could feel more vibration in the steering wheel.

The needle lines up on 85. My hands were clammy. I tried to concentrate on the road but could sense Pat grinning at my obvious discomfort. Finally, 90. We're rolling down the highway like Bachman-Turner Overdrive and I'm thinking if one of my hands slips, we'll flip over eleventy-eight times and end up *Flat as a Pancake*.

At that speed it wasn't driving so much as aiming, just keeping the car centered between the lines. There wasn't any scenery to distract me; the country was so flat you could see the grain silos in the next town 30 minutes before you arrived. After a while Pat piped up again.

"There used to be a tree over there, but they had to take it out. People kept crashing into it."

It was a "you had to be there" moment, but to this day I consider it one of my top 20 favorite jokes of all time. I nearly lost control of the car laughing.

Summer Hire Boom Parties

Oil boomed during all four of my college years, with companies aggressively recruiting engineers the entire time. In July of the previous summer (1979), I drove from Hominy to Oklahoma City to attend the Company's summer hire picnic. High and lowlights of the trip included:

Being "beered and dined" at a barbeque lunch by a number of executives who talked up the Company and explained why I should consider working for them after graduation.

Splitting into small groups, each hosted by a Company rep, for drinks and dinner in a 5-star restaurant. Many of us were not legal drinking age but it didn't come up once the entire night.

Unsuccessfully hitting on Lisa, a summer hire I recognized from TU. I'd like to think I was too drunk, but it was probably my sparkling engineering personality that turned her off.

My first trip to a gentlemen's club, where I learned to be patient during a 3-song dance set.

Nightcaps in the bar of our hotel, where we listened to a fine singer, Sylvester Smith III. I purchased his album during a break and Sylvester signed it for me:

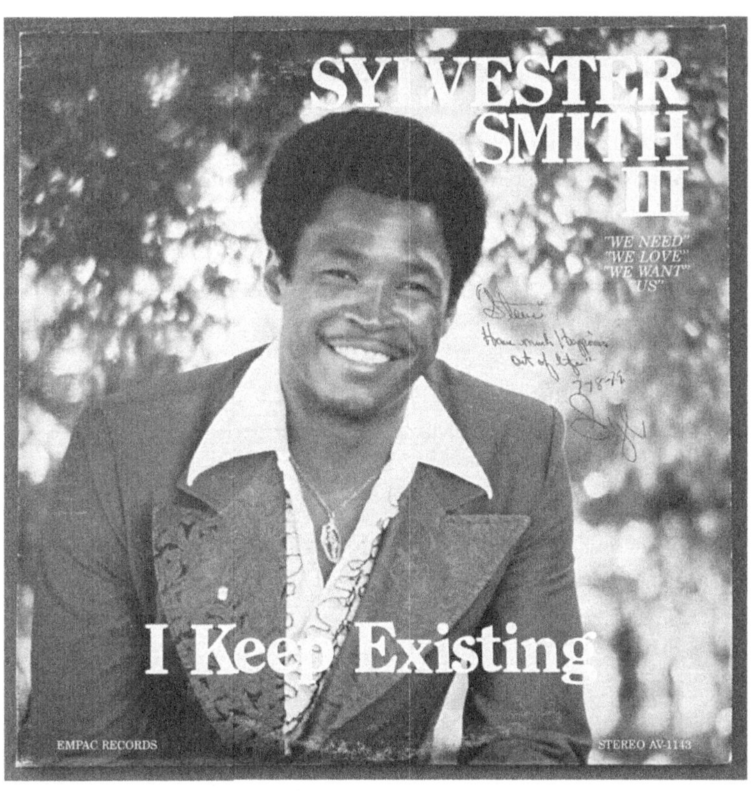

"Steve, Have much happiness out of life – Syl 7-18-79"

In June 1980 the summer hire extravaganza happened to fall on my 21st birthday. I drove to OKC again, this time with Engineer Pat. After the official party ended, Pat took me to a nightclub to celebrate. A woman friend of Pat joined us, and they both encouraged me to have a good time. I was probably drinking whisky sours as it was the only non-beer drink I knew to order at the time. When the song *Funkytown* by Lipps, Inc. started, Pat's friend pulled me up to dance. I promptly fell over onto the next table. The guys set me upright, shoved me towards the girl and yelled, "Go get her, Tiger!"

We joined the crowd and she danced while I gyrated, trying not to fall down. *Funkytown* ended and a slow song started. The girl was a good sport and held me close. Think 1980s rom com: the sad, inebriated nerd leans heavily on a girl who struggles to keep him on his feet while feeling sorry for him. It was not my finest hour.

We ended up in a booth at Denny's about 2am. I wasn't hungry, and when Pat's Mexican omelet arrived I bolted for the men's room.

I wish I remembered more about my 21st birthday, some of it must have been fun.

The Future Looked Bright

At the end of my second summer working for Union, I was given a copy of *Sign of the 76*, a history of the company, and was told the Company would contact me in a few months to discuss opportunities after graduation.

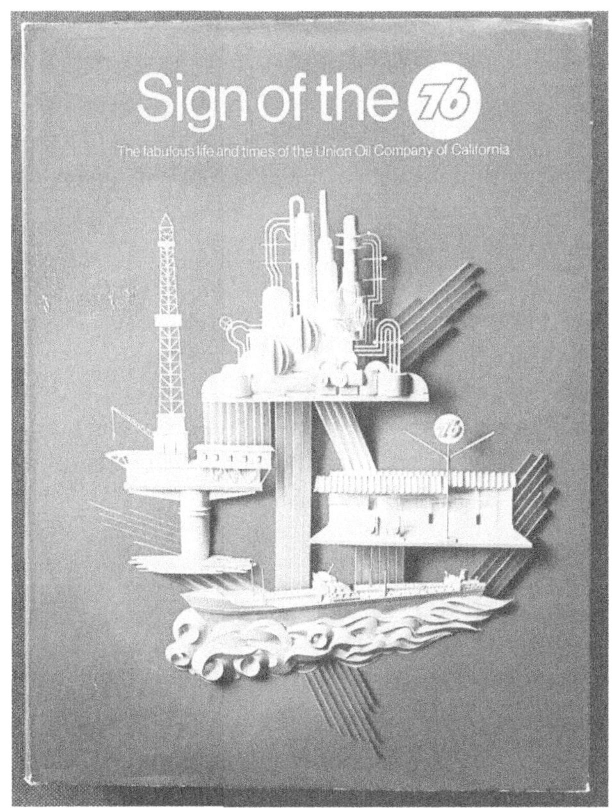

Exxon Recruiter: "Mind doing me a favor?"

In the fall of 1980, oil and gas companies competed furiously to hire graduating engineers. We scrambled to sign up for on-campus interviews the old fashioned way, writing our names on clipboards in the tiny TU Placement office. It was a free-for-all and we all snagged as many slots as possible.

If you were lucky your interview time was between or after classes, but since engineering courses were taught at North Campus and the interviews were in the Student Union on the main campus, we all had to skip a lot of classes to meet with the recruiters. At the time I thought it was ironic to miss a lot of senior level classes that had the most relevant content for our profession and were taught by the best professors.

Some interviews went better than others. I specifically remember my visit with Exxon did not go well. It was clear they were screening for brilliant 4.0 GPAs who wore expensive suits. After the interview I joked with friends that the Exxon recruiter asked me to drop a postcard in the mail slot for him as I left. I glanced at the card, it was a polite rejection note, addressed to me.

Those Exxon guys didn't waste any time.

The Accidental Reservoir Engineer

Three and half-years after receiving a scholarship and Cross pen and pencil set from Tenneco, I sat across the table from the recruiting engineer from Tenneco's Oklahoma City office. By then I had completed a few interviews and had improved my responses to the typical questions. When asked what kind of petroleum engineering work I was most interested in, I was ready. I had no interest in being a drilling engineer, I was shooting for a position in either reservoir or production engineering. I should have considered more carefully the order in which I expressed my preferences.

"I'm interested in opportunities in reservoir—" I didn't get to express my alternate and equal preference for production engineering as the Tenneco guy interrupted.

"Reservoir engineer? Really? That's great! *I'm* a reservoir engineer. All I've heard from Tulsa students all day is production or drilling. You're the first guy who wants to be a reservoir engineer."

Okay, I knew what to do. I wanted a job, and this guy wanted me to want to be a reservoir engineer. I smiled and nodded, and the rest of the interview went very well. A few days later I received a letter inviting me to visit the reservoir engineering department of Tenneco's Pacific Coast Division in Bakersfield, California.

Writer and mythologist Joseph Campbell, in an interview many years ago, described how a person can look back at the seemingly random events of his or her life and discover how easy it is to "connect the dots." You realize with the benefit of hindsight that you really had no choice but to arrive at the place where you are now.

The Tenneco recruiter responded with such enthusiasm to the word "reservoir" that my people-pleasing instinct kicked into high gear, and 40 years later I was forecasting wells for yet another year-end reserves report.

I always wondered how my career would have turned out if I had led with the word *production* instead of reservoir.

Bakersfield Plant Visit

Shortly after the on-campus interviews, PE seniors received offers of plant visits, expense-paid trips to oil and gas company offices at various locations. I was not familiar with the term, but for a research project in high school I toured a refinery plant in Tulsa and talked to a chemical engineer. I assumed a "plant visit" meant I had successfully completed the interview process and the trip would be a low-stress recruiting tour of the division office to meet the staff and scope out Bakersfield as a potential place to live. I was only partially correct.

Tenneco made all the arrangements, including a Monday flight from Tulsa to LAX, followed by a short puddle-jump flight to Bakersfield, arriving late afternoon. It was only the second time I had flown, and I was stunned to discover that my seat was in first class, and I was the only person in the section. I had the complete attention of the first-class flight attendant, who seemed amused at my inexperience as a first-class traveler. I enjoyed a couple of in-flight beers, and was quite impressed by the steak lunch, easily the best meal on a plane I would ever have. I learned later that company policy was first class tickets for business travel, ostensibly to facilitate working on company business during the flight. (First-class travel was discontinued a couple of years later when the Boom went bust.)

My flight landed in Bakersfield's small and easy airport around 4pm, and I was met by three young reservoir engineers who had been with the company for a couple of years. One guy urged us to hurry to get to the restaurant, the Monday night football game started at 5pm on the west coast. We had drinks and a great dinner at Cask & Cleaver, then I was dropped off at the hotel.

The next day the same guys treated me to breakfast before driving to the office. One of them handed me an itinerary, and I glanced at it on the way to the reservoir engineering manager's office. I was startled to learn I had a dozen short interviews scheduled throughout the day, with a break for lunch. I was unprepared for this but there was nothing to do but go for it.

I learned a lot about the Company and the role of the reservoir engineer and became more comfortable as the day went on. My last interview was with Harold, Division Production Manager. He asked if all my questions had been answered, and I complimented his high-quality reservoir engineering team.

Harold said he had heard good things about me. I found out later the reservoir engineer assigned to host me collected opinions from everyone I spoke with and passed them on to Management. Harold pulled a folded note from his shirt pocket and slid it across the table like a scene in a movie. The Company was offering me a reservoir engineering position in the Pacific Coast Division in Bakersfield, at the starting salary written on the note. I was totally surprised and struggled with a quick decision: do I open the note, read the salary, and react? Or do I play it cool like this happens every day and put the note in my pocket unread? I slipped the note into my coat pocket and thanked him as graciously and enthusiastically as possible. He noticed the Tenneco pen and pencil clipped to my shirt pocket and I explained I received it after accepting the Company's petroleum engineering scholarship three years earlier.

The VP handed me back to my host and we headed for the airport. (I peeked at Harold's note and the salary blew my mind.) We made a quick stop on Panarama Drive so I could see the humongous Kern River oil field located just outside of town. It was an incredible sight: thousands of pumping units stretched to the horizon inside a maze of gleaming insulated pipes delivering steam to injection wells for heating the thick, heavy crude in the shallow reservoirs. I thought back to my summer in Hominy helping Eli patch leaky flowlines. The miles of pipe in Kern River Field was a welder's fantasy.

At the airport I thanked my host and boarded the small plane for the short flight to LAX. I was unbelievably jazzed and a bit stunned. I had survived a long day of interviews and after three and a half years studying engineering, the Holy Grail was in my pocket: a job offer. I looked at the note again to confirm my starting salary was $27,000 per year.

Thirty minutes later I was wishing I had some of that money in my pocket. My return trip to Tulsa was anything but smooth.

The Kindness of Strangers

We took off from Meadows Field in Bakersfield for the quick 45-minute flight to LAX. After 20 minutes in the air the captain announced that LAX just shut down due to fog. The pilot explained the options: we could divert to Burbank airport, located on the other side of Los Angeles, then take taxis to LAX and catch our connecting flights when the airport eventually reopened. Or we could return to Bakersfield and book alternate flights from there. Then the captain did something I'd never heard of before (or since): *He asked the passengers to talk it over and let him know what the group decided to do.*

I was stunned by this unusual display of democracy in action, but I was screwed either way. If we landed in Burbank, I had no money for a cross-town taxi. If I missed my connecting flight at LAX, I had no idea how to book another. All of my travel arrangements had been made and paid for by Tenneco. I had about twenty dollars in my wallet and no credit card. (This was many years before college kids qualified for credit by simply having a pulse.)

Imagine yourself in 1980, stuck in a strange city without resources, using pay telephones to ask operators to place collect calls after normal business hours to strangers working for a huge corporation to ask for help modifying travel plans to arrive home in time to take the 10am exam in Secondary Recovery class the next morning. It is so much easier today with the Internet, cell phones, and abundant free-range credit.

The passengers quickly conferred and unanimously voted to land in Burbank (I abstained). I was invited by the guy sitting next to me to share a taxi to LAX with him and another passenger. I explained my situation and that I didn't have enough money to cover my share. They told me not to worry about it.

We landed in Burbank around 6pm, and it took almost two hours to get across town to LAX. I thanked my companions for paying for the ride. The guy who invited me was also traveling on TWA, going to Denver. (TWA was a major airline, back in the day. I am so old...) TWA booked the other guy on a United flight to Denver departing around 10pm, fog permitting. I had no options to get to Tulsa that night; the attendant suggested I swap my ticket for the United flight to Denver too, then book the earliest available flight to Tulsa from there. (Back then the airlines cooperated pretty well in exchanging tickets and vouchers.)

My new friend from Denver had a pass to the United club lounge and invited me to join him. It was Election Day, November 4, 1980, and we could kill time and watch the election returns. It was the first presidential election for which I was old enough to vote, and after scheduling my plant visit to Bakersfield I had scrambled to vote by absentee ballot ahead of my trip.

As we entered the lounge, all eyes were on the television screens. Ronald Reagan had won big, and President Carter had conceded even while polls were still open in California, sparking controversy.

The fog lifted a couple of hours later, and we boarded the flight for Denver. We arrived well after midnight, and I booked a flight to Tulsa departing late the next morning.

I had a single personal check in my wallet for emergencies and figured this qualified. I called the airport Holiday Inn and asked if they had a room available, did they offer a shuttle pickup service at the airport, and did they take personal checks for payment?

Yes, yes, and no. I hung up and the Denver guy, at the next phone calling his wife, asked me what was up. He opened his wallet to take inventory, then told me I could write him a check for $75, enough cash to cover the hotel room. It was incredibly nice of him, and I've thought of his kindness many times since. He wished me luck and walked away.

I called Holiday Inn again and requested shuttle pickup at the airport. The hotel operator asked if I was the same guy who called earlier and only had a personal check. I explained I now had cash and he promised to send the shuttle. It was close to 2am before I checked in and went straight to sleep.

I finally arrived in Tulsa mid-afternoon. I had missed my exam but was okay with that. A month before starting my final semester, I had a job offer with a great salary and the prospect of starting my career the next summer in sunny California.

Senioritis and the Boogie Woogie Flu

I took a half-dozen plant visits around the country the next few weeks, each of which generated another job offer. Boom! The Tenneco offer remained at the top of my list. I liked what I saw in Bakersfield, and the potential of moving to the West Coast and working in Thermal Enhanced Oil Recovery seemed exotic and cool. Plus, Tenneco had called to increase my starting salary offer to "remain competitive" with other companies hiring PE graduates. Boom!

After growing up in Tulsa and then attending TU, I knew it would be good to shake things up. Moving to California would be a bold move and a major break. At the time, the trend in the industry was to work a few years in one location before being transferred to another location. I figured unless I went international my next location after California would be quite a bit closer to home, maybe Denver, Dallas, or Houston.

An hour before taking my first final exam of the fall semester, I called Tenneco to accept their offer of a reservoir engineering position in Bakersfield, then called my parents to let them know my decision. This totally changed my perspective and removed all stress and pressure from the exam.

My final semester in the spring of 1981 was a blast. I decided to make up for lost fun-time during the previous three years and was easily distracted by social events and general goofing off with friends enjoying their own case of Senioritis. My grade point dipped but it didn't matter. Petroleum engineering graduates were still in high demand, a 4.0 was nice but not required. (I changed jobs several times during my career and my college GPA did not come up a single time.)

During my last couple of months at TU a two-song soundtrack was constantly ear-worming through my brain. The guys in the dorm room below mine constantly blasted "Hold on Loosely" by 38 Special and "September" by Earth, Wind & Fire. (I was fine with this, it could have been much worse, like "Funkytown.") Anytime I hear either of those songs I am immediately transported back to my dorm room, singing along and feeling no stress.

My only memory of graduation in May of 1981 is shaking hands with Kermit Brown and Chi Ikoku, my favorite petroleum engineering professors. After the ceremony my grandfather treated my family to a celebration dinner at Spudder's, a terrific steak house. There is an ancient spudding rig set up near the entrance, and the inside is decorated with all manner of oil and gas memorabilia. On the wall I spied something familiar: an old well sign from the Osage Hominy field. It matched the sign I had found in the grass working at the field two summers earlier. As of early 2022, the sign still hangs high on the wall inside Spudder's, partially obscured by an extension cord.

CALIFORNIA

"Go West, Young Mangineer!"

Between graduation in early May 1981 and relocating to California a couple of months later, I continued working part-time at TG&Y and prepared for my move. I also became engaged, and purchased a modest ring with a tiny, almost affordable diamond. I was fortunate to have graduated without any debt (thank you Mom and Dad!), but I was now broke. The Company was paying for my relocation, so I asked for and received an expense advance to cover my out of pocket travel costs. The plan was to move to Bakersfield by myself, start my career, and earn some money. I'd return home in the fall for the wedding.

Since it was late July and very hot, I planned to take it easy on my 1970 Delta 88. Unlike the slogan in the television commercials a few years later, this actually was (formerly) my father's Oldsmobile. I would take my time and cross the country over four days, including a stop overnight in Amarillo to visit a college friend. For navigation I had an awesome AAA Triptik, a wire-bound flip chart that showed my route marked with a highlighter. In the front passenger seat was a jug of iced tea and a cassette case with 24 tapes. I said my goodbyes and hit the road.

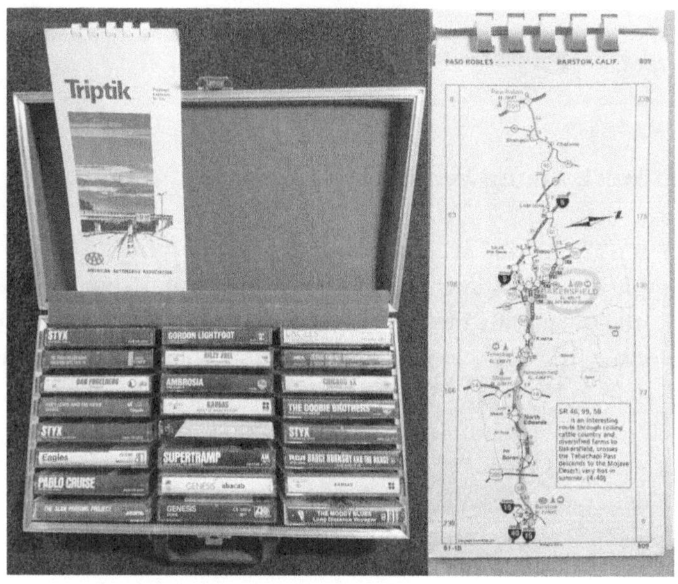

My Grapes of Wrath playlist for my journey to Bakersfield

Compared to the challenging *Grapes of Wrath* Okie migrations during Dust Bowl days, my journey to Bakersfield would not have impressed Steinbeck. Still, there were a few interesting moments. After driving only 100 miles my air conditioning belt noisily started coming apart. I pulled off somewhere in Oklahoma City and used my pocketknife to cut off the frayed belt. It would be a warm ride for the next 1300 miles.

After dinner with my friend in Amarillo I spent the night in a hotel, rising early the next day to drive to Gallup, New Mexico. My plan for the third day was to drive straight to Needles, California, but I turned off at the sign for Meteor Crater. I spent a couple of hours touring the small museum and gazing at the giant hole, trying to appreciate the moment of impact with a cosmic perspective.

I arrived in Needles mid-afternoon and pulled into a Best Western parking lot. The town looked deserted; everyone was inside avoiding the brutal heat. I smelled sulfur and popped the hood of the 88. I stupidly pulled off the caps of my battery and the acid inside seemed to be boiling. I left the hood up to let the engine cool, stepped inside the motel office and dinged the bell to wake the clerk napping in the back. While he set me up I glanced at a large, round thermometer just outside the office window. The scale read 10, 20, 30, 40. The needle pointed at 29. The clerk told me the thermometer started at 100, it was 129 (deg F) outside! No wonder my car was fuming. I told the clerk I planned to check out around 3am to drive the rest of the desert in the relatively cool early morning, so he checked me out right after checking me in.

I left Needles on schedule and about an hour later pulled off to the shoulder for a drink of iced tea and a few minutes of galactic inspiration gazing at the awesome river of stars. I heard a crackling sound, and after my eyes adjusted to the darkness I saw the outline of a pickup truck parked on the other side of the highway, directly opposite. There were four guys sitting around a small campfire that I had completely missed when I parked. They had been shielded in the angle of my approach by cactus and the shadow of the dark truck. I was completely spooked that I had unknowingly parked directly across from four strangers on a deserted highway at 4am. I started the car and left in a hurry. Later, I wondered what those guys thought about the strange car who parked so close to them for five minutes. (Note to self: might be a good idea for a story.)

I crossed the Tehachapi's and arrived in Bakersfield around 9am, much earlier than I had anticipated. The Company had reserved a room for me at the Rodeway Inn. They had a room ready and let me check in early. I promptly slept for several hours, then had Sunday night dinner by myself at a nearby Wendy's.

The next day, Monday, July 27, 1981, would be the first day of my new career as a petroleum engineer.

Newbie Orientation to Corporate Politics

Late in the morning on my first day, after touring the building and meeting everyone, I sat behind the desk in my office and paused to enjoy the moment and appreciate my situation.

I was at *my desk*. In *my office*. My name was on the wall just outside the door. *I had a door.* That very minute, just sitting in *my chair*, I was *earning money*.

It was so cool.

The reservoir engineering department secretary (that's how she introduced herself, it would be a few more years before "administrative assistant" became common) had just dropped off a couple of custom accessories: a shrink-wrapped stack of scratch pad notes with STEVE MOORE printed at the bottom, and a box of business cards that identified my title as "ENGINEER." (After one year of service engineers were promoted to "Petroleum Engineer.")

I was working on HR paperwork when Pat came in and sat down. He had started with the Company a couple of weeks earlier after graduating with an MBA to complement his petroleum engineering degree. Pat noticed the green calculation pad on my desk, a leftover from college.

"Hey, you should use the Company calculation pads, they're in the supply room. And don't forget to order yourself a calculator, the Company will pay for that, too. Most of us got HP-

41Cs, with the card reader and the printer, but get whatever you like." Wow. An HP-41C setup cost several hundred dollars. I had crossed the threshold and was in A Strange New World.

I learned later that Pat was a shrewd operator, and that morning he wasted no time in sizing me up while delivering a mild dose of intimidation.

"So, Steve. What are your career goals?"

A quiz? On my first day? I was unprepared and fumbled out something inane, like be a decent engineer, or help the Company achieve its goals, or live long and prosper. I had already adopted the strategy of deflecting inquiries by quickly flipping things around, so I asked Pat about his goals.

He smiled slightly as though he had been waiting for me to ask. "I want to be president of the Company in five years."

Audacious? Absolutely. And he nearly pulled it off. Not in five years (he admitted at the time he was exaggerating), but he had a very successful career and ultimately stepped off the ladder into an executive position in the corporate headquarters in Houston. Over the next couple of years, I watched Pat make bold political moves with division management and monopolize technician and administrative support for his projects. His efforts paid off, and he was rewarded with choice assignments and high-visibility presentations to Corporate Leadership when they visited from Houston.

AKA: "A Rear-smooching Rear Smoocher"

A couple of weeks later the receptionist called to let me know I had a visitor. A service company rep wanted to meet the new reservoir engineer. The only thing I remember about my first "business meeting" is the weird little joke he made walking to my office. Did I know what an *obsequious sycophant* was? I shook my head.

"An ass-kissing ass kisser," he said. I chuckled to be polite but thought it was an odd way to start a conversation. Still, the phrase had a nice, snarky flavor and catchy repetition, and more than a few times during my career I'd run into a character and would think "what an O.S.!"

Every engineer and technician in the reservoir group acknowledged Pat's skills in engineering, communicating, and engaging with the bosses. I quickly realized I could never emulate his process to achieve personal success, for two reasons. One, I didn't have the experience, insight and political instincts to pull it off if I wanted to. And two, I didn't want to.

Over time my early resentment morphed into low-level admiration for people like Pat, who set clear goals and had a willingness to do whatever was needed to achieve them. Pat showed me a valuable lesson I did not recognize at the time. Not only did engineers with his style get promoted to management, many of them became *my* managers.

Sometime during my second year, I adopted the goal of becoming a competent, professional engineer. High quality work would be my defining characteristic, my "brand." Management would recognize this and Good Things Would Happen, even if I didn't join in those silly political reindeer games.

Overall, my plan worked. Mostly.

"Tell me more about this 'Cap Bud' of which you speak."

The Company had an awesome, 18-month training program. Before I received a reservoir engineering assignment, I spent six months each in Geological Engineering, Production Engineering, and Drilling. I got to know the staff and completed meaningful projects in each department, an excellent experience which laid a solid foundation for interdepartmental teamwork.

My first reservoir engineering assignment was a handful of heavy-oil steamflood and cyclic-steam assets in Kern River Field, plus several lower-value heavy oil properties in two other fields. I set about analyzing injection and production data to identify strategies to optimize production, while simultaneously learning about thermal EOR, which had not been part of my university education.

One morning my manager entered my office and asked me for the list of projects I would be submitting for the Division's annual capital budget request. I froze. I had nothing. I was totally unprepared.

In later years, I would spend an extraordinary amount of my reservoir engineering time engaged in budget activities, even serving as Budget Coordinator many times for multiple companies. But in the fall of 1982, I was completely ignorant about the budget *process*. In hindsight, this seems incredible. I had a four-year degree from a university with a good reputation for Petroleum Engineering, and I had completed 18 months of corporate training. I knew "capital" referred to investment money and I had a good understanding of analyzing investment economics. Somehow I missed the fact that *reservoir* engineers were responsible for identifying new drilling locations and associated facilities, obtaining cost estimates and summarizing details suitable for inclusion in a Division Capital Budget Request.

I quickly tried to recover and told the boss my projects were good, no additional wells or facilities were needed so I was not requesting any capital. I told him I was focused on optimizing steam injection operations. He raised an eyebrow but let it ride. For the next several weeks, whenever the capital budget was reviewed, my area assets were conspicuously absent from the itemized summaries.

Looking back, my first capital budget experience was another early clue that reservoir engineering might not have been an optimum career choice.

Engineers in Company Cars Getting Stupid, Part 2: Stevel Knievel

When I started my petroleum engineering career in the early 1980s oil was still booming, the beginnings of the next bust still a couple of years off. One of the best perks enjoyed by many oil and gas professionals at that time was the use of a company vehicle. My first company had a great policy.

Newly hired drilling and production engineers were immediately assigned a personal company car to travel to the field offices and drilling locations. They were able to take the cars home each day. They were also allowed to use the car for personal use, *at company expense,* up to two hundred miles from the office. I knew several engineers who sold their personal cars after receiving their company vehicles, saving a ton of money by avoiding car payments, maintenance, insurance, and buying gas. The two-hundred-mile limit allowed them to drive as far away as

San Diego for a weekend trip, and gasoline purchases were reimbursed through expense accounts.

For reservoir and geological engineers who did not go to the field often, the policy was different. REs and GEs had to complete two years of employment before receiving a company car with the same privileges, still a nice benefit. New reservoir and geological engineers who did not yet qualify were still able to use a company car on occasion. When someone went on vacation or was out of the office for even a few consecutive days, they were required to give their cars to another employee who did not have one.

All managers had company cars, and the policy applied to them as well. When Harold, the Division Production Manager was out of the office, his practice was to give his Crown Victoria to the most senior technical professional (geologist or engineer) who did not yet have a company car. Occasionally I would be notified by Harold's secretary that I should come to her desk and get his keys. I was nervous and paranoid about commuting to the office each day in Harold's car and parking in his covered parking spot close to the building. I rarely took Harold's car anywhere but home and the office, afraid of picking up a door ding in a grocery store parking lot or worse, damaging the car in an accident.

My fear and paranoia about damaging a company car was not unjustified. For my first solo trip to the field, I checked out one of the pool cars. The drilling site was located near the foothills south of Bakersfield. After turning off the highway I traveled through a fruit orchard and came to a long stretch of dirt road. It was smooth and hard-packed, had been graded recently and was in terrific shape. I could see that I had a few miles of perfect road ahead and no one in sight, so I increased my speed. I had left the orchard behind and had no worries about kicking up a big dust tail. (I had been warned the local farmers would get angry if you dusted their valuable fruit trees.) Soon I was cruising along at 60 miles per hour.

As you no doubt guessed from the title of this section, this was an incredibly dumb thing to do. I'm suddenly horrified to see a ditch a few yards ahead cutting across the road. It was a small drainage or irrigation channel about three or four feet across and maybe a foot and half deep. As a driver familiar with "Dip Ahead" signs all over the country from previous travels, I experienced a half-second of surprise and then I was airborne.

As canyon jumps go, it was not that impressive. I was not Stevel Knievel flying a rocket-bike across the Snake River or jumping a motorcycle across eleventeen buses and a Roman fountain at Caesar's Palace. It was just a freaking four-foot drainage ditch. Still, in not-so-classic *Smokey and the Bandit* style I did manage to get air under all four wheels while simultaneously keeping all fluids inside my body. (For the small chance that a millennial might be reading this: please use the Internet search app of your choice for clarification of my obscure cultural references.)

Bandit One (corporate model: 4-door Olds Cutlass, chocolate brown) bounce-landed on the far side of the ditch. The road had a slight incline and I had been traveling just fast enough that the rear wheels barely cleared the far edge. I still cringe when I think of the horrible sound and the huge jarring thump when the car bottomed out. I hit the brakes and tried to maintain control. Somehow everything worked and the car stopped. I climbed out, shaking a little and waving my hand to clear the swirling dust away from my face.

I was stunned to see no signs of damage. My engineering brain kicked in and I corrected myself: No external signs of damage, but the suspension system must have taken a beating. I looked under the front and back of the car as best I could but saw nothing obviously wrong. I knew the car must have been damaged, but I was not able to confirm it visually.

No cell phones in 1981, and the pool car had no radio. I'd have to wait for someone to come along or walk back to the highway and flag somebody down. I finally decided that since I had been able to control the car when I brought it to a stop, maybe it was still drivable. I probably couldn't make it any worse, so I slowly put the car in gear, crept forward and heard…nothing. No metal-on-metal shrieking, no rhythmical thumping. The car rolled forward and I tested the brakes. Everything seemed okay, so I crawled along at a very reasonable three miles per hour for a bit, then goosed it up to ten.

I was slightly proud of myself for detecting each of the next three drainage ditches in plenty of time to cross them ever-so-gently, keeping my speed low all the way to the well site. I had been lucky and learned a hard lesson. On my return trip to the office, just before I reached the highway, I saw a sign on the left side of the road. I twisted around to read it: CAUTION UNEVEN ROAD SPEED LIMIT 20 MPH. Rookie mistake; I had missed it entirely.

A few months before I reached my two-year employment anniversary and would be assigned my own car, the Company changed the policy. To cut costs, reservoir and geological engineers had to be senior level to qualify for a car (a promotion that typically occurred back then after three to five years of service). I still occasionally got to use Harold's car, and I was extraordinarily careful with it. I also made sure to have it washed and filled with gas before returning it to him. It was the right thing to do, of course, and I thought a few brownie points couldn't hurt.

"Your tainted petrodollars are no good here, sir"

Oil was still booming in 1981, and just a few weeks after I started, Tenneco flew (first class!) all recently hired employees to Houston for a New Hire Orientation seminar. Two days of presentations by HR and Corporate leadership, cocktail parties, and networking.

We stayed at the Hyatt in downtown Houston. Standing in the lobby looking up, I was very impressed with the hollow interior and mesmerized by the brightly lit elevators rising more than 20 floors. From the hallways of the upper floors the view of the lobby below, accompanied by the faint tinkling of a piano, was just as enthralling. Over the years I frequently enjoyed staying at the Hyatt, and never tired of the view from above or below.

Two college buddies also worked for the Company in other divisions, and we met for dinner in the 5-star hotel restaurant. Our meals were a travel expense, so we all ordered expensive steaks and drinks. Our waiter, Dawkins, cleared our plates after the first course of bread and salads, and used one of those shiny metal blades to clear the crumbs from the tablecloth in front of each of us. This was a new experience, and we sat uncomfortably as the man worked to clean up the mess each of us had made.

Dawkins returned with a round metal tray filled with tiny cones topped with perfectly round scoops that resembled ice cream. Rick politely informed Dawkins of his mistake, we hadn't ordered those.

"Yes sir, these are complimentary, fruit sorbet. 'Tis a palate cleanser, to clean the palate before the main course is served."

None of us had experienced palette cleansing before, I'm positive the dorm cafeteria back at TU never served cleansers of any kind between courses of French fries and charburgers.

We each took a lime-flavored sorbet and it worked perfectly, setting us up to enjoy our steaks a few minutes later. When it was time for our check, Rick offered to pay and put it on his expense account. He put a stack of twenty-dollar bills on the table.

Dawkins made a show of reaching past Rick and crumpling the stack into a tiny ball of trash. "Sorry sir, your money's no good here."

Rick stared at Dawkins, then looked around the table, unsure what to do. Dawkins let us sit a few seconds in silence, then grinned big and reached for the ball of cash. "Kidding, sir."

Every time I stayed at the Hyatt, I enjoyed the spectacular views and always remembered our dinner with Dawkins.

Moore's Law of Fruit Salad: It's okay to count apples and oranges together, as long as you are *only concerned about the total fruit inventory.* Otherwise, don't do it.

My first time to handle a field operation was for a drill stem test on a new gas well located near Lodi, California. The test went okay, except I terminated the shut-in phase too early. Back in the office a few days later, I completed the initial reserves booking calculation, filled out the Company form and submitted it to my manager for approval.

The next day he walked in my office and tossed the form on my desk. He said it was fine, but I needed to use a 6:1 MCF/Bbl ratio converting the natural gas reserves to equivalent oil volumes.

Okay Steve, you got this. In a friendly tone I informed my boss that the gas had a high nitrogen content and had only half the usual BTU value. Therefore a 12-to-1 ratio was more accurate in reporting the volumes in equivalent oil barrels.

He leaned over my desk. "Maybe you didn't hear me. I said change it and use 6-to-1!" He spun and walked out.

Nitrogen volumes were counted as reserves, even when there was no market for sales? A cartoon light bulb floating a couple of inches above my head flashed on. Oh, right. Silly rabbit, technical reserves are for kids. All of the fruit in the bowl has to be counted.

Corporate reserves were *political.*

Men's Room Follies, Part 1: A Man in the Can without an Exit Plan

While compiling my notes from the Moorchives, I discovered a surprising amount of interesting (and possibly humorous) anecdotes took place in men's restrooms in corporate buildings. Don't worry, to keep things from becoming waterlogged I'll sprinkle them (heh) throughout the book. Here's the first, from 1981.

It was the first time I put in a few hours of overtime in the evening, and I had the entire office building to myself. Later that evening, sitting in the middle stall of the men's room, I discovered I wasn't alone after all. (That's quite a hook, isn't it?)

I was minding my own business when I heard knuckles rap on the door and a female voice called out "Housekeeping!" I yelled "Just a minute!" and endeavored to wrap things up but heard the door swing open. The woman muttered "okay, okay, very fast" and I heard a mop plop in a bucket, then slosh around the floor.

I sat in silence, embarrassed and wondering why this was happening. The engineering part of my brain was trying to develop an exit strategy that didn't include walking across the clean, wet, floor and ruining the woman's hard work.

The door in the stall next to me banged open and she mopped, water streaming into my foot space. I moved my feet a few inches toward the far side and double checked that my door was locked. I heard "Lift feet, please" and the mop slid under the stall door. I grabbed my pants and lifted my feet, and the mop made several passes around. The floor was wet and slick as she moved to the third and final stall. My shoes were up against the door and I tried to calculate how long it would take for the linoleum to dry, and whether I had the endurance to keep my feet up until it did.

I heard the woman mopping over her own steps as she backed to the door and out without another word. I dropped my feet down carefully but stayed put. When I heard her yell "housekeeping!" at the ladies' room door I made my break. I washed and hustled back to my office without furthering our relationship.

I *knew* I should have P&A'd the swimming pool first!

My reservoir engineering responsibilities included three active steamflood properties in the prolific Kern River Field, first discovered in 1899. Despite my failure to request drilling funds in the 1983 capital budget, late in the year I received approval to drill a replacement well.

The Fee "C" was a typical heavy-oil property developed on tight spacing: 50 producers on 50 acres. Oil prices were still high enough to justify replacing the ancient well that died from casing failure, last producing 10 barrels of oil per day.

The field office had been someone's home decades earlier, and an old, empty swimming pool was in the exact spot where I needed to drill the replacement well. The target reservoir was only 1,200′ deep, directional drilling was not an option.

The Drilling Department did not want to remove the swimming pool, and despite my objections the replacement well was spud only 25 feet away from the original wellbore. After 80 years of production there was a significant amount of depletion in the highly permeable (multiple *Darcies*!) sands, and we lost mud circulation during the entire drilling operation. We put the replacement well on production anyway, and it never produced a drop of oil.

The first well of my career, the "Fee C" 18-R, wasn't worth a shit. I had drilled a dry hole in the middle of one of the most prolific giant oil fields in the country.

On the Other Hand…

I did have a bit of success later on the same Fee "C" property where I drilled that duster. We maintained a steam injection Line Well Agreement with Getty, who operated the offsetting properties. A series of injection wells had been drilled around the perimeter of the lease, we operated about half and Getty operated the rest.

The LWA specified the quality and minimum volume of steam, expressed in BTUs, to be injected each month by each company. Monthly injection summaries were exchanged and subject to annual audits. If a company failed to inject the required minimum number of BTUs, they would incur a financial penalty.

The agreement had been in effect for a few years, but as far as I could tell an audit had never been conducted. I did the calculations and discovered we had injected our share but Getty was seriously short, a cumulative deficit of millions of BTU's over more than a year. The calculated penalty came to just over half a million dollars (roughly $1.4 million today). I double-checked my calculations and, after clearing it with my manager, prepared an invoice and mailed it to Getty.

A couple of months later my boss walked into my office with a letter and a check. Getty had accepted the penalty and paid the fine. The boss gave me a hearty "Good Job!" and took me to lunch to celebrate. It was the largest amount on a check I had seen up to that point in my life.

The lease truck was a tiny car filled with clowns.

The managers at my first company were great at communicating to the staff what was going on in the Company. Several mornings each week the RE manager would lead a meeting with the entire department and summarize current drilling and workover operations. Engineers summarized their work projects and shared plans to visit the field or be out on vacation. Oil was still booming, and at least twice a week the boss would take everyone to lunch, sometimes lasting two or three hours. Sitting next to or across from different people invariably led to friendly relationships and the valuable exchange of personal and professional insights. (Bonus: the first time I attended a department lunch I was introduced to Butterfinger Pie, easily one of the Top 5 Deserts on our planet.)

I also experienced working on a true team with a production engineer, geologic engineer, and occasionally a drilling engineer. We still reported to our functional supervisors, but the supervisors worked well together as their own team, and we all shared common goals and deadlines. I remember being told by my boss that I was expected to spend as much time in the offices of my teammates as my own. I really enjoyed working in a team environment and assumed this was The Way Things Were Done in the industry. This culture made a huge imprint on my professional personality. Later I would learn that not all companies embraced the team concept; many managers ran their engineering and geology departments inside functional silos, often with disparate goals and priorities.

One of the three teams to which I was initially assigned was charged with evaluating the steamflood potential of three leases in the Poso Creek Field: Grimes, Mabry, and New Hope. After studying the reservoirs for a few weeks and concluding steam injection operations were not economic, my geologic engineering teammate Kevin and I renamed the properties: Grim, Maybe, and No Hope.

Getty Oil operated the offsetting lease and a few years earlier initiated large-scale steamflooding in the same reservoir. Kevin and I stuck to our uneconomic conclusion and started calling our team the Poso Bozos.

Later, the Company hired a thermal reservoir engineer from Getty, and we asked him how his former company was able to operate their Poso steamflood. He laughed and said, "big companies make big mistakes." Getty had conducted a thermal simulation study to justify the installation of steam facilities, then launched the project. Subsequently, a major error was discovered in their model, but since the capital funds were already sunk, Getty continued injecting steam to recover as much of their investment as possible. This made the Bozos feel better and our team reputation improved, but only slightly. We were still managing crappy, marginal properties.

"No, you can't wear Steel-Toed Crocs either"

The Kern River oil field is located just outside of Bakersfield, a short 20-minute drive. A rare daytime logging job came up for an infill well on one of my leases, so my geological engineering teammate Jan and I checked out a pool car and drove from the office to the wellsite.

We climbed into the logging truck and Jan moved forward next to the operator to check the data. I stood a couple of feet behind, looking over their shoulders. It was hot in the truck and I was soon sweating in my office clothes. The floor of the logging truck was very hot, and I shuffled from one foot to the other. Jan heard me moving around and glanced back, then covered her mouth and pointed at my feet. The logging guy looked too and they both burst out laughing.

Maple-colored pancakes were spreading below my feet. The hot metal floor of the truck was melting the crepe rubber soles of my business-casual shoes. We came directly from the office, and my boots were at home. Feeling totally embarrassed as my feet were starting to burn, I left the truck to wait outside in the slightly cooler Bakersfield sun. My guess is it took Jan and the logger several minutes to stop laughing and get back to monitoring the log.

Jan enjoyed telling everyone in the office about my hot-foot experience. I leaned into it and proudly displayed my deformed shoes on the bookcase in my office as a cautionary tale for other poor *soles* who considered going to the field wearing inappropriate footwear.

The First Time I Tried to Obtain Quality Production Data

In 1982 well production plots were still being updated by hand. The official monthly production plots were done in ink by technicians, but to optimize steam injection reservoir engineers needed updated well test plots as soon as possible. At times there was a shortage of tech support (Thanks, Pat!) and I'd update the plots myself. This gave me a good feel for the range and nature of the test data.

I came across a well in which several weeks of well tests were identical, like 17 barrels of oil and 63 barrels of water each day. This couldn't be right, production (particularly water) couldn't be that consistent. I discovered this was also the case for a handful of other wells too.

I went to visit my friendly neighborhood production engineer in his office. He had about five years of experience but sighed like an old man. A visit from the team reservoir engineer could only mean something unpleasant. "What?"

I showed him the obviously bad data and asked him to pass along the need for quality test data to his field guys. He looked at me like a teacher staring at the dumbest kid in class, about to explain for the tenth time that the flat earth on which we walk is actually round.

"Look, Steve, if we give the operators a bunch of shit about well tests, they're just going to write down some random numbers and turn 'em in until we get off their backs."

I was surprised. It was the first time I ran into trouble obtaining quality information to do the engineering job I was paid to do. I started to explain that better production data would lead to optimized steam injection, which would increase production and profits and—

The production engineer held up his hand. "I'll take care of it." The conversation was over. The data was not going to get any better.

The challenge of acquiring quality data would turn out to be a recurring theme in my professional life. I would learn that Management almost always requested as much data as possible when reviewing proposals, but were often reluctant to allocate financial, human or system resources to improve the quality of the data that was so critical to their investment decisions.

Dude, It's California!

There is an old joke attributed to Johnny Carson, who described Bakersfield as "the third largest city in Oklahoma" due to the number of transplanted residents from my home state. I found adult life in California to be refreshingly different after growing up in Oklahoma, which was exactly what I wanted after college. Here are a few examples:

"And the rodent from Bakersfield takes second place in the 12-meter butterfly!"

Summers in Bakersfield were hot, dry, and long, and it seemed that every house had a swimming pool, as common as having a driveway. During weekends back in Oklahoma people mowed their grass, changed the oil in their cars, or painted the backyard fence. (Except folks who had a place at the lake; they did their chores on weekday evenings to free up their weekend.) In Bakersfield, weekends meant spending 72 hours poolside or getting wrinkled bobbing in the water and trying not to spill your drink.

Pool parties were a big thing. The Reservoir Engineering department was a friendly, social bunch, and one of the supervisors hosted a welcome pool party for me and a couple of other newbies soon after I started working for the Company. It was a terrific experience and the first time I was introduced to Bartles and Jaymes Wine Coolers.

To encourage others to get in the pool, our host Pat dove in and starting swimming to the far side. One of the engineers laughed and pointed. Pat wore his hair in an impressive super-deluxe comb-over which did not survive his plunge into the water. As he swam past, his hair trailed behind and seemed two or three times longer than one might expect.

"Look at that rat chasing after Pat!" the engineer said, and we all cracked up. Pat reached the other side, climbed out, and furiously finger-combed his hair across his dome. It was one of the funniest things I've ever seen.

No alligator lizards, but still interesting.

Summer, 1982. Time for our first family trip over the mountains to a sandy, sunny beach on the Pacific Ocean. Where to go?

"Ventura Highway," the song by America (written by Dewey Bunnel) popped into my head. The verses included "sunshine," "where the days are longer," and "alligator lizards in the air." That great song with the tantalizing opening guitar riff had been rolling around in my brain since the early 1970s. How cool would it be to hang out at the beach in Ventura?

Extremely cool. We nearly froze. After driving 3 hours, finding a place to park, and hauling coolers, towels and chairs a mile or so to the water's edge, we were all freezing and hadn't even touched the water yet. I had no idea the ocean temperature and breezy weather was so cold at this latitude in early summer. What about sunny California? The Beach Boys had been telling me how great it was for years. Still, we stuck it out and bravely stood ankle deep in the frothy water for fifteen seconds. Plus, there were sticky black tar balls buried in the sand like Satan's Easter eggs. They stuck to your feet (and everything else) and were nearly impossible to clean off. It was a miserable time, and a long drive back to Bakersfield.

Our second trip to the coast was much more pleasant and interesting. My geological engineer friend John hosted me, my wife, and daughter on a day trip to Venice beach. We enjoyed the crazy energy of the place: colorful characters dancing and roller blading, dozens of interesting food options, noisy street musicians and vendors selling sunglasses. Eventually, we picked a nice spot in the sand near the water, which was cold but warmer than it was in Ventura.

As we sprawled on towels and watched the waves, John explained there was a variety of ethnic and international heritages among the people who lived in Venice. At that moment a woman plopped down on a towel just a few yards away and immediately took off her bikini top. Without missing a beat, John casually said, "Like that woman there, she's from France." John and I spent the rest of the afternoon shielding my daughter from the view and pretending not to look. A memorable California day at the beach for sure.

Exchanging Life Lessons

Another family day trip, to the IMAX theater in Los Angeles. We arrived late and the only seats left were on the front row. As I sat down I realized I did not have my wallet, and immediately went outside to retrace my steps. I was filled with dread, knowing I had probably lost my driver's license, credit cards and cash, and there was a big hassle ahead reporting and replacing everything when we got home.

I assumed I dropped it after buying our tickets and didn't even bother looking around with the large crowd of folks milling about. I approached the ticket booth with the absolute minimum amount of optimism and asked the girl if anyone had turned in a lost wallet.

She said yes and asked me my name. She checked the driver's license and handed my wallet to me. I was stunned and grateful and nearly speechless but managed to thank her profusely. She asked if I'd like to have the name and address of the man who turned it in? Absolutely. I thanked her again and returned to the movie.

I slipped into my front row seat just as the movie started, a nature documentary filmed in IMAX format. The lights fell and the opening scene was a huge bolt of lightning crashing down from the top of the screen, with thunder booming for several seconds.

My son thought it was about to start raining, and everyone in the theater heard a three-year-old voice say 'Oh, no!" The entire audience chuckled, a terrific moment of comic relief for me after the stress of temporarily losing my wallet.

At home the next day, I wrote the man a letter, thanking him for turning in my wallet and saving our weekend. I enclosed $30 as a gift of appreciation. A week later I received an extremely nice letter back from the man.

He explained it wasn't him who found my wallet, it was his 8-year-old son, who asked his father what he should do. The father told his son they must leave it at the ticket booth in case the owner came back for it. In his letter, the man pointed out that the girl in the ticket booth also did a good thing holding and returning my wallet to me. This was true, and I wished I had thought to reward her for her kindness at the time.

The man gave his son the cash and told him it was a gift, to thank him for finding and turning in the wallet. *Then the man thanked me for teaching his son an important lesson about doing the right thing.* I was blown away reading this.

A few years later, returning from a well review at a field office near Coalinga, I stopped at a highway rest stop. Walking to the men's room I passed a thin guy with long hair leaning on the hood of his car. It was hot and the car's windows were down. A little girl played with a toy in the front seat. I exchanged nods with the guy as I walked by.

Returning to my car the guy politely stopped me. He said he had just been granted custody of his daughter from his ex-wife someplace in northern California. He was taking her to his home in LA and asked if I could spare some cash so he could buy some gas. I gave him a couple of bucks and he thanked me.

As I got back on the highway I wondered about the guy's story. After I gave him the cash he stayed where he was, presumably to continue asking others for help. Was he really taking his daughter home or was something nefarious going on?

I remembered the father and son who returned my wallet at the IMAX theater a couple of years earlier. I decided that whether the guy had told the truth or not, the girl in the car likely confirmed a genuine need for support. Even if the guy was scamming folks, perhaps some of the cash would help the kid.

I took the next exit and got back on the highway heading back toward Coalinga. I passed the rest stop, then reversed direction again at the first exit. I pulled into a parking spot next to the guy, still standing by his car. I called him over, told him the two bucks I gave him earlier wouldn't get them very far, and gave him a twenty and a five. He thanked me again and asked for my address so he could pay me back. I told him that wasn't necessary, wished him luck, and got back on the road.

These two experiences really stuck with me, and 30 years later inspired me to write a similar scene in my novel, *A Fortune of Reversal*.

The Fog of Moore

If I had to pick one word to describe life in Bakersfield in the 1980s, it would be HOT. If I could use two words, they would be HOT and FOGGY (usually not at the same time). Three words? HOT, FOGGY, and HOT.

Back then, the dry desert heat gave way to serious winter fog. It was so thick and scary Bakersfield schools had "fog delays," running buses two hours later in the morning for safety.

For work reasons it was often necessary to drive through the thick Tule fog on already-dangerous roads to get to a well operation in the field. In the late 1980s, I would commute through the fog to my office at Elk Hills, located midway between Bakersfield and Taft. Navigating through the spooky gray soup inspired a special kind of fear, unique to those who lived and traveled through the southern San Joaquin Valley.

Imagine whiter-than-white-knuckle driving on a two-lane road with visibility asymptotically approaching zero. You're going uncomfortably fast, trying to keep the taillights of the welding truck ahead in sight while being passed on the left by another welding truck that you *know* is two seconds away from colliding head-on with a third welding truck coming the other way. I also hoped the welding truck I was following wouldn't lead me through a four-way stop or off the road into a cow pond.

I asked myself, over and over: if driving a school bus through streets with pole lights and traffic signals is unsafe, why am I risking my life on this dark highway full of sleepy maniacs and *fidiots,* driving to a job I didn't like?

I already knew the answer: I was caught in a monkey trap.

A Special Day

In the fall of 1981, I had lived and worked in Bakersfield for only three months when I experienced a terrific advantage from living in the Golden State. Mark, a fellow reservoir engineer, had received free tickets from a service company representative for a Los Angeles Kings hockey game on Saturday night, November 14th. He invited me and his friend John to go. (John was a geological engineer but Mark invited him anyway.) Mark also suggested we drive to California City for a round of golf in the afternoon before driving to L.A. for dinner before the game. It was a great plan, and before the end of the week would get even better.

In April that same year, NASA successfully completed the first space shuttle mission, with Columbia making a spectacular first-time wheeled landing on the dry lakebed at Edwards Air Force Base. This was a big deal and an estimated crowd of 300,000 watched the historic event. Many people with RV's set up camp days earlier to be in prime viewing location for the landing. After a perfect touchdown and a quick turnaround process which included a cross-country return to Florida mounted on the back of a reconfigured 747 aircraft, Columbia was scheduled for its second mission in October. Technical problems caused delays and the shuttle took off on Thursday, November 12, scheduled for five days in space.

A fuel cell failure caused the mission to be cut short, and the landing was rescheduled for early Saturday morning at Edwards after only two days in space. This landing would also be historic, the first time a manned vehicle had been reused to enter space and return. Large crowds were expected, particularly as the landing would occur on a Saturday.

Edwards AFB was 85 miles from Bakersfield, and not far from California City where we planned to play golf that afternoon. Mark, John, and I easily decided to add the shuttle landing to our plans, and we obtained a car pass from the Bakersfield Chamber of Commerce to access the public viewing site. The plan was to drive to Edwards and watch the landing, then to California City for golf, then on to Los Angeles for dinner and the hockey game.

Mark had a company car, so he was the driver for the trip. After leaving early Saturday morning we were well on our way to Edwards when we heard a radio news report that the shuttle would make an additional three orbits for some reason and the landing would be delayed until early afternoon. We caught a lucky break; as we heard this announcement we came to the turnoff for California City, so Mark made a snap decision, executed a quick one-lane slide-across and took the exit. We would play golf first then head to the shuttle landing.

It was still dark when we arrived at the course and we waited for the clubhouse to open. The pro shop guy let us shift our tee time, we would be the first group to play as soon as there was enough light. It was very cool to be standing on the No. 1 tee box taking practice swings and watching a beautiful desert sunrise light up the virgin golf course laid out nicely ahead of us.

A few hours later we finished our round and enjoyed cold beers standing by the car. I had brought a multi-band radio to listen to the news broadcast during the shuttle landing. I tuned it to the air force band and heard jet pilots aloft reporting that the winds were favorable. Columbia was cleared to land after completing its current orbit.

We threw our clubs in the trunk and headed to Edwards. We cut it close and a massive crowd was already in place. We were directed to park at the far end of the large parking area.

The public viewing area was bounded by several miles of temporary fencing and the crowd stood behind it, fifteen to twenty people deep. Armed security staff patrolled in jeeps to keep people behind the fence. Farther back were numerous large RVs with folks sitting on the roofs in lawn chairs ready with binoculars and cameras. Vendors had set up stands selling drinks, t-shirts, and other shuttle merchandise. I purchased a souvenir coffee mug, thinking it would be a cool memento to display on the bookcase in my office.

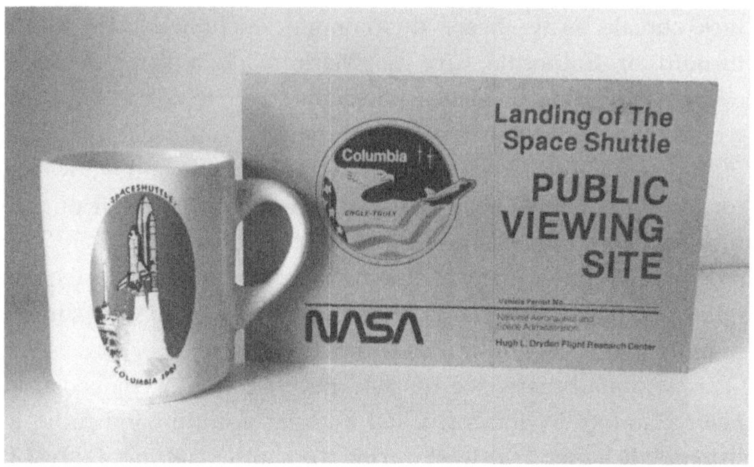

We walked forward as far as we could, somewhat disappointed to be at the end of the viewing area but excited to see the landing. We listened to the news on my radio. The live broadcast originated from the base facilities on the opposite side of the dry lake bed, where NASA was set up and hosting VIPs.

It was getting close to the scheduled landing time when the radio broadcaster announced they had heard the twin sonic booms caused by the shuttle's approach. We looked at each other, we hadn't heard anything. Several seconds later we heard the booms and realized how large the lakebed was that separated us from the news crews on the other side.

Someone yelled and pointed and we spotted the shuttle, a white speck high in the blue sky. It dropped fast and circled, and we discovered we had caught a second lucky break that day. Due to wind speed and direction NASA had switched the landing to an alternate runway. This caused the shuttle to make its approach very close to where we were standing. It was an incredible sight as it flew right in front of us at a high speed, maybe a hundred feet or so in the air. We had a perfect and thrilling view and then it was past. By the time Columbia touched down and rolled to a stop it was far out of sight.

We bolted for the car. Since we were last in, we were first out and hit the road ahead of the crowd, most of which would also be heading to the Los Angeles area. We made it to the city in time for a great Mexican dinner before parking at the Fabulous Forum for the Kings game.

Another lucky break: the free tickets were for great seats a few rows behind the glass close to the rink, in a section where the Forum staff took your food and drink orders and then delivered them right to your seats. We had a great time even though the Kings lost to Winnipeg 2-3. Two and a half hours later we were back in Bakersfield, the end of a fantastic day.

I read a lot of science fiction as a kid, and was a big fan of America's space program, growing up during the Apollo missions. One of the reasons I chose engineering as a profession was my admiration for NASA and the engineers and scientists who made space exploration happen. The space shuttle was a massively complex machine with more than a million components that had to work together in hundreds of systems. I considered the space program to be emblematic of "true engineering" and getting to watch the second space shuttle mission end with the landing at Edwards Air Force Base is one of my favorite life experiences.

A footnote: While writing this essay I discovered my memories were partly wrong. Many times over the years I've thought of that special day and always remembered we attended a Los Angeles Lakers basketball game that night, and I had a fuzzy memory that the opponent was the Houston Rockets. To confirm this, I used Google to check the Lakers schedule in 1981. Sure enough, the

Lakers did play a game on November 14, 1981, but they were not at home, they were in Phoenix playing against the Suns. *Huh.*

Clearly, I made a mistake and decided it must have been a Los Angeles Clippers game instead, perhaps against Houston. I Googled the Clippers schedule for 1981. Yes, the Clippers had a home game that day against Indiana. The SAN DIEGO Clippers. The Clippers did not move to Los Angeles until 1984. *Huh.*

I did some more thinking and Googling and finally realized we had attended an L.A. Kings hockey game that night, not an NBA game. It was my first NHL game, and we had those great seats with personal food and drink service. I had mixed up memories of later trips to LA for Lakers and Clippers games with the memory of the shuttle landing trip. Google also helped me "remember" that the Kings lost that night to the Winnipeg Jets. I didn't remember who won the game but was not surprised the Kings lost; they were mostly terrible in the years before Wayne Gretzky joined the team in 1988. (Thanks again, Google!)

It is interesting to think about the contrast in culture and technology from that day in November 1981 to January 2017 as I write this. We were listening to an FM radio station on the car stereo during the drive to Edwards AFB, which interrupted with a "special news announcement" that the shuttle landing would be delayed a few hours. This was radio-worthy news in 1981 (it was only the second shuttle flight), but it certainly would not be a special bulletin today, except perhaps on websites dedicated to space exploration. By the end of the space shuttle program most people weren't even aware when America had men and women in space.

At Edwards, I used a multi-band portable transistor radio (a Christmas present from Dad) to listen to the Air Force communications and the live news broadcast during the landing.

There were no smart phones delivering Internet broadcasts to your ear buds in 1981.

From transistor radios and space shuttles then, to the Internet and Google today, I am very grateful to the scientists and engineers and for the technology they create.

Challenger

After the Space Shuttle landing I decorated my office with pictures of shuttle launches and landings and other space art. I drank my coffee from my souvenir Columbia mug. I was fortunate to attend another shuttle landing at Edwards a year or two later.

On January 28, 1986, my reservoir engineering manager walked into my office and sat down. He knew I was a space fan and told me about the Challenger explosion that happened a few minutes earlier. It was awful news, and a horrible day. It kind of set the tone in the office for the next few months as oil prices continued to fall.

My Epic Choke

I often played tennis with James, a fellow reservoir engineer. We played at his apartment complex early in the morning before the Bakersfield heat melted the courts. In 1984 he encouraged me to play in the Company tennis tournament. I had played tennis on my high school team and thought I was still half-decent so I signed up, thinking it might be fun.

The tournament was a round-robin format: doubles play, one set, a point for each game won, tie-breaker as needed. Winners stayed on the court and split partners, losers moved to the next court. At the end of the evening the four players with the most points would pair up and play one set for the championship.

I played okay and drew some good partners. Somehow, I ended up number one with the most points. I was paired with Bob, who finished fourth. Bob was Vice President and General Manager of the Division, the highest-ranking executive in our office. I'd met Bob before and was impressed that he hosted a regular lunch at the Stockdale Country Club for all employees who had birthdays that month. It was a nice perk, and Bob encouraged everyone to ask him any question they liked. It was a cool opportunity for the staff to engage with senior management.

Bob was also a tennis enthusiast who did not like losing. Just before walking on the court, someone told me he was the defending champion from the previous year.

As I write this, I'm trying to come up with a word or phrase that is a thousand times worse than *choke,* but just like I played that night, I'm having trouble making a point.

It was Truly Magnificent, the stuff of legends. We're talking a Peter Jackson 68-hour *Lord of the Rings* Marathon Epic level of failure. I was nearly frozen with nerves. I don't think I returned a single serve or made a shot that cleared the net. I double-faulted my entire service game.

Colleagues, spouses, and kids were crowded around the court watching my debacle. I could hear mutterings of pity, an occasional chuckle, and the synchronized gasp when I nailed Bob in the back with a ball. He just shrugged it off and encouraged me to "come on!"

At some level I realized I would survive the disaster still breathing, but I also knew it wasn't a solid career move to win every game in the early rounds of the Company tournament, then lose every point in the Final while partnered with the Division

General Manager. *Let's keep an eye on Moore, that kid's a winner! He's going right to the top, yessiree Bob!*

It was the most brutal, humiliating tennis defeat I had experienced since the high school summer when I lost a set to Tim Boyles, who was wearing cutoff shorts, dark socks, and *dress shoes,* for crying out loud.

Losing in the Final still meant Robert and I "won" second place. I failed again trying to smile for pictures holding our runner-up trophy mugs. Mine sits on a bookshelf in my writing studio, metaphorically filled with the tears of a loser. Next to the trophy is a souvenir Tenneco tennis ball, now as flat as my performance was in the championship match four decades ago.

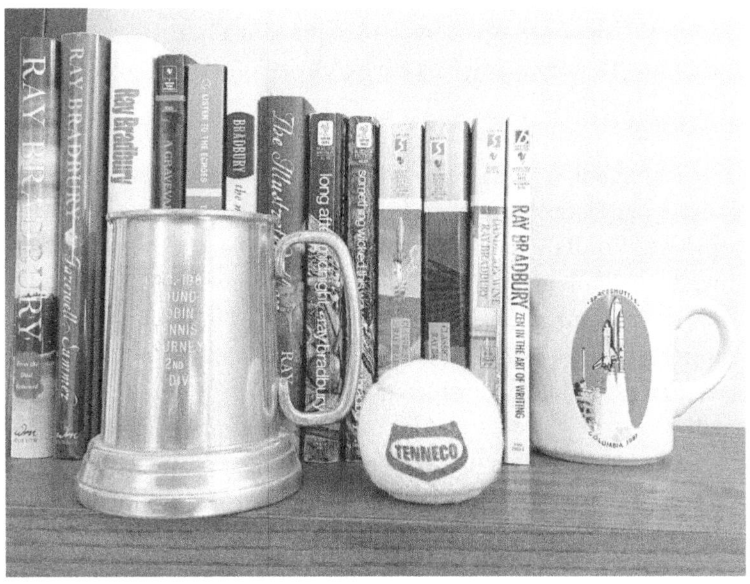

An Innovative Experiment in Innovation

In 1985 the Harvard Business Review published an article by Peter Drucker, "The Discipline of Innovation." Shortly after reading the article, the Division Production Manager called all engineers, geologists, and supervisors to the main conference room. The PM explained key points from the article, and he directed the staff to engage in an innovation project.

For the rest of the morning, we were to meet in small groups with other technical professionals who were not on our functional or area teams. A waterflood production engineer might meet with a thermal geologist and a drilling engineer. A thermal reservoir engineer could visit with a facilities engineer and an exploration geologist. The meetings were to take place in a borrowed office, or the coffee bar or outside, anywhere but an office belonging to one of the participants.

We were told to start out talking about a recent ski trip, or a sporting event, or a new movie. The idea was to put different people together in new surroundings and talk about non-business topics to stimulate new thinking patterns. Eventually, we were to introduce challenges or problems each of us faced in our work, and brainstorm creative ways to tackle them with our new temporary team. The production manager requested someone in each group record the problems and solutions, no matter how far-fetched or crazy. We were to do this for an hour or so, then wander around, join a new group, and repeat the process. At the end of the morning everyone would be treated to a catered lunch.

I met with three people I knew but did not work with directly. I summarized a challenge from one of my projects, and a geologist recalled his previous company had faced something similar. He suggested I visit with another engineer who had also worked on that project and now worked for our company. Someone else introduced another problem and we tossed around various solutions. After a while everyone rotated to another group for more discussions.

Despite the somewhat forced nature of the assignment, the blend of geology and engineering minds conversing in unfamiliar office environments sparked a rush of brainstorming and what-if creativity in all groups. Supervisors collected over 200 ideas and later whittled them down to about 50 that were actionable.

I really enjoyed the innovation experience, and it wasn't long before I started diving deeper into similar topics like excellence, creativity, and business psychology.

"Merry Christmas! And this is what Senior Management really thinks of you."

Communication, especially from Management to the staff, would become a dominant theme in my professional life, and inspire multiple entries on my list of Moore's Laws, presented later and in Appendix 1.

(Note: most of the time I capitalize Management, because I'm pretty sure that's how Management would prefer to be portrayed, as Important. Pro tip: Write for the job you want, not the job you have.)

At my first company in the early 1980s, feedback on personal performance was universally desired and rarely received. Consequently, the annual personalized Christmas card each of us received from the Division Production Manager took on special but probably undeserved significance. The staff would meet in break rooms or hallways and ask "did you get yours? What did it say?"

The DPM's short, handwritten note began with your first name. The message that followed was assumed to be a Major Clue as to how you were perceived by Senior Management. If you were wished a generic "Merry Christmas" or "Have a Great New Year," you were pretty much screwed. The Big Guy did not know who you were, or what you did.

If the message included a reference of any kind to your assignment or project, it was considered a positive sign. Management knew both your name and the work you were doing. The more specific the reference, the better: "Steve, Nice work on the Fee C line well agreement."

If you received the dreaded "We have many challenges ahead in 198_," it was interpreted as "Uh oh. You should update your resume and activate Steve-Net to find a new opportunity, and soon."

Sending personalized Christmas cards to the staff was certainly a nice thing to do, and I can think of only a couple of other managers who took the time to do this.

Still, it seemed to me one shouldn't have to wait until the holidays or your annual performance review to get feedback from Management.

I should have known my Manager was good at Playing the Game

After the CEO had octuple-bypass surgery (that's an 8, followed by uple zeros), the Company built a state-of-the-art employee health and fitness facility at a cost of more than $40 million (that's a 4, followed by 89 reservoir engineering salaries).

It was located in the Company's headquarters in downtown Houston and was truly incredible: A gym loaded with weights and Nautilus machines, racquetball courts, fully stocked locker rooms, and a plethora of personal fitness trainers. There was an indoor running track, studios for exercise classes, and a partially subsidized cafeteria where you could order food by the ounce. You brought your own shoes, all other clothing, towels, and sports equipment was provided.

I was in Houston to attend a week-long training course with a small group from Bakersfield including Pat, my supervisor. Pat was excited to learn the facility included handball courts. I told him my grandfather played handball, and when my brother, sister and I were kids we used to play with his old balls that had lost most of their bounce. (Yes, I'm fully aware of the last sentence. Context, people! Let's keep things professional.)

I had never played handball, and Pat offered to teach me the game. Late in the afternoon we checked in at the fitness desk and were given shorts, socks, t-shirts, handballs, and gloves. We changed in the locker room, then started slapping the ball around. I was terrible and just whacked at the ball, trying to send it back to the wall. Pat taught me the rules but not the proper technique, and after 20 minutes my hands were swollen hunks of useless raw meat hanging from my arms. Pat enjoyed our game, but it was a miserable experience for me.

In the locker room, Pat helped me peel off my gloves. I couldn't bend my huge sausage fingers at all, so I removed my shirt and shorts using only my thumbs. After showering, I managed to slip on my underwear, socks, and polo shirt, but I could not grip the zipper of my pants with my fingers. Fastening the button was impossible; I didn't even try.

Pat laughed so hard his butt fell off, leaving him with his own pants problem. There was no way I was going to ask my boss for assistance, the situation was bad enough already. I wasn't about to ask a stranger, either. "Excuse me, Mr. Vice President of North American Production. Would you mind zipping up my trousers? Why, yes, I am a reservoir engineer. Why do you ask?"

Picture yourself in my situation: You manage to pull your pants up to your waist, and you spread your legs apart to keep them from falling while you work on the zipper. You have four wieners and an opposable Plump When You Cook 'em Ballpark Frank on each hand. Your reservoir engineering supervisor is a giggling ball of jello, rolling around the floor of the locker room without an ass. Your mission (and you must accept it): raise the zipper to a minimum height sufficient to hold your pants together and avoid scaring people as you walk back to your hotel. What do you do?

You bend over for a gravity assist so the zipper tab hangs free. You work the tip of a wiener-finger underneath the tab and try to hold it steady while you maneuver a wiener tip from the opposite hand to the other side of the tab. Friction is your friend, and you mash your wiener tips together and try to raise the flag. Both fingers slip off immediately, and you note with satisfaction that your boss is now choking on his own tongue. Repeat as many times as necessary.

Eventually, I switched to my frankfurter thumbs, inched the zipper about halfway up and declared Victory. I slipped into my shoes, not bothering with the laces, and slunk back to my hotel room. It was my first and last time to play handball.

"I always gave my job 125%."

Management held asset reviews with all teams each quarter. At one meeting I pointed out to the Production Manager it was my fifth quarterly review of the calendar year and asked if he could change my dollar bill into quarters for the vending machine. He didn't seem to get the joke.

Now that I think of it, this might have been the start of the "performance issues" I had with Management…

"We believe there was a second presenting engineer located behind the glassy partition."

One of the supervisors must have had narcolepsy. He would be sitting at his desk listening to you speak, and then mid-sentence his eyes would flutter and his head would drop, then he'd shake himself awake. The poor guy always fell asleep during meetings, inspiring the staff to break down the Zapruder film:

"In frame 92 we see the supervisor's eye lids begin to close and the first downward tilt of the skull occurs. Skipping ahead to frame 97, the body jerks violently and the head snaps up and back as the manager appears to regain consciousness with appropriate embarrassment…"

What if your boss is a Climate Survey Denier?

During my third year, all employees were asked to complete a company-wide "Climate Survey," consisting of dozens of questions on topics like corporate culture, HR policies, management styles, and communication. It almost seemed like the Company might actually *care* what the employees thought of their employer.

The survey was almost anonymous. It did not ask for your name, but required the names of your division and department, and the number of years you had been with the company. Anyone with rudimentary math skills and a roster of employees by department could figure out whose answers they were reading, give or take a person or two. And there were more than a few people with the requisite skills working for the company (even in HR). Pat and I were the only reservoir engineers in our division with three years of experience and based on the way Pat behaved around management, it was going to be easy to distinguish my answers from his. I shrugged it off and filled out the survey with honest opinions. From conversations with the RE group later, it seemed like most everyone gave the Company serious, thoughtful feedback.

A few months later Management shared the results of the Climate Survey, compiled by a third-party consulting firm. The Pacific Coast Division, which was the *top performing division* during the year in which the survey was conducted, had the lowest morale score of all the divisions. I did the math: Low morale equals top performance. *That can't be good.*

It got worse: The Reservoir Engineering Department had the lowest morale score in our division. *Uh oh.* The two reservoir engineering supervisors squirmed in their chairs. The morale of the group was kinda sorta on them, right?

Division Management appeared genuinely concerned. A mediator from the consulting group came to Bakersfield and met with each department without supervisors or managers present. He encouraged frank discussions and eventually the reservoir engineers opened up and told him what we thought could be done to improve communication and morale issues.

The meeting lasted a couple of hours. On the way back to my office, I passed by my supervisor's office and he called me in. He asked how the meeting went; I told him fine.

"So, what kind of issues do we have in the reservoir department?"

I was surprised by his question but not by his concern. He was a first-line supervisor of the staff with the crappiest morale in the company. The consultant had made it clear we could be honest in our discussion and the feedback he'd provide to Management would not use specific examples or anyone's name.

I wasn't going to give my boss any details and muttered something innocuous. "You know, the usual stuff." He continued prompting me and after a couple of minutes realized I wasn't going to give him anything. He leaned back in his chair.

"Well, I can't believe it. I had no idea morale was so low in our group."

I stared at him and used my telepathic powers to silently think-scream at him: "YES! EXACTLY! YOU DON'T ENGAGE WITH YOUR STAFF ENOUGH TO NOTICE THEIR MORALE!"

That encounter with Clueless really stuck with me. I experienced variations of this behavior many times over the years, and eventually summarized the issue as:

Moore's Law of Communication:
You must first have *communication,* before you can have a communication *problem.*

The manager who hears no problems, doesn't have to deal with any problems. If morale had been on his weekly list of Things To Do, the boss might have checked it out with his staff. I think most of us would have been grateful for the opportunity, and cheerfully offered up potential solutions, too. All he had to do was ask.

One last Baskin Robbins thing

One Bakersfield summer evening my family and I stepped inside a Baskin Robbins shop for ice cream after a movie. As the teenage boy behind the counter filled orders, I flashed back to my own experience with BR years earlier. When it was my turn to order I remembered one of my favorites.

"Can you make a milkshake out of chocolate mint ice cream?"

Without hesitation the kid nodded and calmly said, "Yes. I have the knowledge."

I've thought of that moment often, and still admire how adroitly he answered my stupid question with a perfect, snappy retort. I assume he was sharp enough to avoid a long-term career in frozen desert sales, and I sincerely hope he went on to have a great life.

My First Performance Review

The first year of my career was all training, spending several months each in the production, geological, and drilling engineering departments. I started my first reservoir engineering assignment in August 1982, managing several heavy-oil thermal leases.

In May of 1983 I had my first annual performance review with the Reservoir Engineering Manager. The written appraisal form listed my strengths as "generally gets projects done on time, good work ethic," and "inquisitive."

In the section marked "Employee Development" (not-so-loosely translated as "Weaknesses") my boss had written: "Needs to gain more experience." I had to agree; after one year on the job it sure would be nice to get some more experience. Check, I'll get right on that. I understood that my first review was a low-expectations freebie.

There was at least one sign of Things To Come. In my handwritten notes from that first review is this piece of advice to myself: *"Put out brush fires as quickly as possible!!!"* Note the use of three exclamation points. Extinguishing metaphorical flames would turn out to be a recurring theme throughout my career. (Yeah right. For me and every other human on the planet for all of time.)

"Steve is overly concerned with the use of the word 'overly.'"

My second performance review in 1984 did not go well. It turned out to be the worst review of my career, and it occurred just three years after I graduated from college.

I had a different supervisor this time. Pat transferred from another division six months earlier. Naturally, he started with the positives. "Does good detailed analytical work. Good technical background. *Has good written and verbal communication skills."* (Emphasis added. I received this complement from managers many times over the years. This was a significant Clue, unnoticed at the time, revealing the One True Path to Self-Actualization.)

Next up, Employee Development: "Poor time management skills – cannot set workable goals and meet them, gets stalled due to perfectionism." *Yikes! What the hell? And why am I suddenly thinking about my father?*

Then the Middle-Finger Death Punch I did not see coming: "Overly sensitive to superior/subordinate roles with colleagues. Overly concerned with political implications rather than getting job done." *Boss used "overly" twice in consecutive sentences!* It was immediately clear I would have to act much more *underly* if I was to have a future with the Company.

Obviously rehearsed and choreographed to perfection, the District Reservoir Engineering Manager stepped through the door. My supervisor smoothly tossed him the spiked club with which he'd verbally pounded me, now covered with dripping, sticky bits of oozing flesh ripped from the still-warm corpse of my engineering career.

The District Manager choked up and continued pummeling the overly-dead horse. I was not where I should be as a developing engineer, and I needed to get my act together. Then he told me I was on Double Secret Probation. (Okay, he just called it "probation," but it's impossible for anyone my age who has seen Animal House more than once to not automatically add "double secret" anytime he hears or sees that word.)

I didn't know what was meant by "...overly concerned with political implications." I was an engineer for crying out loud, I didn't have an MBA! I had no interest in feeding the egos of managers and colleagues. It was all about solving technical problems, as efficiently and economically as possible. That's what engineering was all about, right?

Wrong, you Mooron! You, dear reader, of course know the answer: It absolutely was about playing The Game, saying the right thing at the right time, and appearing to be totally impressed when you were actually skeptical. After a few stressful days of serious introspection and analysis, I realized I'd made two huge mistakes:

1) The Company was collaborating with a third party to test a surfactant steam additive, and the pilot project was located on one of the leases I had been assigned to manage as Area Reservoir Engineer. A senior engineer with many years of experience was also involved in the project. I pushed back at him on a couple of issues, thinking I had decision-making authority. It was my area and I was responsible for meeting my performance targets, so I felt justified in expressing my opinions. I didn't read it correctly at all, and my sword-crossing with the senior engineer percolated up to management. I'm positive if my Boss had explained the senior engineer was the Lead for the project and was effectively in charge of the lease, I would have understood and complied. Instead, I blew it by assuming it was still my lease and my project, and that the senior engineer was actually assisting me.

2) The thermal (heavy oil) reservoir staff had recently completed a year of significant in-house training conducted by two experienced engineers formerly employed by Shell and Getty. They convinced Management that critical improvements in the Company's thermal EOR operations were needed, and competently mentored the rest of the staff in the latest technologies and strategies. The program was a success; expenses were reduced and production and profits went up.

Enter my new supervisor, who did not have a petroleum engineering degree and was not present for the training and implementation of the Thermal Revitalization program. A few months before my performance review I debated a technical issue with him, confident I was right as the topic had been thoroughly covered during the in-house seminars. I was certain that for this issue I had more relevant experience and training than my boss, who should respect my recommendation. He insisted on another approach, and after a tense exchange I agreed to comply with his decision.

My motivation for arguing with my boss (yeah, that sounds pretty stupid to me too) was partly derived from my understanding of my responsibilities as Area Reservoir Engineer, to apply correct technical solutions to problems on *my* leases. Later, I realized my supervisor may have thought I was questioning his management-hood by defending my position.

It was ironic: I had been judged "overly sensitive to superior/subordinate roles" and "overly concerned with political implications," yet it was clear I was unable to translate those concerns into positive political results. (And, perhaps, the Boss was a wee bit concerned about his own superior/subordinate situation?) When I boiled it down, the real problem was I did not conduct myself in a politically acceptable manner, resulting in the "does not work or play well with others" criticism in my review.

I was devastated. I worried about losing my job and being able to support my family. I immediately started coming in early each morning, making the first pot of coffee for the department. I stayed late in the evening and worked 11-hour days, cranking out proposals and memos in a show of productivity. Over Thanksgiving weekend, I set up a card table in the living room of our apartment and manually updated well test production plots during football games to identify cyclic steam stimulation candidates. In conversations with my supervisor, I was friendly, polite, and agreeable, frequently nodding my head and listening intently. I hated much of it, but I felt I had no choice other than to embrace my new role as "obsequious sycophant."

The next year flew by, and my strategy seemed to be working. At my next annual review, both managers took me to lunch and said I had recovered nicely. I was no longer on Double Secret Probation, and they appreciated my extra work effort and attitude. The written appraisal form includes, "did a good job this year working on superior/subordinate roles" and "job attitude improved significantly." Also, "continues to do good analytical work, complemented by *good communication skills.*" (There it is again.) I was relieved, of course, and happy I had found a way to reanimate my petroleum engineering career.

Ten months later I was terminated when oil prices crashed.

Black Friday Special: Free Cardboard Boxes

In 1986, the Saudis flooded the markets. Oil prices and many companies collapsed. Everyone had heard the rumors and was worried. I assumed the Company would implement several cost-cutting measures before they would cut staff. Surely Management would cancel perks like personal use of company cars, reduce or eliminate travel and training classes, maybe even cut salaries and benefits to protect people's jobs. If layoffs happened at all, they would be months away.

I was naive and wrong.

When prices started falling, the thermal asset teams were requested to evaluate and run cash flows for various scenarios in which steam injection was reduced or suspended. I remember several long days making dozens of economic runs, waiting at the printer room long after midnight for summary reports, and preparing slides and handouts for presentations to Management.

My team's presentation was Wednesday afternoon, and at the end I distinctly remember the VP of Engineering thanking each of us for the hard work and long hours. Later, I remembered how tired he looked, and that his tone and words of appreciation were a bit off. He knew what was coming.

Black Friday was March 14, 1986, and it left a mark. I arrived around 7am, my usual time, and headed for coffee. As I turned the corner, I had to step around stacks of brand-new cardboard boxes and shrink-wrapped rolls of packing tape in the hall next to the break room. *Shit. It's happening.*

It was quiet and eerie, everyone sitting in their office waiting to see how it would play out. I heard the phone ring in the office next to mine, then Alex was at my door.

"Harold wants to see me in his office. I guess this is it." His voice was shaky. I just nodded, unsure what to say. He returned in five minutes. "I'm out of here," he said, then went to his office and slammed the door.

I remember this very clearly: At the *exact* moment Alex's door banged shut, my phone rang. Later, I fantasized that I answered the phone and yelled, "Come get me, you sonsabitches!" then barricaded myself in my office, armed with a stapler and a letter opener.

It was Pat, Harold's secretary. Her voice was low and sad. "Steve, Harold would like to see you in his office." I took a couple of deep breaths and walked to the executive suite, my mind already leaping ahead and wondering how I was going to regroup and support my family. Pat didn't look up as I walked by her desk. I learned later those who survived the layoff started calling her "Norm" from the *Cheers* episode in which Norm is tasked with delivering termination news to coworkers because of his sympathetic, comforting style.

I sat across from Harold at a round table. The reservoir engineering manager sat on a couch nearby. Harold delivered the news and handed me a stuffed legal envelope. I don't remember the conversation except that it was completely one-sided. I had no idea what to say or how to react.

The Company laid off 25% of the Division staff. Most were involved with heavy-oil thermal operations, which went belly-up first from falling oil prices due to the high cost of production. We would receive severance pay and be provided with "outplacement" services, a term I had never heard before. Harold, who had handed me a job offer at the end of my plant visit 4.63 years earlier in November 1980, thanked me for my service and requested I pack and leave the office by mid-afternoon.

Sure, you bet. No reason to drag out the agony. I wouldn't want to cause a morale problem in the reservoir department. I packed my office and hauled the boxes to my car. On my last trip out, I paused for a moment, then slipped my nameplate from the bracket by the door and tossed it in the box.

I was 26 years old, and my wife was seven months pregnant with our second child. I distinctly remember thinking the whole "petroleum engineering" thing might not work out.

What the Heck is Outplacement?

Despite being laid off by my first company in less than five years, I still consider Tenneco to be at or near the top of my list of favorite employers. A big reason for this was the severance package and other termination benefits they provided to all who were terminated in March 1986.

I received six months' salary as severance pay, and three months of extended medical insurance benefits which would cover the birth of my son in May. This gave me some much-needed breathing room and time to evaluate options.

There were also "outplacement" services. The Company leased a handful of off-site offices with a large conference room for all to use for two months. We had access to a bank of telephones and unlimited long-distance service (a huge benefit back then). A typing service was available for resumes and cover letters, and the place was well-stocked with office supplies, coffee and snacks. A representative from the local chamber of commerce gave a presentation on small businesses for sale in Bakersfield to those who might consider changing careers.

The Company seemed sincere and committed to helping all of us land on our feet. Each week for several months I received a weekly jobs packet in the mail, sent from corporate HR. Inside were many pages of industry job opportunities culled from ads in *Oil and Gas Journal* and newspapers in energy towns like Houston, Midland and Denver.

A Lesson in Perspective

All of us were encouraged to attend a group therapy session with an occupational counselor to work through issues and strategies for getting our lives back on track. I still remember two thought-provoking exercises from the session. Both were very helpful in maintaining a proper, healthy perspective on what just happened to each of us.

The counselor told us to use a clean sheet of paper and draw a line down the middle, top to bottom. We labeled the bottom of the line zero and wrote our current age at the top (I was 26). She asked us to recall major events and meaningful experiences, such as key relationships, marriages, births, deaths, graduations, vacation trips, anything we considered personally significant. We made tick marks and labeled the events in relative order on our life line. Naturally, each of us marked an event at the top labeled "Terminated" or "Shit-canned" or "Released from Bondage" depending on our outlook.

The counselor told us to look at our life lines and consider the nature of the events we had noted. They had emotional impact at the time they occurred, but the significance and relevance for most of them had probably faded. They were still important memories but likely did not affect our current feelings and thoughts as they once did. They were now just part of our history.

She asked us to imagine the line extending up from the top of the page and, depending on our current age, stretching two, three, or even four times its current length to represent our total life expectancy. The age at the top might be 75, 90, or 100. She encouraged us to think of the many significant life events we would experience in the future and to imagine them marked on our lines. Could we realize the layoff was just one of many events that would appear on our final life line? I thought this was a terrific thought experiment, and very helpful.

For the second exercise the counselor asked us to imagine that we had died at the end of our extended life line. How would we inscribe our own gravestone to indicate we had lived a successful life? We each gave it some thought and scribbled our responses. The counselor surprised us by requesting we read our descriptions of success out loud to the group. There was quite a mix of answers. Many had to do with family: "He was a good father." "Successfully raised three kids to be responsible adults." Some were religious, and a couple were materialistic: "Traveled the world," or "Retired rich and died debt free."

After all twenty-five of us read our descriptions of a successful life, the counselor pointed out not one of us had said anything at all about working for the company that just ended our employment. No one even mentioned the oil and gas industry. Our vision for success in life was not tied to working as engineers or geologists or accountants.

This exercise really helped me, I now had a much better perspective on what had happened. It was a big deal now, but in the long run it would be just another tick mark on my life line.

Terminating Unemployment

The outplacement counselor distributed a handy little booklet called *How to Find Work in the New Economy,* which I still have. One of the valuable tips in the book recommended keeping track of your work history, previous addresses, salary information, and other personal information that would be required filling out job applications, unemployment forms, and other government applications. I wrote my information in the forms provided in the booklet.

It is easy to keep track of information digitally now, but in 1986, before personal computers, cell phones, and the Internet were common, compiling the information in the booklet turned out to be handy. A few years ago, I attempted to set up access to my social security account with the U.S. government and had to answer a handful of questions such as "which one of the following was not an address at which you lived." I dug *How to Find Work* from my files to verify a couple of Bakersfield street addresses from 30+ years earlier.

Tenneco encouraged each of us to file for unemployment benefits due to the "forced reduction in staff." I took the book along with me when I went to the unemployment office. I remember waiting in line with a geologist friend, feeling awkward and depressed.

Shortly after receiving my first weekly unemployment check, I got another call from "Norm" with a much happier outcome. Pat patched me through to Harold, who gave me a name to contact about a job opportunity. He had spoken with the general manager at Elk Hills and recommended me for a reservoir engineering position. He did the same for a laid-off drilling engineer. We both interviewed and were offered jobs. I gleefully terminated my unemployment benefits and started working again on April 14, 1986, exactly one month after the layoff. Six weeks later my son was born.

Somehow, I had bounced. We were able to save the severance pay and a year later used it for a down payment on our first house. I eventually concluded—with great relief—that I didn't totally wash out of my first engineering job, not if an executive manager was personally recommending me to a peer at another company. I remain eternally grateful to Harold, who hired me, fired me, and helped me get hired again. It was a huge help to me and my family.

Thank you.

THE MUDDLE

A seemingly endless collection of humorous anecdotes, office misadventures, and amazing stories of professionals behaving badly. Plus, commentary and a bit of philosophy, all presented in much the same way memories appear in my mind these days: mostly at random, occasionally clustered.

"Meet Steve, our new reservoir engineer and government policy analyst."

I worked the next four years as a reservoir engineer for a large private company hired by Chevron and the U.S. Department of Energy to operating the humongous Elk Hills Field. I spent 3.99 of those years trying to find a way to escape to a "real" job with a conventional oil and gas company.

As an operator without an ownership stake, the Company made money by keeping the DOE staff happy and, to a lesser degree, Chevron managers. Each month the Company received an Award Fee calculated from a complicated formula that included performance scores and ratings in a wide variety of areas. I still have a copy of the NPRC - CPAF Functional Monitor Report for February 1989. It is 61 pages long and summarized nicely on the cover page with a simple overall rating: Good. The report is chock full of government jargon describing metrics and contractor performance, everything you'd imagine a 1980s government report would include.

To be sure, production of oil and gas and drilling operations were included in the report, sandwiched in between Safety ("the number of backing accidents involving Unit vehicles declined 0.3% from the previous reporting period") and Human Resources ("Personnel action reports were submitted late for the 3rd straight month.")

On my third day, I was assigned a task which would be the strangest reservoir engineering project of my entire career: Write a political "position paper" which explained that continued production of Elk Hills crude oil was inconsistent with public statements made by Vice President George H.W. Bush. The VP had urged countries in the Middle East to reduce production to stabilize oil prices, while the U.S. Government maintained production levels at the giant Elk Hills field.

This was clearly beyond my purview, but I did my best. I drafted a one-page memo summarizing the issue and suggesting it might be politically expedient for the Reagan Administration to "consider shutting in a portion of the Elk Hills production in a symbolic gesture of support." My supervisor passed it along to Senior Management with a post-it note: "it looks good, and could use some closing verbiage." Management returned it to my boss three weeks later, and he gave the original back to me. The issue faded quietly; I never heard that any action was seriously contemplated and did not receive any other feedback.

I gained valuable experience working on world-class reservoirs while surrounded by a rich tapestry of quirky characters (Moore about them later), but I couldn't wait to leave Elk Hills. I wanted to work in a more conventional corporate culture and add value through economic development of oil and gas assets. Exactly four years to the day after starting, I resigned to accept a thermal reservoir engineering position with a company in Bakersfield.

Geologists prefer faults to vaults.

For most of my time at Elk Hills, my office was in one of the overflow trailers scattered around the main building. As part of a task force, I shared a bullpen with a reservoir engineer, two geologists, and a draftsman. I think we all preferred to be in the trailer, we were far away from our managers and could open a door or window for fresh air. When the boss paid us a visit, we heard the trailer door open in time to stop bullshitting, turn down the music, and pretend to be hard at work.

The two production engineers on the team shared a cramped office inside the main building. Their space was tight and limited to accommodate the opening of a large steel door, the entrance to the main file room. It was an actual vault like those used in banks, strong enough to survive a fire, earthquake, or accidental bombing from the Air Force jets that occasionally buzzed the field. Elk Hills was a government facility, so the well files were locked up at the end of the workday. It was not unusual to hear frustrated geologists pounding on the door and yelling "Let me in, dammit!" or "Let me out, dammit!" at least once a week.

HR Puffing about Stuff

When I accepted the job offer over the phone, the nice HR lady told me there would be a drug test. I was in a good mood. "Sure thing. What drugs do you want me to bring?" I could tell from her silence she did not think this was funny.

Months later the same HR rep and the corporate attorney, in a mandatory all-hands meeting, announced a new drug policy. Security could come to your office at any time and request you step away from your desk while they searched your office and personal belongings. During the Q&A session, I raised my hand.

"Let's say I take a restroom break and leave my office for a few minutes. A production engineer in a nearby office sees the Drug Interdiction Task Force coming. He grabs a fistful of doobies from his backpack, ducks into my office and drops them in my bottom desk drawer. Security finds it and I'm in trouble. What is my protection against something like that? Will we be provided with keys so we can lock our desks and doors?" I knew the new policy was a legal thing, and it was stupid of me to pipe up during the meeting. Still, I thought I had made a good hypothetical point.

The HR rep was clearly flustered and came up with this stunning jewel in response: "Well, we're all professionals here and we'd like to think something like that wouldn't happen."

If that was true, then why did we need a drug-search policy in the first place?

Safety first. Mostly

Safety, of course, was a big priority. Especially at a government-owned field where the number of monthly "backing accidents" in Company vehicles was an important performance metric, on par with successfully drilling a 10,000′ oil well.

At one monthly meeting, the Safety Engineer warned the office staff not to open fully-loaded top drawers of file cabinets if the lower drawers were empty. He cited a statistic like "every 17.3 minutes a worker is injured by a toppling file cabinet." I whispered to my neighbor, "After it fell on him 3 or 4 times, seems like the geologist would've figured it out." The Safety Engineer went on to say, "If you don't believe a file cabinet will fall on you, try it sometime." Solid advice.

The safety guy also proudly reported the number of days since the last lost-time accident. I wondered: did death from a diabolical file cabinet loaded with reserves reports count as a lost-time accident, or was it a simple case of "involuntary termination of employment?"

There was one safety issue that I thought perfectly captured the flavor of working at a government facility. The winter fog in the Bakersfield area frequently caused condensation to form on the metal doorsteps of the trailers. During an occasional cold snap, they could even become a bit icy. Rather than replace or modify the metal stairs with a safe non-slip material, the Company posted signs warning "SLIPPERY WHEN WET." For a company whose profit was partially derived from safety performance, I thought it was a half-assed solution. Didn't the trailer staff deserve a total-ass effort?

And what was up with all those belt buckles handed out in the 80s and 90s? It wasn't like we were all counting on this year's safety award to keep our pants from falling down.

Lunches with Buddy

The nearest place to eat lunch was the golf course snack shop across the highway. The other options were in the small town of Taft, a 20-minute drive curving around ancient wooden oil derricks scattered between dusty clusters of roadside trailer homes. My friend Buddy and I would get chicken sandwiches at Leonard's, or kung pao something-or-other at a tiny Chinese restaurant.

Frequently we ended up at Pizza Hut. We talked about how much we enjoyed our jobs, marveled at the high-quality communication we received from managers, and exchanged examples of professionalism by coworkers. We were pleased with how our petroleum engineering careers were going, and easily saw ourselves retiring from the Company in another 30 years or so.

Nope. We dissected and analyzed the micro-management behaviors and absurdities we had experienced that morning in the office. We discussed plans to someday escape from oil and gas and spend the rest of our lives writing novels. We wanted to live like Hemingway, not like (insert the name of your favorite Reservoir Engineering Legend here. Right, I can't think of one either.) Our lunches were highly cathartic therapy sessions over salads and personal pan pizzas.

I have a very distinct memory of sitting in a booth at Pizza Hut with Buddy on a hot afternoon in August 1988. On a wall-mounted television a Los Angeles news station announced a breaking sports story: A Canadian newspaper had reported the Edmonton Oilers had traded Wayne Gretsky to the (then) lowly Los Angeles Kings. The sports guy sounded skeptical and so was I, but the story was confirmed the next day.

Gretsky is also known for wisely saying *you miss 100% of the shots you don't take.* I thought of this quote often over the years trying to manage my career. I don't remember where I was when JFK was assassinated (I was only four), but I will always remember where I was when I heard The Great One was migrating south to L.A.

Déjà Interview

In 1988 I wanted a better opportunity and managed to get a job interview with a reservoir engineering manager at a large independent company. It was my first interview in two years, and I was serious about improving my career prospects. I was also realistic about my chances for getting an offer but knew the interview would be great practice.

It was a sunny afternoon when I met with Pat in his office. I recall the weather because the window blinds were down but partially open, and the sun was in a perfect position to set up a dazzling slotted-light pattern directly behind Pat's chair.

Pat's interview style today would be considered "old school" but in 1988 it was just "school." He pulled out a legal pad and told me he was going to ask some specific questions. I stifled an urge to promise to give specific answers and said I was ready.

I only remember a few of his questions, but they were typical. What was your greatest accomplishment in your previous job? What do you feel are your strengths? What are your weaknesses? If you were an endangered native California species, which one would you be?

No, he didn't actually ask that last one. After I responded to each question, Pat wrote a note on his pad. I attempted to maintain eye contact and speak with confidence, but as the interview progressed I realized I was getting an ocular migraine. That angled light/dark pattern from the window blinds behind Pat was really bothering me. It was developing into one of my typical migraine headaches, complete with temporary vision and speech problems and numbness in my face and fingers. I did my best during the discussion but fumbled some words and my train of thought was derailed a couple of times. Pat must have noticed my difficulty but gave no indication.

We finished our meeting and I thanked him for the opportunity. Before I left the parking lot, I wrote in my notebook every question Pat asked, as well as the answers I gave. After struggling through the headache I didn't feel confident about the way things went, but I had obtained some good empirical data and planned to use the notes to prepare for future interviews and develop better responses.

As expected, I didn't receive an offer. I continued looking for opportunities, but the industry was still in a downturn. Two years later in 1990, the same company had another opening for a reservoir engineer. I contacted the HR department and was somewhat surprised when they invited me back for another meeting with Pat.

The night before the second interview, I studied the notes from our discussion two years earlier. I was impressed with—and thankful for—the level of detail I had captured and carefully reviewed the questions and my answers. The notes helped me remember Pat's personality and style, and that I had fumbled some questions due to the headache. I was confident I would perform better this time.

I met with Pat in the same office, and this time there was no problem with the window light. After exchanging pleasantries, Pat pulled a file from his desk labeled with my name. He said he had made notes from my first interview and would update them during our conversation.

He asked me a question and I recognized it as the same first question from our previous session. I gave my answer and Pat looked at his notes. He paused, then asked another half-dozen questions. During my answers he studied his sheet. Finally Pat chuckled and said my responses were "remarkably similar" to those I had given two years earlier. He seemed impressed with my consistency, and apparently it never occurred to him that I might have used my own notes from our previous conversation.

I felt much better about this interview, but still took time to write detailed notes before driving home. A few days later I received an offer which I accepted. Pat was my manager for the next three years.

At a writing seminar several years ago, a guest speaker recommended that everyone "be good to your future self." The idea was to take actions today that will make things easier for yourself in the future, a form of being your own best friend. Writing everything I could remember after that first interview with Pat clearly helped me two years later. I continued writing detailed post-interview notes for the rest of my career.

"I don't know, what are YOU most proud of?"

Long ago I came across a terrific suggestion for a question to ask your potential boss during a job interview: "Let's say one year from now you're telling me I'm the best performer on your staff. What will I have done during the year for you to tell me that?" I thought this was an excellent question to which few managers would be able to give a ready response. And if they did, it would be extremely useful and set clear expectations.

In 2008 I had a series of short interviews with managers and technical staff, and my last session was with the Division General Manager. I was planning to ask my clever "one year from now" question but got derailed when he asked, "What is the one thing you are most proud of?"

I was unprepared and stalled by asking if he meant professionally or personally. He shrugged. "Answer however you like." I realized I was stumped in either category. I not only didn't have a good answer, I didn't seem to have any answer at all. Of course there were things in my life and career for which I was proud, but at that red-hot moment nothing came to mind.

On the personal side, I imagined people would typically be proud of their family (except free-wheeling singles with no kids). I decided to skip that common response and go with a professional answer. I knew I couldn't tell the GM that I was proud of maintaining continuous reservoir engineering employment for 27 years while deriving no joy or satisfaction from doing actual reservoir engineering work.

I finally chose to describe a special team project from a few years earlier, in which we significantly improved the collection, analysis and reporting of real-time production data to quickly respond to problems and facilitate corporate decision making. It was a genuine accomplishment of which I was proud, but it seemed a weak answer to a "most proud" job interview question.

It was also more evidence that I was still struggling to find My Path. I wished my younger self had been a better friend and sprinkled a few more metaphysical breadcrumbs for me to follow.

Despite my experience of that interview, I was unprepared when it happened again several years later. This time the question was "What do you enjoy most?" I struggled to produce a good, quick answer, one that either 1) impressed the manager as an excellent response, or 2) expressed the truth. What, in fact, did I enjoy? I don't recall what I said but I remember I took way too long to answer.

Today I'd respond, "Finding the humor in Life, then writing about it."

"Okay...how do you feel about Ted Nugent?"

I was listening to "La Grange" on the radio while working at my desk when Brad walked in. I reached over to turn down the volume and Brad leaned over my desk and jabbed a finger at me.

"Don't EVER turn down ZZ Top!"

That perfect response is etched in my memory. To this day, every time I hear the opening riff of "La Grange" I hear Brad yelling at me.

A Small Constellation of Management Stars, Part 1: Dave and Don

A few years ago, I made a list of every supervisor to whom I reported during my career. I also included a handful of names from senior management if I had a significant working relationship with them. There were 40 names on the list.

I reviewed the list and considered my experience with each manager. I put a check mark next to those managers I'd be happy to work for again. I checked 5 names, 12.5% of the total. This says much more about me than the people on the list. I realized long ago that *I was the common denominator in every single one of my problems.*

Dave Kilpatrick and **Don DeCarlo** are two of my favorite managers, and I continue to have the highest respect for each of them. Both were regional leaders for a company I worked for in the early 1990s. If either of them contacted me today and invited me to relocate across the country to join them in a new venture, I'd try hard to find a way to accept. Both men were friendly and projected easy confidence without a hint of arrogance. They stayed abreast of all operations and actively engaged with the staff, always ready to discuss your project.

Dave and Don each had a terrific sense of humor and were instrumental in creating and sustaining a terrific office culture.

Everyone in the Office is on the Party Planning Committee

The Company Summer Picnic was a great example. Every employee participated, including Dave and Don and the rest of the management team. There were committees for the Santa Maria style barbeque, kid games, party favors, food, drinks, ice, entertainment, horseshoe contests, and cleanup. By design, each committee was a blend of folks from different departments so we would get to know each other better.

I remember working a shift at the fishing booth, crouched down out of site behind a wooden barricade. Kids would dangle their plastic fishing poles over the wall, and we'd attach a toy and give their line a tug. Working the booth with me was the regional vice president, an accountant, a production engineer, and an HR rep. The picnics fostered a sense of community and teamwork and were a great success.

At 4pm on the last Friday of each month, the entire office staff (including senior managers) gathered in the main conference room. Those with birthdays that month were celebrated with jocularity and cake. Over time the parties grew into creative mini-roasts of the birthday folks, hosted by those who had birthdays the previous month. It became a competition, each host group trying to top the previous party with a creative twist or crazy theme.

Someone would re-write song lyrics to poke fun at one of the birthday people and a group would sing it to them, karaoke-style. Another month (years before cell phone cameras), an engineer with a video rig conducted man-on-the-street style interviews of coworkers telling funny stories about the birthday folks. Cake soon became cake and ice cream, then cake and pizza and ice cream floats. It was a great time, partly because Dave and Don urged everyone in the office to participate.

Lonnie and I had June birthdays, so we were the Party Planning Committee and hosts for the July party. One year we shook things up, moved the party to 8am, and arranged a biscuits-and-gravy breakfast from a popular diner for the entire office.

I picked up the order early from Carrows and set up the spread in the break room. Instead of sausage gravy for the biscuits, the restaurant had given me chicken gravy by mistake. I left Lonnie in charge, drove back to Carrows for a couple of containers of the good stuff, then hustled back to the office. I was too late and missed all the fun. No one cared a bit about the chicken gravy. No one saved me a biscuit, either.

And contrary to expectations, I did not eat the sausage gravy anyway. Without biscuits it just doesn't work.

"How do you like your eggs, flame-broiled or over crispy?"

I had another breakfast adventure with Lonnie a couple of years earlier. We carpooled one day to Elk Hills and drove through Carl's Jr. for a couple of Sunrise sandwiches. At the office we dropped by the break room and Lonnie put the bag of breakfast in the microwave after our 30-minute commute.

The sandwiches were wrapped in foil. Sparks commenced and the bag caught fire. I thought we had just set the building on fire but Lonnie just laughed, grabbed a handful of paper towels and tamped out the flames. I stood nearby, a tear rolling down my face. The sandwiches were a total loss.

By silent agreement, neither of us filed an Incident Report.

Putting the P in PC

As technology and software evolved in the early 1990s, it became impractical for engineers and geologists to use shared computers in tiny auxiliary offices. Eventually, individual computers were installed in the offices of all technical professionals, confirming that the P in PC stood for Personal.

Our first office computers were dumb network devices without hard drives. Our contract IT guy told us not to worry, there was plenty of storage on the servers. We ran out of space in one month.

Dave not only helped us get individual PCs, he urged Corporate to approve the installation of hard drives: "It's like hiring the best carpenters in the world to build your house, then giving them plastic tools to work with." The upgrades were approved.

Thank you, Don

Before I joined the Dave and Don company, I really wanted to escape from my previous job. I was very happy to receive an offer after my interviews. The vacation benefit was the standard two weeks per year.

Even though I had less than 10 years of experience, I was aware that many engineers changing jobs at the time were negotiating three weeks of vacation if they had five years of industry experience. I asked HR for three weeks of vacation, and the answer was no. I accepted the offer anyway.

During the next year the Company hired two or three engineers with similar years of experience, and all successfully held out for three weeks of vacation. I realized I should have been more assertive negotiating my deal but shrugged it off.

One morning Don walked into my office and shut the door. Don knew I hadn't held out for three weeks of vacation like the new guys. He told me to go ahead and plan on taking three weeks, and to let him know when I was taking the extra week. We'd keep it just between us.

I was completely surprised and thanked him enthusiastically. My respect for Don jumped a level or two. It was the nicest thing a manager had done for me since Harold recommended me for a job after the Tenneco layoff nine years earlier.

About six months later, Don dropped by again. He said he was in Houston the previous week and talked to HR. My third week of vacation was now official.

"It's a Major Award!"

In mid-December, Don walked into my office again and closed the door. He pulled an envelope from his coat pocket and tossed it on my desk.

I was the reservoir engineer on a team working the Company's heavy oil assets near the town of Coalinga, California. Oil prices combined with high operating steam-oil ratios resulted in marginal economics for thermal EOR projects in the Coalinga area.

Don said the Coalinga Team had done well, working hard to cut costs and improve production and profitability. He and Dave were giving a "Significant Contributor Award" to each member of the Team, along with a check for $1,500 just in time for Christmas.

I'd worked marginal properties before (as a Poso Bozo), it was not fun. The bonus check was much appreciated, but the fact that Don and Dave recognized our Team's efforts meant more than the money. Their actions and support matched my own philosophy regarding the Mission of a Manager: to get the most *and best* from each person on your staff.

Don is also the only boss to whom I gave notice of my resignation twice. In March of 2006, Don hired me for a second time to work for a company in Oklahoma City. Family issues prevented me from making the move from Tulsa, and I had to resign after only two months. Telling Don I was leaving was difficult, but he couldn't have been more gracious and understanding.

Dave and Don: thank you. It was a pleasure working for you both.

"Dads Deceiving Daughters for $200, Alex"

When my daughter was about six years old, she was the victim of a despicable hoax. I derive only a small amount of joy from the fact that I was the perpetrator.

She was the perfect age for this particular prank, young enough to still believe Dad could do anything. My powers of persuasion and influence were never greater.

It was a weeknight, 6:30pm. Just home after a long day at the office, I plopped on the couch and caught the beginning of the syndicated television game show *Jeopardy!* on a local station. I watched the entire show while my wife gave my daughter a bath.

Thirty minutes later Final Jeopardy was over. I surfed channels and found another *Jeopardy!* show starting on a different cable channel. My daughter joined me on the couch in her pajamas, fresh and clean from her bath.

I realized it was the same *Jeopardy!* episode I had just watched. I decided to have a little fun and started giving the correct questions before the contestants had a chance to respond. Sometimes even before Alex finished reading the answers.

"What is a Triceratops?"

"Who was Sir Isaac Newton?"

"What is Beethoven's Fifth Symphony"

I gave the correct response to every challenge, even wagering a gazillion dollars and winning Double Jeopardy. My daughter was super impressed that I finished Final Jeopardy with a perfect score. She said I was really smart and should go on the show and win a lot of money.

Okay, I know this was a tiny bit evil. I admit I enjoyed my little girl thinking I was the smartest man in the world, or at least in our apartment.

Ten years later, my daughter recalled that magical evening when I aced *Jeopardy!* I decided to come clean and told her how I knew all the correct responses. She was surprised, disappointed, and justifiably miffed. I suggested she could at least continue to respect my power of memorization, pointing out that I had memorized the correct questions after only hearing them once, 30 minutes earlier. She was not impressed.

What is "The End of a Family Legend?"

Men's Room Follies, Part 2: "Don't tell me what to do, I've got a Pee-hD!"

At one company there was a highly respected technical professional with multiple degrees, including a PhD. Many of us noticed this brilliant gentleman never washed his hands after visiting the men's room. Once you heard this or observed it yourself, any time you saw the guy around the office you remembered his nasty quirk.

One morning, a production engineer and I walked into the break room together. Dr. Hands was making a fresh pot of coffee. The production engineer impulsively confronted the guy, pointing out he shouldn't be making community coffee since he never washed his hands in the bathroom.

The guy smirked and childishly delivered the old, lame classic: "My mother taught me not to pee on myself." He seemed proud to acknowledge he didn't wash. I stayed out of it, but thought: *did your mother teach you anything about common courtesy? During your long academic journey, you couldn't pick up a little knowledge on germ theory?*

After that exchange, each time I saw Dr. Hands I remembered his stupid retort and reminded myself to avoid shaking his hand if we ever met sometime in the future.

"And on his deathbed, a geologist will have eternal optimism, which is gneiss."

After parking in the visitor's lot, my wife and I walked toward the rim of the Grand Canyon for our first spectacular view. As we approached the viewing area, we saw a crowd of people clustered around a body lying on the sidewalk, convulsing. EMTs were working on him, trying to stop the seizure.

Turns out he was a geologist on his first trip to the Canyon. He took one look and collapsed from a full-body orgasm lasting several minutes.

Geologists are a special breed of cat. High-functioning optimists, they look at a pile of rocks and ask, "How high can I fly?"

My Hero's Journey of Certification: The Professional Petroleum Engineering Examination

In the summer of 1988, I and several engineers in my company began preparing to take the professional license examination for petroleum engineers in October. I had passed the prerequisite Engineer-in-Training exam in ludicrous fashion as a junior in college. It would not go so easy this time.

Bing Wines, a consulting engineer from Oklahoma City, offered a review course for the exam. Topics included casing design, water drive material balance calculations, project economics and—yeah, boring stuff like that. Bing was well connected to the industry advisors that designed the tests each year. He explained the pass rate for the petroleum exam had soared in recent years to greater than 90%. The national engineering board was not happy, so the petroleum subcommittee made changes to the test and scoring methods. The 1988 test we were preparing for would be the first exam to use the new format and scoring process.

A clue about Reservoir Engineering and how it was perceived by the industry consultants designing the test: Bing said historically the reservoir engineering questions on the exam were the "least attempted" problems apart from the single economics problem which nearly every PE tackled. Drilling problems such as casing design were the most popular, followed by production engineering problems.

We took the review course, purchased a bunch of petroleum engineering textbooks (the exam was open book, you could bring in as many references as you could carry in one trip), and studied every night for several months.

The 8-hour exam was held at the Fresno fairgrounds, a two-hour drive from Bakersfield. Most of us went down the night before and stayed at a hotel. My friend Steve Thomas and I treated ourselves to a terrific steak dinner; others ordered take-out food for last-minute studying in their rooms.

Early Saturday morning we parked Steve's pickup truck and used two-wheeler dollies purchased specifically to haul three cartons each of reference books to the auditorium. My pre-exam stress was high. I had studied nearly every night for several months but had only a vague idea what to expect other than a very long day.

The new test format was a total of twenty problems. You chose four problems to work in the four-hour morning session, and four more in the afternoon session. Lunch was a peanut butter sandwich and a soda sitting on the tailgate of our truck in the parking lot.

As predicted, everyone worked the casing design problem as it was straightforward. I worked the economics and water influx material balance problems but don't remember the rest. It was a long day.

Four months later I received my exam results in the mail. I failed with a dismal score, well below the 70% needed to pass. Nearly everyone in the 1988 Bakersfield group failed. We learned later the national engineering board got the results they wanted; the overall pass rate for the PE exam dropped from a high of over 90% to just 15% for the 1988 exam.

Our tests were available for review in March 1989 in downtown Los Angeles. Scorers usually wrote useful notes on the tests indicating what was incorrect. Everyone had committed to take the exam again in 1989, so Steve and I took another road trip to LA. Mary Ann, our host from the State Board, passed out our exams and proctored our review. We were not allowed to make photocopies so we reviewed the notes in great detail, and as soon as she collected the tests we wrote down everything we could remember before returning to Bakersfield.

Most of us took Bing Wines' review course again, and he told us the low petroleum pass rate sparked great joy for the Test Committee. Steve and I studied every night for several weeks, traveled to Fresno again in October 1989, enjoyed our steak dinner, took the test with a PB sandwich lunch, and got our results four months later. We both failed again and repeated our Score Trek to LA to review the exam. Mary Ann remembered us from the year before.

Third exam, October 1990. Same result. This time Mary Ann said she was happy to see the "boys from Bakersfield" had returned. We took Bing's course again. Evidently it was not that helpful, but it did put our minds in study mode. I told Bing that other than my wife, he was the only person in America who wanted me to pass the PE exam.

1991: If it's October, I must be in Fresno. Fourth test, and I almost passed. Mary Ann greeted us cheerfully in March 1992 but didn't even pretend to be surprised. I noticed a bit of gray in her hair I didn't remember from the year before. We took Bing's class one more time just to contribute to his retirement fund. By then Steve had started an engineering consulting business. We studied every evening in the office he rented in a small business park, fortifying ourselves with Arby's sandwiches and buckets of coffee.

October 1992. We're on Highway 99 rolling toward Fresno, and without warning Steve shouts a long, drawn-out "F___ Meeeee!!" This perfectly captured our mood; we were getting burned out on the Professional Engineering license thing.

I thought back to high school in 1976. I took the ACT and scored a 28. This was a decent score, but with a 29 I would have qualified for a scholarship or grant at a state school, so I took the test again. My score was 28. I took the damn test a third time and scored another 28. I accepted it as The One True Measure of my academic performance and moved on with my life.

Of course, I also remembered how ridiculously easy it was to pass the EIT exam in college. Maybe by failing the PE exam multiple times I was experiencing the natural Karmaquences for breezing through the EIT test?

Steve and I agreed this would be the last time we took the PE test. If we failed again, we would accept defeat and take our place on top of the pile of Unprofessional Engineers.

In March 1993 I received my fifth exam score in the mail; I finally passed. Steve passed too, and There Was Much Rejoicing Throughout the Land. We took our wives to a celebratory dinner at Cask and Cleaver, the same restaurant where I had dinner my first night in Bakersfield in November 1980.

A couple of weeks later a fellow engineer named Brian dropped by to chat. On my desk was the custom stamp I had purchased to validate documentation as a Professional Engineer in the State of California. Brian picked it up and said, "Neat! How much did this cost?"

Five years of study. A huge stack of textbooks and a two-wheeler to haul them around. Taking Bing's review course four times. Gallons of coffee, stacks of sandwiches, and piles of pizzas. Five overnight trips to Fresno, four days of paid vacation spent driving to LA to review tests. Brian seemed surprised by my answer.

"About six thousand dollars."

The Opening Lines of a Reservoir Engineering Thriller I Plan to Write Someday:

Wiping the bloody knife on his Friday jeans, the engineer shoved the body behind the copy machine. "How's that for a budget cut?" he mumbled.

The Wrath of Grapes

In 1993, an independent company in Oklahoma needed engineers to work California oil and gas properties they had recently acquired. Since the jobs were in Tulsa, they were having trouble hiring engineers with California experience.

My wife's family and mine were in Tulsa, and after 12 years in California we recognized the opportunity to move to our hometown and put our kids back in touch with their grandparents. I interviewed with the company and my experience was a good fit. I received an offer that included a relocation package and a whopping 20% increase in salary. It was much cheaper to live in Tulsa, and it looked like a no-brainer decision. In a reverse migration, this Okie was leaving Bakersfield to move back to Oklahoma.

I hated the idea of leaving the Company after only three years. I thought Division Management was excellent, I had been treated very well, and enjoyed working on a strong team. When I discussed my resignation with Dave, the Division General Manager, I asked how a small company in Tulsa could pay me such a high salary. Without hesitation he answered, "you're underpaid here." He explained HR had extended a customary lowball offer after my interviews. I was more than ready to leave my previous company and instead of negotiating, I accepted their first offer. I was grateful to Dave for the honest explanation. Another lesson learned too late.

At my farewell party, coworkers really embraced my *Wrath of Grapes* theme, and I received several thoughtful gifts, including:

A pair of massive bookends made from damaged tubing pulled from two super-expensive steam breakthrough workovers from my leases in Coalinga field.

A jar of "really heavy" Coalinga crude oil.

A Dwight Yoakum CD including the song "Streets of Bakersfield."

A paperback copy of Steinbeck's *Grapes of Wrath*

A custom vortex-busting anti-tornado hardhat, redundantly labeled STEVE-BOB and BUBBA.

I had a small surprise of my own. I've always liked reversals and twisting things around. I purchased an extra-long "Goodbye from the Gang" card and modified the message to read from me to the group. I wrote a signed, personal message to everyone in the Division office, a total of 74 people. I think it was a hit. A year or two later my friend Mike mailed the card to me with a note:

"You can run, but you can't hide. Your past will always catch up with you! Thought you might have some use for this. Lord knows I don't."

Thanks, Mike. You were right.

Geo Jeff with Kung Fu Grip!

For several projects I was teamed up with Pat, an interesting variety of reservoir engineer. He threw off a vibe that I thought of as "quiet reluctance." He was affable enough but quirky.

At an offsite meeting I introduced Pat to Jeff, a geologist and former teammate with a great sense of humor. A couple of years earlier Jeff and I and a couple of others helped an engineer friend move to a new house on a Saturday morning. The engineer hadn't spent any time doing what veteran movers call "packing." At one point I carried a crock pot with no lid and a shoe box protecting a single sock to the rental truck. Jeff was ahead of me and got tangled up in a garden hose on the garage floor. He dropped his load and started wrestling with the hose, narrating the action in a loud TV-announcer voice:

"Jim wrestles with the Great Anaconda waist-deep in the river while Marlin sits in the air-conditioned broadcast studio." We all cracked up.

(I stole Jeff's bit and successfully used this joke on at least two other occasions years later. Note: it does not work on folks too young to remember Jim Fowler and Marlin Perkins from *Mutual of Omaha's Wild Kingdom*.)

The first time I met Jeff, he shook my hand with a knuckle-crushing grip. Pain shot up my arm and I realized I was meeting a Real Man. I stifled a whimper, increased my grip to a more respectable level, and hoped Geo Jeff with Kung Fu grip wouldn't notice the two-second delay.

So when I made the introduction I watched for Pat's reaction when they shook hands. To Pat's credit, his expression didn't change at all. Jeff said it was nice to meet, and Pat replied in a normal conversational tone that was completely at odds with his words: "Good God man, you nearly broke my hand."

Jeff looked surprised as Pat calmly massaged his sore hand. When Jeff looked at me, I turned and walked away so neither would see me laughing. Jeff told me later he hated it when a guy offered up a "limp fish" to shake.

The Cat Story

One afternoon I got a call at home from Geo Jeff. He knew we had just moved into our new house and gave me a "lost kitten crying in the rain" story. He wanted to bring it over and promised to take it away if we didn't want it. He knew all too well that my kids would beg to keep it. Our daughter named it Kathy, a name I could not bring myself to use. I just called it Cat.

Flash forward a couple of years. My wife's parents were visiting from Oklahoma. We were having dinner one evening and I saw through the window that the cat was outside in our back yard. Since we kept her indoors all the time, I figured someone accidentally left a door open. I excused myself and went out through the back patio door. I cornered the cat against the fence and she freaked out. It took quite a bit of effort and I suffered third-degree scratches on my arms but finally got her mostly under control. All four of her claws pierced my flesh through my shirt as I carried her into the dining room.

My wife, son, daughter, and in-laws stared at me with open mouths, forks suspended. Nonchalantly sitting upright on the floor near my chair was the cat some called Kathy. She looked up at me as if saying, "Dude, seriously? Another cat?" I had somehow managed to capture a stray copycat in our backyard and brought it inside the house.

"Oh," I said calmly to my family. *Holy effin' cow!* I thought to myself. My family laughed and laughed. I barked a sharp "No!" when my daughter asked if we could keep the new cat. I let it out the front door and it raced away so fast it turned red from the Doppler shift.

The Time Dad Caught the Stray Cat became one of those "family stories." I didn't mind. If you've ever tried to catch a stray cat outdoors and bring it inside your home, you know it's actually an incredible accomplishment.

The Engineer's Credo: Solve the Problem

I found an odd device lying on top of a cabinet in the cubicle where the community printer was installed. My supervisor walked by and must have noticed my puzzled expression.

"That's Pat's remote control light switch."

Pat was a contract petroleum engineer who commuted each week from Houston to Tulsa. He worked in a spare office long into the evening Monday through Thursday, then flew home Friday afternoons.

The lights on our floor went off automatically at 6pm. The manual reactivation switch was located near the elevator lobby door. Each night Pat trudged to the end of the hall, turned past two cubicles, made another turn, and walked another 20 feet to the control panel to flip the lights back on. After one hour the lights would go off again, and he'd repeat the process.

Pat was an Engineer, and Engineers Solve Problems. He duct-taped three presentation pointers together to make a 9-foot extension pole. My supervisor demonstrated the technique. He stepped into the printer cubicle, leaned over the top and extended the 3X-pointer to the far wall. It just reached the light button and saved Pat several dozen steps every evening.

Crude, but brilliant. And a wee bit lazy.

"We'll be right back after this break."

When I worked in California, smoking had been mostly banished from the workplace, and I only knew of a handful of coworkers who smoked. When I moved back to Oklahoma in 1993, I noticed the percentage of people who smoked was much higher, and I had to recalibrate my senses a bit and adjust to everyone's schedule. Frequently I'd walk into someone's office and they would be outside on a break. Some folks were pretty regular and I could check my watch each day to know if it was a good time to visit. Certain people seemed to take a lot of breaks, and one day I took one of my own and scribbled some calculations:

5 breaks/day x 10 min = 50 minutes each day

50 minutes/day x 4.5 days = 225 minutes/week
(We worked 40 hours in 4.5 days, with Friday afternoons off)

225 minutes/week x 48 weeks = 10,800 minutes/year

10,800 minutes/year / 60 minutes = 180 hours/year

180 hours/year / 40 hours = <u>4.5 weeks per year</u>

I was stunned. More than a person-month of time spent each year outside the office, smoking on the job? I shared the numbers with some coworkers and most were surprised. Someone pointed out 10 minutes per break was probably conservative; another pointed out some people seemed to take 8 to 10 breaks each day.

One guy said non-smokers took breaks too, talking about football or TV shows (or smoke breaks!) Another person pointed out that smokers participated in those discussions too, implying lots of folks took lots of breaks during the work day.

Building management had just implemented a "no smoking indoors" policy a few weeks before I started working for the Company. I assumed smokers thought if they could smoke at their desks as before, productivity wouldn't have suffered. I could understand that logic; everyone was adjusting to the new rules.

After doing the smoke math, I never worried about taking a break at the office again. Besides, over my entire career I averaged way more than forty hours of work each week, especially during reserves cycles.

He was right, too

One morning I shared an elevator with Larry, a production engineer. As we split toward our offices, I told him to have a great day. He paused and looked at me with great seriousness.

"Anything's possible."

Since that morning, every time someone tells me to have a great day I think of Larry and his perfect reply.

Delays and Demons

After a Geographix training course in Houston, my buddy Kyle and I were flying back to Tulsa. Our flight from Houston was delayed due to thunderstorms, and the airport announced a change in takeoff direction. Our plane taxied from one end of the airport to the other, then sat on the tarmac for an hour. Kyle had the window seat, I was in the aisle, and a quiet woman sat between us engrossed in a book. To pass the time, I tried to discretely read over her shoulder until I saw the title: *Everyone's Guide to Demons and Spiritual Warfare: Simple, Powerful Tools for Outmaneuvering Satan in your Daily Life* by Ron Phillips.

I breathed easier knowing if there was an outbreak of demonic monkey-fighting serpents on the plane, our seatmate was prepared to handle the situation.

A Massive Write-off

My reservoir supervisor asked me to come up with a friendly roast for the 3rd-party petroleum engineer who annually audited our corporate reserves. "Pat Smith" was a popular guy who worked for a major consulting firm and about to turn 50. I wrote the following press release and mocked it up to match his company's format. (The company's name has been changed and, frankly, improved.)

For Immediate Release
Tuesday, December 5, 1998

STINGY, SOUR AND ASSOCIATES, INC. ANNOUNCES DRASTIC REDUCTION IN SMITH RESERVES

Investment Community in "Shocked Disbelief"

Stingy, Sour and Associates, Inc. (SSAI) announced today that reserves for one of its premier senior properties have been dramatically reduced, leaving leaders of the petroleum and investment communities reeling in shocked disbelief and laughter.

Reserves for the "Smith" property near Ft. Worth, Texas have fallen a whopping 365.25 units over the last year, according to company insiders. While the exact amount of producing reserves remains unknown, it is widely believed that the 50-year-old Smith property, or the "Shiny Big Guy" as it is affectionately known, is well past its producing half-life.

"It remains to be seen whether this property can be maintained in top producing condition," said a stunned company spokesperson who wished to remain anonymous. "Over the years we noted erratic production trends, and usually these were attributed to questionable data. Now, we're not so sure."

SSAI officials plan a full, internal investigation, and the search to replace the lost production units has already been initiated. "Once old Smith finally peters out, it will be very difficult to replace," the company official said. "We do, however, expect to get at least a couple of productive years out of this valuable company asset, no matter how difficult it is to operate."

This release includes certain statements that may be deemed "incredibly optimistic forward-looking statements" within the meaning of the Private Securities Litigation Reform Act of 1995. All statements in this release may or may not have any validity in the court of public opinion, and serve no purposes other than severe humiliation and embarrassment. Although SSAI believes the expectations expressed in such ridiculous statements are based on reasonable yet fictional assumptions, the use of management buzz words to fully cloud the integrity of issues not-yet-defined requires a complete and thorough incompetence in the use of the English language.

The Vice President of Mind Sweeping

One of the Vice Presidents finally slipped past his use-by date and was kinda sorta demoted. Pat's new title was something like "Senior Vice President and Consulting Staff Director Specialist." He was relocated to a large, next-to-the-corner office to while away the days until he vested in trazillions of stock options. IT set him up with what engineers called Geology Monitors; two huge screens each larger than my car. (Back then, engineers upsized their own monitors by hot-wiring HP-48SX calculators to previously-owned Sony Watchmans.)

Pat didn't even pretend to be working. He openly played The World's Largest Game of Minesweeper on his computer all day, with thousands of squares using every pixel of real estate on his screens. He had lightning-quick skills unmatched by any other displaced VP, zipping his cursor around and clearing so many mines he developed a mouse-click callus on his finger. We all wanted to be Pat when we grew up.

"No, I'm not that happy to see you. And yes, I do have a mouse in my pocket."

By mid-1993, various flavors of Windows 3.0 had been released and major software was transitioning to the new graphical user interface format. Naturally, corporate hardware and software upgrades were delayed for security, testing, bug-squashing, etc. I had purchased a Gateway 2000 computer for home use a couple of years earlier, and my computer at home was more advanced than the desktop model provided by the Company.

My friend Steve and I wrote a memo to our manager recommending a handful of steps to improve computer and software skills among the technical staff. Included was a brief discussion on manipulating software windows on the monitor (open, maximize, arrange, etc.), cumbersome to do using only the keyboard. We stated that a computer mouse was "required technology" for working in a Windows environment, and recommended the Company purchase a mouse for every computer.

A day later our manager reported back. The CFO had not approved our recommendation because "a mouse is only used for playing games." Steve and I and every other technical professional knew that was dead wrong, but okay. I knew what to do.

Each morning before I left home for work, I unplugged the mouse from my computer and packed it in my briefcase. At the office I connected the mouse to my PC and it provided a huge boost to my productivity. If I didn't forget, at the end of the day I'd take my mouse home to use that evening (yes, sometimes to play games. Remember Duke Nukem?)

Of course, the tech world advanced quickly and it wasn't long before everyone had their own mouse in the office, even the CFO. Steve and I joked we were geniuses ahead of our time, but we knew it was actually the Company lagging behind.

Have Mouse, Will Travel.

Flash forward a quarter of a century to 2019. I accepted some contract engineering work and was assigned a workspace cubicle. The computer equipment the Company provided was "contractor grade," old and dirty. I knew it was nothing personal, it was the setup they had handy. The two monitors presented mismatched images; a spreadsheet extended across both screens had a somewhat disturbing shift in position, clarity, and color. It was an interesting challenge.

The computer mouse was shaped like a Volkswagen Beetle and nearly as large. I almost needed two hands to shove it around the pad. I contacted the IT person and after rummaging around a cardboard box found a slightly smaller model, but I was unable to get it to work. Okay, I knew what to do: Solve The Problem.

It was déjà vu all over again. I started carpooling every day to work with a spare mouse from home, just as I had 26 years earlier.

"Must hide faster!"

From the impact tremors rippling in my coffee, I knew Pat was T-Rexing his way down the hall to my office. He gave me a medium-size project to complete. A couple of days later, I took the finished product to his office and handed it to him.

"What's this?"

"It's the Blarney evaluation you asked me to do Monday."

Pat shook his head and handed the report back. "Jack already did this." Pat often gave the same assignment to two (sometimes three) engineers, forgetting his first (and second) request. After we figured this out, the reservoir engineers adopted a Rule of 3 Strategy: don't start working on any request until Pat brought it up at least 3 times.

We also used a Rule of 3 variant to address Pat's consistency issues. Two or three of us would conspire to ask Pat the same question a minimum of three times spaced a minimum two hours apart. Then we would meet and calculate the average of his answers to determine exactly what was going on.

We Solved the Problem.

The MOASS

Budget cycles were Fun with a capital NOT, and always generated a multitude of complex Excel files. We called one monster spreadsheet The MOASS (The Mother of All Spreadsheets, pronounced "mo ass"). The name stuck and was still being used by the staff a couple of years later.

During a presentation to Corporate Management one of the engineers used the term MOASS in one his slides, prompting a question from one of the executives. Division managers simultaneously cleared their throats while the staff snickered at the back of the room.

Later, a larger, more complex spreadsheet was created by the Budgeteers: the DOTMOASS (The Daddy of the Mother of All Spreadsheets, pronounced "dot mo ass"). I shudder to think of the Lovecraftian horror the world may soon face from spreadsheets developed by future next-gen reservoir engineers. May Bill Gates have mercy on us all.

It's Always Sunny in Geodelphia: Gilman's Coin of Excellence

I met Jesse at McNellie's for a beer after work. He was my Team's geologist, and it promised to be an interesting evening. Jesse liked to discuss fascinating, arcane technology from articles he'd read on the Interwebs. Stories with titles like *Anti-Gravity Drones Airlift Festivus Poles to Drilling Crews in Remote Wyoming Just in Time for Airing of Grievances.*

This time he slid a small plastic case across the table. It was a large coin with the image of a derrick spouting oil, crossed with a geologist's pick and spade. The edge of the coin was inscribed: GILMAN'S GEOLOGY COIN OF EXCELLENCE - NEVER A DRY HOLE. On the flip side was an image of a granite mountain and the words YOU ROCK.

It was the coolest piece of swag I had ever seen. I complimented Jesse and handed it back. He shook his head and said it was a gift, in appreciation of our work and friendship.

I keep the coin displayed on my desk in my writing studio. Thank you, Jesse. That moment in McNellie's is one of the best of my career.

A Small Constellation of Management Stars, Part 2: Paul

I enjoyed working for managers who had a good sense of humor, an awareness of pop culture, and were comfortable in their own skin. Paul was a favorite.

On Thursday mornings in the main conference room, the operations meeting was open to all technical staff. It was a good opportunity to get the latest information on drilling activities, recompletions, and other Company business. The room was full, a couple of folks standing in the doorway.

A proposed well location stimulated a brief discussion about the nature and quantity of the hydrocarbons in place, specifically how much of the shale gas was "free," and how much was adsorbed in the rock. After a couple of the geologists had their say, Paul, the regional vice president, thought it was time to move on.

"Guys, I will choose..." he paused and looked around with a small smile. "Free gas."

Kyle and I both grinned. No one else recognized what he'd done, so Paul moved on to the next operations report.

After the meeting Kyle and I hung around. We complimented Paul on his use of Rush lyrics to make his point. He had changed the line from "I will choose free will" to "I will choose free gas."

"I thought you two would appreciate that," Paul said.

"Next week I expect you to work a little Jethro Tull into the discussion," I replied. I don't know why Jethro Tull popped into my head, perhaps a loose association with Rush from the music I liked in high school and college.

A week later, same meeting. A well completion report included some operational challenges. At the end of the discussion, Paul leaned forward and said, "Guys, I'm just trying to avoid a *bungle in the jungle*." He shot us a grin and Kyle and I cracked up.

Paul was cool. It was a pleasure working for him.

"Rectum? Damn near cracked him up!"

Ten years ago I had a prostate cancer thing. It turned out fine, but there were some interesting moments, beginning with the urologist describing the biopsy procedure. I warned him he'd likely need to perform a managerectomy first to gain access.

After the diagnosis I informed my reservoir engineering manager I'd need a few weeks off, the first and only time I went on short-term disability. I asked him not to mention the specific reason for my planned leave of absence to anyone. Less than an hour later the Division Manager was standing in my door expressing his concern and asking about the surgery. I appreciated his support but was disappointed my supervisor couldn't remain discrete for more than 20 minutes.

My primary goal was to make sure my wife got through it all okay. She was terrific, I was very glad to have her love and support.

My second goal was to find the best doctor. After a couple of consultations, I switched from the doc who did the biopsy to Dr. Marc Milsten, an excellent urologist who had done over 800 prostatectomies. That turned out to be an outstanding decision.

My third goal was to somehow make my new doctor laugh. Urologists are a special breed, and they've heard every clever and lame joke imaginable, probably hundreds of times each. During a pre-op ultrasound, Doc said he heard my first urologist could be kind of rough.

"Yeah, little bit," I agreed. "He knocked a couple of my back teeth loose during the biopsy." That got a laugh from my doctor and the technician.

The procedure went well, and I had to use a catheter for 7 days following the surgery. My 7th-day appointment fell on July 4th, so it was pushed to the 5th and I endured an extra fun-filled tubular day. Before removing the device, Doc mentioned a bit of leakage could occur, and for a short time I might need to wear some additional protection.

"Well, that's just great," I said. "I'm going from Independence Day to In Depends Day."

Big laugh, mission accomplished. I'm pretty sure he hadn't heard that one before.

"And our cardboard boxes and packing tape are of the highest quality, second to none."

During a bust cycle for the industry, Company Management bluntly warned employees by email that tough times were ahead, including reduced cash flow, potential failures meeting corporate goals, and possible reductions in staff. At the same time, Company reps were still actively recruiting college graduates and attending university job fairs.

The Executive Leadership Team reassured us all the Company had "very competitive severance packages," leading many of us to speculate whether that little nugget was included as a kicker in the brochures they were handing out to college kids.

"Quick, hand me that shovel!"

The Company launched an internal corporate website full of useful information, like 1-800 telephone numbers for disgruntled employees to visit with highly sympathetic counselors. You could also access do-it-yourself performance review forms and enjoy the latest Dilbert cartoon. One morning I read the Quote of the Day and was inspired to offer an update:

"If you find yourself in a hole, the first thing to do is stop digging."
- Will Rogers (1879 - 1935) American cowboy, comedian, and humorist

"Unless, that is, you find yourself in an (insert your favorite term for unpleasant hole). Then the first thing to do is start digging. Frantically.
- Steve Moore (1959 -) American writer, former reservoir engineer, and self-described humorist

Author's note: I should have followed my own advice.

Engineers in Company Cars Getting Stupid, Part 3: The Cow

A production engineer I knew in the 1980s shared this story:

Pat is driving a company pool car on a lease road when he pops over a rise and runs smack into a cow-sized cow. He pulls the car back a bit and jumps out. The cow is lying motionless on the road, and there's a huge dent in the grill and front bumper. Holy crap, he's killed a cow with a company car! Now what?

Pat leaves the scene and walks the road for a while, looking for a house, a lease office, another driver, anyone to whom he can report the accident and assume responsibility. No such luck. He returns to the car and the cow has disappeared. Apparently, it was only stunned and wandered off.

The car is dinged up pretty good and there are no witnesses. Pat has no way to prove what happened. He examines the car and finds cowhide hairs stuck in the damaged grill. After carefully extracting several strands, he tucks them into his notebook to show he "only hit a cow," and no other humans were involved. I wondered how long he saved the cow hairs "just in case."

I like this story. Pat was a high-quality individual who first tried to do the right thing, then morphed into a Crime Scene Investigator to save his own butt.

iPhone Notification

"Good morning, Steve. Today is Thursday, February 25, 2016.
You have one item scheduled this morning at 730am:
FOUR HOURS OF STRESS

Your next item begins at 1pm:
FOUR HOURS OF BOREDOM

There is a 98% chance of significant frustration early in the day, followed by a cloudy disposition during the noon hour. Chances for despair increase throughout the afternoon. Some despair may be SEVERE.

You have one item scheduled for tomorrow, 3pm, at McNellie's:
MEMORIAL SERVICE FOR STEVE'S CAREER

How about *below* the surface?

My boss was out of the office but communicating by email. I sent him a request to take a half day off on Friday to visit my dad on his birthday. Here was his email reply:

"Let's talk. *On the surface* I think it's a great idea."

Emphasis added, with bewilderment. Interesting choice of words. I skipped the discussion and took the afternoon off anyway.

Men's Room Follies, Part 3: A Sprinkling of Shorts

"But how do you *really* feel?"

I was in Calgary, Alberta attending a week-long training course in 1989. At a restaurant one evening I entered the men's room to pay back some of the beer I'd borrowed. Two guys walked in, set up on either side of me, and we all made it rain. The guy to my left announced in a too-loud voice that they were from Edmonton, and where in the hell was I from?

I said I was from California but grew up in Oklahoma.

"Oklahoma? Oooh, I *hate* Oklahoma," the guy on my left says. "Hey, Vince! Tell this guy how much I hate Oklahoma!"

From my right, Vince vigorously agreed. "Oh yeah, you know, he *really* hates Oklahoma."

I thought it was an unusual choice for urinal conversation, but I was a stranger in a strange land. The first guy piped up again.

"The machine hasn't been invented yet that can measure my hatred for Oklahoma!" We all three cracked up carefully, trying to maintain control. I accepted their invitation and joined them for a beer.

A Real-Life Pat

A coworker told me he was working on a Saturday afternoon at the office. As he was about to enter the men's room he ran into Pat, the IT lady, coming out. She offered no explanation, and he didn't ask.

The next time he needed to go, he took the stairs to the men's room *two* floors up to make sure he didn't run into her again. The mystery remains unsolved to this day.

Here's something you don't see every day.

During a visit to Las Vegas, I took a picture of a urinal in the men's room of New York New York casino. Mounted on the wall within easy arm's reach was a handy cup holder designed for not one but *two* beverages. I had to admire the forward-thinking architect, as well as the dedicated drinker who would take full advantage of this amenity to free up both hands for the relief process.

Apparently no one makes a 3-cup holder.

Take your piddly-ass problem somewhere else!

Someone with extra time on their hands posted this message in the men's room on the first floor of the corporate headquarters building: "Please respect others using this restroom, stand closer to urinal to avoid peeing on floor."

The Gift of the Managi

My boss asks me to join him in the Production Manager's office for a briefing on an acquisition project. I take a chair across the desk from the Manager and my boss sits on the couch against the wall to my left. (The PM has a couch in his office? Nice!)

During the discussion the Manager sneezes a couple of times and explains he has a summer cold. He blows his nose with a tissue from a box on a table behind his desk.

A couple of minutes later there's a sneeze from the couch. The Manager asks my boss, who is fumbling through his pockets, how he is feeling. My boss says he has a cold too, and he thought he had a handkerchief but apparently does not.

The Manager holds out the tissue box and my boss takes one and says thanks. "Better take two," the PM says in a soft voice, "They're kind of thin." Boss takes another, says thanks again, then blows and wipes his nose.

I'm watching this touching moment of humanity and starting to feel a little queasy. This was a side of the Manager no one had seen or suspected. It was a sweet, tender moment of managers supporting managers, one I hope to never see again.

"Be flexible, except for change."

A nice lady came to my office asking for a five-dollar donation for a coworker's retirement gift. All I had was a twenty, and she hadn't collected enough yet to make change. I told her I'd catch her later in the afternoon.

There was a CrossFirst Bank next door, on my lunch break I walked over and stepped inside the lobby. It was nearly noon on a weekday, but the lobby was empty.

I was greeted by two employees sitting behind the customer service counter. One woman asked how they could help me. I just needed change, could they please break a twenty?

The other woman asked, "Do you have an account with us?"

"No, I work in the office next door."

"I'm sorry, we can't help you if you don't have an account here."

I was tempted to say, "Sure, let's open a new checking account with this twenty-dollar bill." Instead, I spun and left. I hoofed it across the street to Schlotsky's, where the store manager cheerfully changed my twenty even though I didn't buy anything.

The irony wasn't lost on me: *CrossFirst* tossed the money changer out of their bank.

Looks about right

Around the time of peak frenzy over fracturing, my wife and I traveled to her hometown several miles west of Pittsburgh, PA. In a small pub one evening we watched a spirited Halloween costume contest. One outfit caught my attention: A young man wearing a hat labeled "Chesapeake Land Dept" and a vest stuffed with leasing documents. As he sauntered around the tables, he pulled fistfuls of play money from a plastic pumpkin and tossed them in the air.

I was really glad I did not hear the end of this elevator conversation

Woman: "I had to drop off his hamster at his apartment this morning, he forgot it last night."

Second woman, as they stepped off at the 3rd floor: "Hamster?"

The Chair: A True Office Horror Story

The following are actual emails I stored in the Moorchives, even though (for once) I had nothing to do with the situation. I edited the emails slightly for clarity and to ensure anonymity for those involved.

****

From:	Manager - Office Services
To:	All Employees
CC:	CFO
Date:	Jan 16, 1:54pm
Subject:	FACILITIES: FURNITURE & EQUIPMENT

This is to remind you that under **no circumstances** should furniture (including chairs, telephones, or other pieces of equipment) be removed or switched out for your use from **what may seem an unoccupied office/cubical or conference room.**

If you are in need of a certain piece of furniture, chair or telephone, please contact me directly at x### and I'll be happy to help you with your requisitions. Your immediate attention to this matter is appreciated.

Thank you,

Manager - Office Services

****

From: Reservoir Engineering Technician
To: Reservoir Engineering Supervisor
Date: Jan 17, 9:53am
Subject: CHAIR

Here's something you don't want to hear but I better keep you informed.

[Manager – Office Services] noticed that I was using one of the "cubical" chairs in my office and informed me that that (sic) wasn't allowed (not the policy of [Manager – Office Services]). I told [Manager - Office Services] that the chair works better for my job because it has an adjustable height high enough to comfortably work on the computer.

So, as long as I continue to use this chair, I am in defiance of company policy. I will either get a doctor's note, as [Manager - Office Services] requested, so that they can decide whether I need a different chair or I'll just buy my own.

****

From: Reservoir Engineering Supervisor
To: Manager - Office Services
Date: Jan 17, 10:21am
Subject: YUK

Sorry to bother you, can you please clarify this issue?
Thanks,
Reservoir Engineering Supervisor

****

From: Manager - Office Services
To: Reservoir Engineering Supervisor
CC: CFO, Manager - Human Resources, Reservoir Engineering Technician
Date: Jan 17, 12:04pm
Subject: Re: YUK

I said that it was "company policy" and if [Reservoir Engineering Technician] needed additional support, I could (1) give [Reservoir Engineering Technician] a task chair that has adjustable height, (which [Reservoir Engineering Technician] told [Office Services Assistant] [Reservoir Engineering Technician] really didn't want) or if [Reservoir Engineering Technician] could give me a doctors prescription for a chair according to his specifications and I would be happy purchase (sic) one for [Reservoir Engineering Technician].

[Office Services Assistant] is on his way down to give [Reservoir Engineering Technician] the task chair that is height adjustable with lumbar support and arms. These are kept in stock for those in need of certain specifications. Just for the record. The company doesn't decided (sic) whether or not an employee gets a new chair if there is a doctor's written recommendations (sic). We have our furniture dealer read the instructions and order the proper chair, exactly to specifications. There are many examples of this throughout the company.

I thought I handled my conversation with [Reservoir Engineering Technician] with concern, giving him options to handle his request for a new chair without taking a chair from a cubical work area.

I think "defiance" is a pretty strong word in view of the conversation that took place between Mr. [Reservoir Engineering

Technician] and I. I hope this new chair works out for him. If not, please let me know.

Thank you,
Manager - Office Services

One month later:
****

From:	Manager - Reservoir Engineering
To:	Exploitation Staff
Date:	Feb 19, 6:10pm
Subject:	CHAIRS

I need everyone in an outside office to **not** put the black/gray chairs that are in the empty cubicles into your offices. [Manager - Office Services] and I are both working this issue, but I need you to leave them where they are for now, even if it's not being used. It causes a problem for [Manager - Office Services] and consistency in the office. I'll keep you updated, please be patient.

Three months later:
****

From:	Manager - Reservoir Engineering
To:	Exploitation Staff
CC:	Manager - Office Services, Vice President - Production
Date:	May 10, 3:26pm
Subject:	WORK CHAIRS

Several of you have expressed your desire to have a different chair in your office. I have been dealing with [Manager - Office Services] concerning this issue and I now have a specific response.

The company provides a chair for each employee which includes three choices. Those choices are: 1) high back St. Timothy, 2) low back St. Timothy, or 3) blue task chair. There have been some new chairs purchased recently for our floor cubes that some of you prefer, but these are not one of your options. The blue task chair is the closest alternative to the new chairs, but I've not personally compared them. I would encourage you to give this task chair an adequate time to grow on you before condemning it.

I'm sorry to say that I'm unable to help you with this and if you can't live with the company provided chairs, your only option is to provide your own. I would also add that this isn't [Manager - Office Services] decision, so don't blame [Manager - Office Services]. I wish I could provide a perfect world, but I can't. [Manager - Office Services] will be glad to work with any of you in trying to sort out your best option. Please get with me if you want to discuss further.

Uh-oh...

Five days later:
****

From:	Manager - Office Services
To:	All Employees
Date:	May 15, 12:51pm
Subject:	Missing Plant

Tropical Plant Design had placed a plant in [Production Engineer's] old office. It is missing. If this was moved to another office, please return the plant. [Company] rents these plants and special care is taken to maintain them. Each plant is coded &

cataloged. I would like to save TPD from searching 6 floors for their plant.

Thank you for your immediate attention to this matter.

Manager - Office Services

To the 62-year-old marketing guy in the office down the hall:

That fracking "duck quack" ring tone on your cell phone is not as fracking funny as you fracking think it is. You need to fracking change it, and you need to change it RIGHT. FRACKING. NOW!

(Written with the utmost respect for the great Steve Martin in the rental car scene in *Planes, Trains and Automobiles* (1987), and for John Hughes, writer and director.)

Hunting for a Headhunter

During various boom times in the industry, it was not unusual to receive several calls a day from recruiters looking to fill reservoir engineering positions. Many of the opportunities were in Houston, and the recruiters always seemed a bit miffed when I had no interest at all in moving to that huge, humid metropolis.

I always wanted to respond like this: "No, thank you, but hey, our company just posted an opening for a recruiter in one of our satellite offices. Would you have any interest in relocating to Weed Pit, Oklahoma?"

Alternative Career Idea No. 37: Launch New Superhero Comic Book Series

CAPTAIN RESERVOIR

"Protecting the Integrity of America's Oil and Gas Reserves"

- A Positive Role Model for Kids of All Ages
- Never books P50 reserves as "Proved"
- Complies with all SEC and FASBY regulations
- Uses Forecasting Powers for Good, never evil
- Ably supported by sidekick "Little Tek" Nician
- Embarrassingly snug business casual Superhero costume conceals vast stores of energy converted from Chick-fil-A and Whataburger lunches.

Flaws and Weaknesses:

- Unhealthy fetish for expressing numbers with 17 decimal places
- Over-reliance on Excel spreadsheets
- Inability to suppress lame sense of humor and overly fond of reservoir-based Dad jokes.
- Micro-management tactics effectively neutralize Captain Reservoir's spirit and deplete his energy reserves.
- Reservoir engineering grit and spinal integrity dissolve in the presence of Senior Corporate Management.

The Right Hand of Drool

I was flying back from Denver after an SPE conference. The prepare-for-landing announcement blared at full volume, waking a guy sitting across the aisle three rows ahead. As he lifted his head a thick line of drool fell from his mouth. He caught it instinctively with his right hand before it reached his shirt. He wiped his hand on his jeans and looked casually left and right as if to see if anyone noticed. Nope, only me.

The plane stopped at the gate, and the guy quickly stood and reached for his bag in the overhead compartment. I recognized him as a coworker from a former company a few years earlier. I grinned, thinking how he nearly slimed himself, then realized if he recognized me, he'd surely extend his hand in greeting. *That* hand. The Right Hand of Drool.

I hung back as we exited the plane, staying several feet behind and keeping a crowd between us. I thought he might go straight to the men's room, then I could greet him later in baggage claim. But I wasn't lucky that day, he turned left so I dropped back a little more.

He joined the rest of the passengers waiting at the baggage carousel and thumbed his phone. I mingled with a group of passengers from another flight at a different carousel and kept my eyes on Drooler.

The second suitcase to tumble from the chute was mine. I stayed where I was and let it circle around. I *really* didn't want to shake that hand. It was several minutes before Drooler got his luggage and walked away. I picked up my case, then stalled a few more minutes to give him time to drive off. Finally, I headed for the parking lot, mission accomplished. No hands were clasped.

Word of the Day: Trouser-Load

Definition: Surplus space in butt and leg coverings filled with extraneous material, usually unpleasant.

Usage: "Alex considered the manager's email regarding changes to the reserves process to be a ***trouser-load*** of leadership."

So, what happens if there are *two* misfilings?

I was conducting a phone interview with Rajeesh, a candidate from a temp agency for a filing project. I described how the documents would need to be sorted by technical data type before filing, and asked whether I had explained the job clearly. He responded perfectly, and for many years I kept his answer tacked to my office wall for inspiration:

"Absolutely," he said. ***"One misfiling will spoil your happiness forever."***

"So, you're saying there's a chance..."

I was visiting with a super-sharp simulation engineer named Don one afternoon. The California lottery had recently started, and Don mentioned he and his wife purchased a couple of tickets every Friday for the weekend drawing.

Don's boss Larry overheard this and joined the conversation. Larry launched into a rant on how stupid the lottery was, the tremendous odds against winning, and how could an educated person like Don waste his money like that?

Don just listened calmly without interrupting. When Larry finally ran out of air Don said, "Larry, how likely is it I'll become a multi-millionaire by working for this company? Buying two lottery tickets every week significantly improves my odds, right?"

It was a perfect come-back. Larry said nothing and walked out.

A Tie for Second Place

Getting ready for work one morning I noticed a medium-sized spider skittering across the bathroom floor. I scooped it up with a tissue, dropped it in the toilet and left for work.

That evening, after a typical day of office drudgery, I discovered I forgot to flush the spider. Eleven hours after splashdown it was still dog-paddling around in circles searching for a way out. As I reached for the handle to put it out of its misery, I considered which of us had the worst day. It was a surprisingly close call, but I finally declared, "I win!" and flushed the spider.

Then a tiny shadow of doubt started to grow in the back of my mind…

Humor as a Coping Strategy

To inject a bit of humor into a somewhat tense drilling decision, I used some graphics tools in MS Word to add a brightly colored thought bubble above the rate of return: DRILL ME! It prompted a few smiles during the meeting.

Twelve years later, I ran into my former reservoir engineering manager in a parking garage, and we caught up with each other. He recalled my Drill Me stunt (which I had forgotten until that moment) and told me he always appreciated the humor I added to our team. It was very nice to hear; I was surprised and pleased that he remembered my attempt to be clever so many years later.

It made my day. Thank you, Chris.

Stupid or Jerk?

IT had removed all individual printers from offices and transitioned everyone to shared printer/copier machines on each floor. A couple of days later, I sent a routine print job to the nearest machine and left my desk immediately to retrieve it.

Usually, the pages were waiting for me in the output tray by the time I arrived but not this time. I waited for the job to print, but the machine stayed silent with no error messages displayed. I looked around and found my pages in the waste basket.

In the 30 seconds it took me to walk from my office to the printer station, someone had picked up their job ahead of me and tossed my copies in the trash.

RAULS OF THUMB

My Most Important Lesson in Communication

I remember as I child my mother correcting my grammar often. This was a good thing, and along with my love of reading gave me a solid start at developing decent communication skills.

One incident when I was about 12 left a mark. Our next-door neighbor Ethel was visiting with Mom, and I was sitting nearby at our kitchen table. Ethel said her daughter and family "come up from Pawhuska." Mom's training kicked in, and I immediately piped up with a confident, one-word correction: "Came."

Mom looked horrified. I could actually hear her brain silently shout OH YOU LITTLE SHIT! I immediately recognized my childhood-ending mistake and feared the thrashing that would *come up* as soon as Mom and I were alone. Ethel stopped speaking and looked at me with annoyed disdain. (Today her expression would be translated as "Dude! WTF?")

Ethel went home and Mom lit into me. I was never ever NEVER EVER to correct an adult like that again. I vigorously agreed and apologized, but I was also confused. It was okay for adults to speak poorly with bad grammar, but not okay for me?

Eventually I learned about idioms, colloquialisms, and regional dialects. During my career there were many occasions when I helped a coworker or manager rewrite a report, email, or presentation slide, but I never corrected the verbal communication errors of an adult again.

But I did enjoy them.

The First of Many

To minimize communication problems in business environments, you must use clear, concise language, avoid mixed metaphors, and run your emails—and your mind—through logic, grammar, and spell checkers before transmitting.

In 1983, I was doing a stint as Budget Guy. I heard the reservoir engineering manager tell his boss the budget was "far from final, but damn close!" I thought this was funny and jotted it down on a memo slip. I found it recently in the Moorchives:

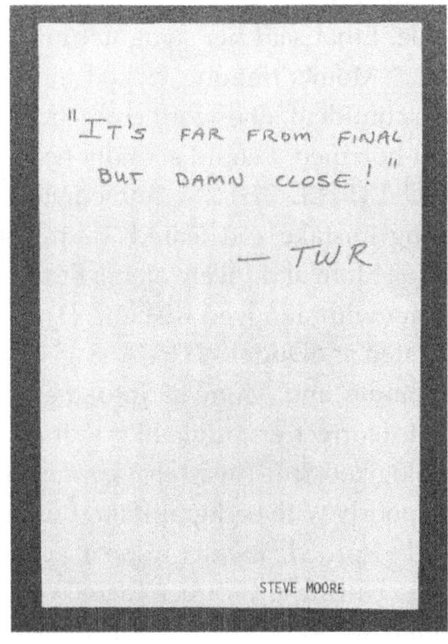

I continued to write down goofy, mixed-up things people said or wrote at the office. Many coworker friends liked the idea and passed along additional gaffes they said or heard. The list grew long over the years and eventually I named it ***Raul's of Thumb***.

The Top 25

My favorite ROTs—both verbal and written—are presented below in no particular order. (See Appendix 2 for the complete list.) Except for my own mistakes, I've included attributions by title only, but the Master List of ROTs sealed in the Moorchives identifies the actual perpetrators. If you would like to know who said what, buy me a drink sometime and we'll talk.

"I called this meeting to make sure all of our pulses are beating in the same direction."
- Engineering Manager

"Be flexible, except for change."
- Production Engineer

"Enthisize" (emphasize)
- Engineering Manager

"The doctor reached in with his biceps and pulled the tubes out of her ear."
- Engineering Technician

"You don't know what's going on behind the screens"
- Engineering Manager

"All you have left over is the residual residue…"
- Production Engineering Manager

" PF " (abbreviation for Petrophysics on meeting agenda)
- Engineering Manager

3rd-Party Reservoir Engineer, pointing to erratic production data on a graph during a reserves audit:
"Were those little who-knows-whats?"
Me: "Yes."

"It fell on death ears." (deaf ears)
- Engineering Manager

"First, we will figure out which road we will take, then we will figure out how to climb it."
- Engineering Manager

"He listens with one ear and thinks with the other. His mind is in the ghetto."
- Engineering Manager

"I'm surprised Linn is taking it up the annulus."
- Reservoir Engineering Manager, during morning operations meeting

"Be sure to include cave outs" (caveats)
- Engineering Manager

"That's a plus in its favor."
- Steve Moore, Reservoir Engineer

"That was earth-to-ground lightning."
- Steve Moore, Reservoir Engineer

"Conthrable" (comfortable)
- Engineering Manager

"Least path of resistance"
- Engineering Manager

(Author's note: There is little truth to the rumor it was I who started referring to managers who denied staff requests for support as "sociopaths of least resistance.")

"It gassed out quickly due to gas."
- Production Engineer

"Just a vacation" (justification)
- Engineering Manager

"We want to ensure that everyone has the ability to do their work and access all necessary information; however, if need be we will consider limiting the individuals that can work in the backside."

- Email (and just good common sense) from Corporate Reserves Coordinator, after a large volume of data was deleted from the master database

"Voluminous volumes"
- Engineering Manager

"It's a lesson in futility, but it can be done."
- Reservoir Engineering Manager

"I have served as a roll model…" (Sausage roll? Dinner roll?)
- Engineering Manager

"Remaining Reserves"

- EVERYONE (As a writer, this repetitive redundancy always bugged, annoyed, and irritated me.)

"Truth is stranger than friction."

- Paul Veatch, Division Manager

Gratefully used with special permission:

"Truth is stranger than friction"

9/23/10

I hereby release Steve Moore from any future claims on royalties for use of the above quote in his upcoming book.

In exchange for this release I require one signed copy of above mentioned book

"Thank you, from the heart of my bottom"

At a going-away lunch celebration before I started a job with another company, my friend Buddy gave me a nice gift: a hard-cover collection of Bloom County cartoons. Opus, a penguin and main character of the comic strip, frequently mixed-up expressions, such as "Ain't no skin off my stiff upper lip." The book was signed by the author, Berkeley Breathed. It was the first in my collection of what is now more than a hundred autographed books.

Thank you, Buddy. A perfect gift, then and now.

In Front of the Screens

One of my favorite moments occurred in February 2004 during my presentation on data integrity and workflows. I introduced Moore's Law of Fruit Salad to Company Management on a PowerPoint slide. At least one VP was amused, and later made a reference to "Steve's fruit" at the end of the meeting.

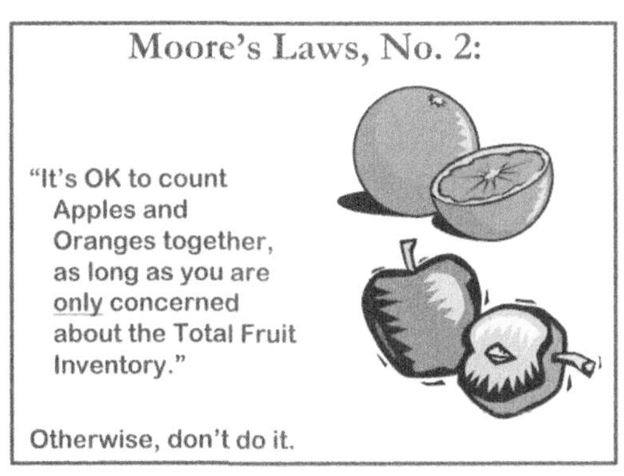

Most of my dramatic or flat-out funny presentation memories are associated with project or budget reviews with Senior Corporate Management. Naturally, my first few presentations to the executives from Houston were very stressful.

"Now we travel back, to a time before PowerPoint..."

Welcome to 1982 everyone! Please, mind your heads as you exit the capsule. This afternoon from our parallel time dimension we will observe a young reservoir engineer named Steve prepare for his very first presentation to Corporate Management. This is the same engineer we visited this morning, the one who melted his shoes into pancakes *solely* to entertain his coworkers. As before, we will hear no sound, so I'll provide narration and context.

Steve is meeting with the senior draftsman to discuss revisions to the reservoir map he will use in the presentation. Drafting personnel were used to prepare inked masters of maps and cross-sections used to make blueline copies. Drafting resources were almost always monopolized by geologists and management, so we are seeing a rare example of drafting support for a reservoir engineer. Steve has cultivated a special relationship with this draftsman by taking him to lunch twice in recent weeks and this morning he brought a dozen donuts for the entire drafting department. This was a smart move and significantly increases the odds Steve will get his maps barely in time to prepare for his presentation.

Skipping ahead a bit, Steve has the new map and is using the copy machine—nicknamed Z-Rocks, for some reason—to reduce key portions of the map to a size small enough for slides. Okay, wait—I love this part—Whoops! The whole map slides down behind Z-Rocks and Steve can't reach it. He'll have to get a "pointer stick" from the conference room to fish out the map, as the copy machine is much too heavy to move.

Skipping again…Steve has managed to make a reduced copy suitable for the presentation. Now he's loading special film called "transparencies" into the paper tray. This always cracks me up; Steve has optimistically loaded only one page of film. He should know the copier always jams and eats three or four pages anytime the paper tray is restocked.

Okay, after six iterations Steve has copied his map onto the slide. But he also has several pages of key points typed by the department secretary that also need to be copied to film. Here's a Pro Tip from back in the day: *always* proofread your originals before you convert them to film slides.

Z-Rocks is particularly cranky today, and it takes Steve nearly an hour to get his slides copied. Now Steve is going the "extra mile" to make his presentation special. See how he is carefully using red and green Sharpies to add color to his slides and highlight key points? Steve believes this will make his slides professionally distinct from those of other engineers and will impress the Senior Leadership Team. Steve is wrong.

Now he's reached a critical decision point in his preparation. Does our intrepid engineer take time to scotch tape the slides to cardboard frames? Frames are a safer choice and make the slide deck easier to handle. They also allow for "cheating," writing notes on the frame in case you get stuck during the presentation. On the other hand, if last-minute changes are required, Steve will lose valuable practice time by having to re-frame his slides. Let's jump ahead to…

Showtime! Those round, grumpy-looking gentlemen sitting at the conference table are the Executive Leadership Team from Houston. Don't they all look Supremely Confident? They should, they each wield Great Power. Steve looks uncomfortable, doesn't he, tugging at his tie. He's elected not to use the cardboard frames and, wait for it, 3...2...1! He dropped the slippery stack of transparencies all over the floor. Notice none of his coworkers or managers have stepped forward to help, they're just laughing in the back of the room. Okay, looks like he's got his exhibits back in order and the title slide is in place. I wonder if the light bulb in the overhead projector will burn out?

Just kidding, folks. Looks like he's ready to start. That's the Vice-President of Production leaning forward and whispering to Steve. Our lip-reading team has already translated; the VP is asking Steve whether he's starting with the dog, or the pony?

In a brilliant, potentially career-enhancing quick response Steve says, "whichever you prefer, sir." See the VP smile as he sits back in his chair? Unfortunately, we see Steve is making the classic rookie mistake of standing in front of the screen during his entire presentation. Half the room can't see the information he's trying to convey.

Don't worry about Steve, though. He'll go on to make nearly two hundred presentations over the next four decades and often does well, even if he thinks so all by himself.

"This project is so economic, it's not even funny."

Early in my career I was assigned to an exploration "E-Team" to provide reservoir engineering support and economic analysis for wildcat drilling prospects. The experience gave me valuable insight into the fluid, variable nature of geologic mapping.

The exploration geologist gave me copies of isopach and structure maps for the project. I completed the volumetric and reserves calculations and tossed everything into an economic case. The heavily risked economics resulted in the profit to investment indicator (internally called PVI) nicely exceeding the minimum funding value of 1.25.

The Exploration Manager was not satisfied. A couple of hours later the geologist brought me a new set of maps, updated with "new information." Sure enough, the prospect area nearly doubled in size, and reserves were of course much greater. The project PVI was now a ridiculous 4.5, and easily exceeded the funding hurdle rate even in low price sensitivity runs.

The day before the Capital Budget presentations to the Executive Team from Houston we had a dry run with division management. I attempted to use humor to keep the absurdly positive economics in perspective.

"And this chart shows that even if oil prices drop to negative values, the PVI *still* exceeds 1.25."

Nothing. Not even crickets. I moved on to the next slide but before I could speak the production manager stirred and said, "Wait. What?" I explained I was joking. The exploration manager did not look happy, but my reservoir engineering manager grinned.

Houston did fund the prospect, and the wildcat was drilled several months later. It was a dry hole. I was not provided with updated geologic maps.

The exploration manager did have a sense of humor. He served as emcee at the next company Christmas party and encouraged everyone to have a good time:

"And if anyone has too much party and needs a ride, we've arranged for a van and a driver to get everyone home safe. All I ask is please don't step on me when you climb in."

"I'd like to substitute toast for the fruit, please."

During a practice session prepping for yet another Houston Budget Tour, the engineer ahead of me had a slide with a reservoir map that resembled a slice of bread. Someone called it the "toast" reservoir and there was minor chuckling from the division managers.

With the stage set, it wasn't much of a surprise a few minutes later when I showed a slide of an isopach map that could be interpreted—and was—as somewhat phallic, complete with a proportional pouch-like shape at the base suitable for containment of one or two small spheres. Please note: while it was my slide, the suggestive map was drawn by my geological engineer teammate. Before that moment, no one in the office suspected the GE of having even the tiniest sense of humor.

Of course, now that my reservoir slide had been publicly recognized as a banana and grapes, it was impossible for anyone to see the image any other way. Word got around, and by the time I started my presentation for the Houston execs the next day it was SRO in the conference room. I had already come to terms with my fate, and without hesitation I flashed Willy and the Twins to the audience.

To their credit, I heard only quiet snickering from the Houston Leadership, who mostly managed to keep things professional. But one of the engineers in the back of the room really lost it. He fell to the floor and laughed so hard his butt separated itself from his body. This nicely shifted the focus from me to him in that moment.

Years later I would think of that fool when I first encountered ROFLMAO in an email.

The Heart of Presentation Darkness

Some people handled the stress of Corporate Executives visiting the Division offices well. Others, not so much.

Sunday evening. I'm working on the final touches to my slides and practicing my delivery for a presentation the next morning. My boss is working on his presentation in the office next door. From the steady stream of cursing, it was not going well.

I hear Pat mumbling to himself as he walks past my door, then thumping and banging and more cursing from down the hall. I check it out and find Pat rifling through my geology teammate's office. He yanks a cross-section from the map rack, unrolls it to read the label, then tosses it on the floor and grabs another.

"Hey, Pat, can I help you find something?"

Pat's eyes are wild. He barks, "Call Fred Baker!" and throws another map. "Ask him how to turn on the blue line machine." Fred was the one-man drafting department.

"Sure," I say as cheerfully as possible. "Do you have Fred's number?"

Pat stops in mid-toss and glares at me, his face twice as red as it was five seconds earlier. "If I had his number, I'D CALL HIM!" He shakes his head as if to say *see what I have to put up with?* I back out and return to my office. I call another engineer to get Fred's number, then reach him at home.

"Sorry to bother you, Fred. Pat wants to know how to turn on the blue line copy machine. We're working on presentations for tomorrow." Fred chuckles as though he's seen this movie before, knows how it ends, and is glad to be safe at home. He tells me where the power switch is located and to let the machine warm up a few minutes before making copies.

In the drafting room I turn the machine on, then find Pat standing motionless in his office, staring out the window. This time of night it's too dark to see out through the tinted windows; all he can see is the reflection of his office with me in the doorway.

"Pat, the blue line machine is warming up now." Pat nods his head slightly. I decide I'm as ready for my presentation as I need to be tonight. I pack up and leave the building. As I get in my car, I look up to the 4th floor and Pat is still standing at the window, seeing only what's inside his mind.

Sometimes we study history and are still doomed to repeat it.

One CEO was a bit of a hard-asset for the Company. He was infamous for being cranky and mean to engineers, geologists, and even division managers during their presentations. I was mid-way through a practice session when my supervisor told me to stop.

"You need to use the same Y-scale on all of your lease production graphs. The CEO ripped me a new one a couple of years ago for using different scales from one slide to the next. He likes everything consistent."

I said thanks, but if I made them all the same, some production would be unreadable with the trend line crawling along the bottom of the chart. My boss got irritated and said he didn't care; he wasn't going to receive another butt-kicking from the CEO and told me to change the graphs. I wasn't *conthrable* with this but modified all the plots using the same production axis. You can guess what happened.

When I flipped to the first of the low-crawling production graphs, the CEO lit up. "Why the f___ are you showing me a worthless graph? The production is smashed to the bottom, why would you use that stupid scale?"

I didn't say anything but looked to the back of the room at my boss, who was studying his shoes. I apologized, skipped to the next slide, and hurried to finish my talk. It did not go well.

When I saw my boss later, he just shrugged and said everyone goes through something like this with the CEO. He said it was my day in the barrel, and to forget about it.

Lessoned learned. But I didn't forget.

"Things get a little hairy during the acquisition briefing."

A group of 7 or 8 managers and technical staff are waiting for the CEO to enter the conference room and take his usual seat at the head of the table. The COO and the Senior VP are engaged in conversation; the rest of us are waiting silently.

The CEO arrives several minutes late and sits. No one greets him. The COO and VP continue their conversation but are winding things down. It feels like the meeting is finally about to start.

I'm sitting at the right hand of the CEO, who suddenly stands and leaves the room. We look at each other, no one says a word. The CEO returns in two minutes with a cup of coffee. As he settles into his chair, he turns towards me and lets out a quiet yet forceful belch, impolitely letting me know he ate Mexican food for lunch. I make a snap decision not to share what I had for lunch and say nothing.

The project geologist starts the presentation by spreading a large map on the table in front of the CEO. The CEO leans forward to scan the map and cough-belches, smaller in magnitude than the previous release. I'm looking at the white map directly in front of the CEO and as he coughs, a small, wiry-looking mustache hair lands on the map directly in front of me. It is black and gray and has a little bend near one end.

I pretend I didn't see it and struggle not to laugh. Apparently, no one else saw the executive hair stick the landing. I have a strong urge to lean forward, pucker up, and blow the damn thing off the map and out of my life. Somehow, I manage to suppress this career-ending impulse.

The geologist is making a solid pitch. I try to focus on his presentation and not The Hair, but I feel trapped like a character in an Edgar Allan Poe story. I realize I don't actually know that it's a *mustache* hair. I assumed it was because the color matches the hair on the Chief Executive Lip, but that little bend in it has me thinking. It could be a nose hair, who's to say?

The geologist finishes his presentation and rolls up his map. The hair is finally out of sight, but not forgotten.

"Okay, we're a little bit ahead of schedule now..."

A geologist teammate asked me to give his presentation at an in-house technical conference so he could stay home for the birth of his child. I agreed to sub for him only if he promised to name the baby "Marcellus."

The time allocated for his topic was nearly an hour, but he only gave me six slides to present. I saw an opportunity and added page numbers in the bottom corner of each slide: 1 of 246, 2 of 246. As I opened the third slide a hand went up in the audience.

"Excuse me, do you really have 246 slides?"

"Yes," I said. "I was told I only had 45 minutes, so I had to cut the presentation in half." Big laughs. I talked through the remaining slides in about 30 seconds and returned to my seat. This surprised the exploration manager who was hosting, and he announced we would all take an unscheduled but very popular break.

PROFESSIONALS BEHAVING BADLY

Managers are encouraged to delegate the reading of this section to someone on their staff.

Inevitably, in my semi-professional memoir I must include anecdotes and commentary from my experiences with the powerful collective force known as Management. I never became a manager; I didn't even manage my own career well. It was an early failure on my part not to recognize the value of ladder ascension and modify my Plan accordingly. Even if I had figured it out, I suspect my personality would not have fit well in the supervisory positions available at the time.

I don't have anything against Management. In fact, some of my favorite managers were managers, and more than a few of them were people, too. But, like every sentient life form on the planet, managers occasionally do goofy stuff that screws with others. Early on I started taking notes for future reference.

This section includes many notable and—at least to me—humorous stories of Managers and other professionals behaving badly.

First, a couple of thoughtful quotes from two of my favorite authors:

"Most people can't think, most of the remainder won't think, the small fraction who do think mostly can't do it very well. The extremely tiny fraction who think regularly, accurately, creatively, and without self-delusion - in the long run, these are the only people who count.

- Robert A. Heinlein, Grand Master Science Fiction Author *Time Enough for Love* (1973)

You can lead a manager to the conference table, but you can't make him think.

- Steve Moore, Former Reservoir Engineer and Self-Described Humorist

"Normally, an office this size would go to someone we valued."

Due to my new role as Budget Guy and a logistical quirk when the Company moved to a new building, I was assigned a larger office that would normally have been assigned to a supervisor. While I was unpacking and thinking I might need to get some more stuff, my boss walked in. He made a point of telling me not to read anything into the bigger office, saying "it doesn't mean anything."

Message received. If my manager had filed an After-Action report, it might have included this: *"Basic demotivation tactic deployed successfully. Target was subdued, appeared depressed, and was later observed taking a three-hour lunch break."*

Drive-by Management *While Actually Driving*

I'm steadily working on a quiet Friday morning. I cc my boss, Pat, on an email and click send. Within 30 seconds he gives me a call. He's driving on a highway somewhere.

Pat tells me to search the Internet for a particular company's web site, find their most recent earnings release, and locate the summary of their Marcellus operations. *Then he has me read it to him over the phone.*

Next, Pat asks me to search the company's web site for a map of their drilling locations, which I don't find. He tells me to get a certain notebook from his office, flip through it until I find the location map, then scan and email it to him. He ends the call.

I'm unable to locate the map, and before I can call Pat to tell him, he calls me again. *He asks if Alex is in the office today.* Heck if I know. I casually suggest that perhaps Pat could call Alex direct and speak to him?

Pat says he received some files last night that he wants Alex to review, but *maybe he won't bother him until Monday,* and ends the call.

The line from a Mel Brooks movie pops into my head: "It's good to be the King." This wasn't the first time Pat called me from the road to search the Internet or read something to him over the phone. On one hand, I can appreciate the dynamics of the situation: Pat is my boss, and I was hired to serve. He's doing the multitasking magic that helped him reach his current position in Management.

On the other hand, the pleasure of reading financial reports to my boss over the phone is not why I worked so hard to obtain my degree in petroleum engineering.

"Successful applicants for the position of Reservoir Engineering Supervisor will display exceptional levels of exclamatory enthusiasm."

One of my managers was unusually fond of using exclamation points in his emails:

Steve, would you mind updating the capital budget spreadsheet with the latest projections?
Thanks!!!!!!!!

Why would he do this? Was it a mystical technique for getting ahead in Corporate World? Naturally, my friends and I adopted our manager's style in our personal communications:

Me: Want to go to lunch today?
Alex: Sounds good!!!!!!!!!!!!!!!!!!!!

Flash forward several years later to February 2019. I'm watching the television show *Corporate* on Comedy Central (Season 2, Episode 4). The exclamation key stops working on the main character's keyboard, and Management interprets the absence of exclamations in his emails as personal attacks, evidence of a bad attitude and a lack of morality. Hilarity ensues. The episode was titled (no joke): "Thanks!"

Brilliant!

Men's Room Follies, Part 4:
Boy's Rooms will be Boy's Rooms

A few weeks after the Company relocated to a brand-new office building, the Engineering Manager sent this email to 56 professionals:

Subject: Restrooms

Every day when I go to the restroom I notice that there is either paper towels or toilet paper strewn on the floor. I don't really understand why this happens other than it must be people from other floors doing this because I know we all have enough pride not to trash up our restrooms. If you drop a paper towel on the floor, pick it up and put it in the trash. If you drop toilet paper on the floor, pick it up and flush it down the toilet. Also, when you wash your hands, don't leave a lake of water on the counter top. Get a paper towel and wipe up your mess. Please.

I was appalled. The Engineering Manager was justifiably lecturing the staff on common decency and hygiene. He was right; guys were trashing the bathroom and constantly missing the waste can tossing door-handle towels on their way out.

It wasn't really a new problem, just new to the Manager who was now located on the same floor as the engineering and geological staff. In the old building, the men's room on the 6th floor—three floors below the Management Suite—was a disgusting mess by mid-morning every single day. This was partly from individuals failing to keep it clean, but also from a *flawed dispenser design and an inappropriate custodial replenishment process.* (Boom!)

First, the towel dispenser was mounted at eye level on the wall. You had to reach up to get a towel, which meant if you weren't quick water would run down your arms and get your sleeves wet. And it was impossible to be quick; the dispenser was jam-packed with towels of the wrong fold style and size. Instead of a flap extending from the slot to grasp, the towels were individually folded in a stack. You reached in with wet fingers and instead of pulling out a towel, tiny fingertip-sized pieces would tear off and flutter to the floor. You'd try again with the same result, then force your entire hand inside, yank out a fist full of towels and drop them on the wet sink counter. You could then pry off a mostly dry towel or two from the top of the stack, and invariably a stray would float to the floor. The towels left on the counter were now tainted with dampness, so the next guy would leave them there and repeat the process with the dispenser.

The trash bin was way too small for the number of visitors and was overflowing after a couple of hours each morning. When you entered the men's room you were greeted with a mess of towels and wet confetti scattered around the floor, the trash bin completely full, and several stacks of damp towels on the counter. After 3pm the dispenser was likely to be empty, so you gingerly selected a towel from one of the wet stacks or air-dried your hands by waving them in the air.

This always bothered me, like finding the remnants of a burrito detonated in the microwave. Years earlier I read about the "broken windows" theory of reducing crime; the idea was to maintain neighborhoods in good shape by clearing away trash and repairing broken doors and windows. This created a positive environment, improved cultural awareness, lifted spirits, and even reduced certain kinds of crime. I thought this strategy would work well in a corporate setting. If we all acted like professionals and cleaned up our own messes, perhaps morale would improve along with productivity.

After receiving the Email of Admonishment from the Engineering Manager, one of the supervisors was compelled to respond, also by email:

Subject: RE: Restrooms
Will do, and I agree. Thanks for the note.

The manager used Reply All, so 55 people read his hearty response to the Boss.

Our Learless Feeder

After an afternoon of data room presentations in Houston, the acquisition team had time for a couple of beers before heading to the airport. We were all appalled when our manager cheerfully told our server the more he drank, the cuter she looked. Then he tried to pay our tab using his driver's license instead of a credit card.

What a bunch of leadership!

A Spree of Unauthorized Nuggetectomies

Service companies frequently delivered treats for the staff to the coffee break rooms. Donuts, fruit, cookies and occasionally a veggie tray were almost daily occurrences when times were good in the Patch. Chick-fil-A platters were always popular, buttery bite-size biscuits stuffed with seasoned chicken nuggets.

But you had to get there early: someone had been snatching the chicken and leaving empty biscuits behind. Seeing the sad, doughy remains, one could easily picture evil, gnarled fingers wrenching the chicken tot away from its helpless biscuit parents. It was universally agreed that chick-napping was a despicable crime unlike any other committed in a corporate break room.

After an eyewitness courageously came forward, the culprit was identified and immediately shamed. She confessed, admitting she didn't like the biscuit, only the chicken. It was clear she needed help, and someone compassionately gave her the hotline number of the Employee Assistance Program.

Everything was cool for a couple of weeks, until someone started plugging the donut holes with carrots…

"Yes, really. You can look him up on BaceFook."

Usually after a meeting or presentation a few engineers and technicians would gather to compare notes and go over next actions. During one of these bull sessions, I joked that one of the managers—we'll call him "Joe Peterson"—posted on Facebook using the obvious alias "Poe Jeterson". Without hesitation, one of the reservoir engineers asked, "Really?"

He actually thought it was plausible that Joe was dim enough to use a stupidly transparent fake name to remain anonymous on Facebook. And now the rest of us knew the reservoir engineer was just as dim.

Grins all around.

"I agree with your lack of disagreement"

I knew a senior engineering professional whose favorite reply was, "I don't disagree." This was both a cop-out and kind of brilliant. It gave him plausible deniability if a project went pear shaped: "I never agreed with that." And if things worked out well, he was on board from the beginning. It was probably a decent strategy, but I thought it was a weasel move and too slick.

And now, a rare appearance by the CEO in your inbox:

Rumors swirled that one of the senior exec's email had been hacked and compromised the entire company network. A couple of days later everyone received this email:

Date:	May 1, 2xxx
From:	CEO
To:	All Employees
Re:	Survey email - do not open

Evidently there is an e-Mail circulating from myself concerning taking another survey. I did not send that out, so please do not open it.

Thanks,

[First name of CEO]

I had worked for the company for three years, and this was the first time I had received any direct communication from the Leader of Our Company. No "Message from the CEO" regarding company news, acquisitions, or mergers. No announcements of promotions, departures, or staff reductions. No mention of company performance. Not even a "Happy Holidays" message at the end of the year.

It took an enterprising hacker to spur our Fearless Leader to open up and get in touch with his people. And the way he signed the message let us all know we were now on a first-name basis, which was nice.

Now, fixing my *width* is another thing entirely.

I'm sure everyone has experienced managers who set unrealistic target dates that had no chance of being met. After several years I started thinking of impossible deadlines as the equivalent of, "Steve, you're not tall enough. Fix it."

Nothing I could do about it, so just get back to work. I realized it was almost always better to submit high-quality work even if it was late. Meeting a deadline with low-quality work often meant revisions and iterations before submitting it late anyway.

It wasn't exactly an "Ayn Rand" moment, but when I started shrugging off arbitrary deadlines my attitude improved, and I started sleeping better.

I'm delaying things as fast as I can!

I was working a couple of hours late one night in the 1980s when my boss Pat stopped in my door. He asked what was taking so long to complete a particular project.

Even though I had only 6 years of experience, I had already developed a tendency to become annoyed with *engineering* managers who seemed to have no idea (or had conveniently forgotten) how long it took to process and analyze data. Unrealistic deadlines were frequently set by management without any input from the technical professionals who were tasked with getting the work done.

I'm positive I am biased, but it seemed as though geologists were usually given plenty of time to complete their project work. Everyone "knew" it took days or weeks to compile geologic data, construct maps and cross-sections, interpret the geologic potential and share the results. As soon as the geologic work was complete, the reservoir engineer would be told "let's show the reserves and economics to the VP tomorrow afternoon," without regard to the time required for a thorough evaluation to support the best decision. (I have a still-vivid memory of one engineering manager literally describing economic analysis as "just punching a button.")

But on this particular night I was in a mood, and asked Pat if I could have a couple of minutes of his time. He agreed and I pulled a chair around so he could see the computer screen.

I demonstrated the complete workflow for the project: data gathering, correcting errors, manual data entry into the software database, setting up the calculations and generating the iso-data maps needed for the evaluation. I told Pat much of it was slow, tedious work, and I would love to get it done faster. I asked him if he had any suggestions on how to speed up the process.

Pat took his time before admitting he did not have a better idea. He said he appreciated that I had enlightened him on the process, gave me an encouraging complement, and left my office. Pat never questioned my project time estimates again, and it felt as though I had earned a little respect from the boss.

That 20-minute exchange is still one of my favorite interactions with any manager.

There's Always a Choice

About a year after our second child was born, my manager informed me there was a new opportunity for the Company, and that I might be a candidate for transferring to a new post in a South American country. I responded that I wasn't interested.

"You might not have a choice," Pat said.

"No, I'm not going to South America."

"Hey, if the Company wants you to go, you'll go."

"Nope, not going to happen," I said.

We went through several iterations of this, and I kept repeating that of course I had a choice. It apparently was inconceivable to my manager that an engineer might resign from the Company rather than relocate to an undesirable location. This made Pat an excellent member of Corporate Group A: Future Senior Manager.

My attitude, however, meant I was solidly entrenched in Corporate Group B: Never Going to BE a Manager.

"Looks like he picked the wrong week to quit being on time."

I arrived at my usual time one morning and was told all asset teams were to meet in the conference room at 8am. This was not previously scheduled and had to be related to the presentations made to Corporate Leadership the day before.

Pat was already seated at the head of the table and did not look happy. The teams quickly filled the seats, and many stood against the walls. At 8 o'clock sharp Pat began speaking in a low voice, clearly struggling to remain calm.

"Yesterday was a disaster. If you can't do better than that, you can all just GET THE F___ OUT!" Total, stunned silence. We'd never seen or heard Pat like this. I'm paraphrasing his comments, but the four-word kicker at the end is exact, burned into my brain.

"Geologists, you were piss-poor. The maps were difficult to see, and you didn't have basic, relevant information on your projects. If you can't review your work professionally with the management team, you can GET THE F___ OUT!"

"Production engineers couldn't answer simple questions about their wells or field ops. It was embarrassing. If you're not going to do your job, you can GET THE F___ OUT!"

At that moment a production engineer walked in, five minutes late. Pat glared at him. "Office hours start at 7:45. If you can't get here on time, GET THE F___ OUT!" The engineer froze and turned Maserati red. Pat jabbed a finger at him, then to the door. The engineer walked out, looking mystified and miserable.

It was our turn. "The reservoir engineers were disorganized and unprepared," Pat said. "If you can't be professional in your presentations, then you can GET THE F___ OUT."

Pat went on for quite a while and eventually ran out of gas. He dismissed everyone except the reservoir engineers, and I wondered how it could get any worse.

Pat seemed to relax a bit, and said he was mostly okay with the performance of the reservoir group. He apologized for including us in his rant, saying it was necessary for all teams to hear a consistent message. He recognized much of the reservoir engineering content was dependent on information and source material from the other groups, who apparently had not taken the presentations seriously.

I'm sure everyone who was at the GTFO meeting never forgot the experience, but the reservoir engineers don't remember it in quite the same way.

"*Huge* difference, actually."

Warning: a bit of bawdy banter ahead.

During a team meeting, someone repeated the old, tired joke: "It's not the size of the boat, but the motion of the ocean."

Our manager spoke right up. "That's what all you guys with little @$%* say." It was a Moby Dickensian moment I couldn't resist.

"Hey boss, you might be confused. There's a big difference between *having* a big @$%* and *being* one."

This got a laugh from the team and a tight smile from my boss. As I write this, it's starting to become clear why I never made it to supervisor…

"I've read *How to Be a Star at Work* six times, so I've got that going for me."

I noticed managers returning to their office after the morning meeting, all carrying a small paperback book titled *Who Relocated the Cheese Whiz?* or something like that. The COO had read the book and liked it enough to give a copy to everyone on his management team.

Two weeks later at our department staff meeting, the boss entered the room and placed a cardboard box on the conference table. After a short pep talk sprinkled with redundancies (doing a good job for the sake of doing a good job, be all you can be), Pat opened the box and handed out copies of *How to Be a Star at Work* by Robert E. Kelly. He closed the meeting with this inspirational message: "I encourage you not to limit yourself to what you're responsible for and what you're not." (Yeah, it made the ROT list.)

I was always interested in improving myself, so I read the book. It wasn't bad and included some common-sense best practices. I know of at least one other reservoir engineer who also read the entire book.

One dark morning not long after our mandatory book club meeting, the Company laid off several folks. Later, walking by the office of one of the terminated reservoir engineers, I noticed he left behind his copy of *How to be a Star*. It was centered neatly by itself on the otherwise empty desktop, perhaps the literary equivalent of an extended middle finger. A few days later it was still there, so I took it and placed it alongside my copy on the bookshelf in my office.

Another engineer saw the books and I told him how I found the extra copy. When he left the company a few weeks later for another opportunity, he gave me his copy of *Star* on his last day, "for your collection."

Word got around, more engineers gave me their books, and at one point I had 8 copies stacked neatly on my bookshelf. After *literally* being encouraged to improve their performance and become stars at work, the painful terminations drastically diluted the boss's motivational message.

I re-gifted several of the books to others over the years, but still have three copies. Let me know if you'd like to have one.

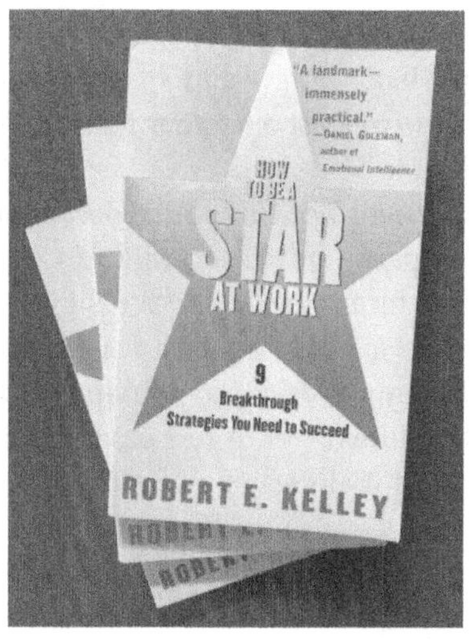

10X your performance by reading this book 10 times

Meet the New Boss, Not Quite the Same as the Old Boss.

I was the reservoir engineer on an acquisition team when our boss resigned for another opportunity. Senior Leadership moved quickly and named Pat the new manager of A&D. Everyone was a bit surprised by the announcement, saying things like "interesting choice" to each other while inside silently asking *what the…?*

On Pat's first day as leader of our group, I presented updated project economics for a development drilling plan to the Regional Management Team. After the meeting, Pat followed me into my office.

"Nice job on the presentation, Steve, but I have a couple of questions. What does 'P W' mean on your economic summaries?

I tried to keep it together. The new Manager of Business Development for a medium-sized oil and gas company had just asked me to explain a commonly used abbreviation for a well-known economic term. "It stands for Present Worth," I said.

Pat nodded. "Right. What about the number 10 right next to PW?" *Uh-oh. It's worse than I thought.* Mentally, I unsheathed the Sword of Knowledge and prepared to battle the Dragon of Ignorance.

"PW10 means the present worth of the project calculated using a discount rate of 10%." The unspoken definition of Discount Rate floated ominously overhead, threatening a brainstorm of additional questions. Pat started to speak, then stroked his chin for a second and walked away muttering his thanks.

We would not skirmish further this day, but our encounter was an omen, a portent, an Orange Cone of Warning: the journey ahead would often be delayed by the Power of Confusion.

"You're under arrest for violating Moore's Laws 1, 3, 4 and 6."

What do we want? CLEAR DIRECTION! When do we want it? YESTERDAY!

I was reassigned to become the reservoir engineer on yet another asset team and passed my budget and variance reporting responsibilities to a new hire. Alex was very bright, highly educated, and had no industry experience. (I gently engineer-splained that BBL was the abbreviation for barrel despite the superfluous "B".) Alex made a serious effort and put in a lot of overtime, but things weren't working out. Finally, Alex's supervisor decided to deliver some constructive criticism. To me.

Pat sat on the other side of my desk and read a list of Alex's needs-to-improves. I took notes and agreed things weren't going well. As Budget Guy there were many times when I had to iterate and struggle to meet the expectations of managers. It would be even tougher for Alex, new to both the Company and the industry. I defended Alex while silently questioning why management hired a budget and planning coordinator without relevant experience.

Pat made it clear I was expected to Solve The Problem. I picked up my pen. "Okay, what exactly do you need, and by when?"

This caught Pat off guard. "You know what's needed."

I nodded. "Yeah, in general. But for today, what is the top priority? Also, who else is it for?"

"What do you mean 'who else'?"

"Well, if the variance analysis is for (I named the VP of production), he likes to have hard copies of all the graphs down to the field level. That takes a bit of time. If it's for the CFO, she prefers an executive summary and an Excel file with all the details for her financial models. So, what we do depends on who it's for."

This seemed to be news to Pat. "Just get it done." He started to get up from his chair, so I tried again.

"Hey, really. What do you want, when do you need it, and who is it for?"

Now Pat looked irritated. "I'm picking up a bit of hostility here, Steve." It went downhill from there. It was my fault; I had failed to communicate effectively and control my frustration.

Eventually I got as much information from Pat as I was going to get and assumed the rest. Alex and I worked a couple of long days and nights and produced everything for everybody, but the damage was done. Alex was terminated a few days later.

A month later the company hired another budget coordinator who also had no relevant industry experience.

Sometimes the best communication is no communication.

The CEO told his Manager of Geology that the company had too many geologists and specifically mentioned one by name who he planned to terminate.

The reason I knew this: The Geology Manager then told a District Production Manager about the termination plan, also identifying the geologist by name. (The geologist was not involved with the assets managed by the Production Manager; there was no reason for the PM to be told the name.)

And the reason I knew that: I was the reservoir engineer for the Production Manager's district, and for some reason the PM felt compelled to tell me about the plan to radically upset the life of the geologist—who the PM named but admitted he had never met—and his family.

I was appalled. It was an unprofessional gossip pyramid scheme, kicked off by the CEO and inappropriately continued by two managers who should know better.

"If you choose not to accept this mission, your career will self-destruct in five seconds..."

In the late 1980s personal computers were not yet common and not all that personal, either. Usually, they were set up in separate rooms and shared by all. Our group had received approval to purchase a new PC exclusively for our team, to be set up in our bullpen trailer office. At Elk Hills, trucks entered the field through a manned security gate before making deliveries at a separate warehouse facility located some distance from the main office complex. It could take several days for Office Services to sort and deliver the packages, and computers were a hot item. If our PC ended up in the wrong place, we'd have to repeat the requisition process from the beginning. It was a government facility and there were protocols and procedures to follow.

My team and I probably shouldn't have been surprised when Pat, our manager, instructed me to intercept the delivery truck at the gate, remove our PC and printer, then haul it to our office and set it up.

I stared at my boss, pondering exactly how one would pull off this stupid heist. Wait around for days at the gate, sipping coffee and chatting with the security guard? Inspect the cargo of every delivery truck that came through until I found our PC and printer boxes? Convince the driver to allow me to offload our equipment, then carry it up the hill to our office?

I told Pat I didn't believe it was possible to hijack a truck at the gate. Then one of my teammates described this scenario: I would cling to the outside wall of the guard shack, high out of sight, wearing a black, skin-tight ninja suit complete with hood and high-tech suction gloves. When the delivery truck arrived I would swing down and subdue the guard with a sleeper hold. After warning the driver to stay put and not cause any trouble, I'd break into the cargo hold, locate our computer with my spidey-sense, and use my super-strength to carry the boxes to our office.

I told the guy his plan wouldn't work; I didn't know any sleeper holds. Plus, it had been 40 pounds since I last wore my ninja suit and significant alterations would be needed.

Eventually, we got our computer, but the Team never forgot the staff meeting when Pat assigned me the Mission Improbable.

"Wait...what?"

The Boss was taking a candidate for an engineering technician position to lunch, and since my friend and I knew the guy from a previous company, we were invited along.

After we were seated, the Boss described our company culture, bragged about his high-quality team, and described how everyone strove for excellence. Management expected hard work, he said, then added, "But we're not slave drivers."

The guy interviewing for the position was African American. I immediately leaned back so my lower jaw wouldn't smack the top of the table. My friend stared at our boss in amazement. It felt like we were trapped in a scene from that old TV documentary about the paper company.

Understandably, our friend accepted an opportunity with another company.

Saturday Night's Alright for Writing

My boss Pat called me at home around dinner time on a Saturday. He had reviewed a reservoir engineering report written by my teammate and found it unacceptable. The deadline was Monday, so he requested I come to his house that evening, *to discuss the other guy's report.*

After greeting me at the door he introduced me to his girlfriend lounging on the couch in the living room. We sat nearby at the dining room table and Pat started railing at the poor quality of the report. It was immediately obvious he was putting on a show for his girl, a superior chewing out a subordinate for shoddy work. I recognized this immediately and let him go on for a while, then quietly reminded him it wasn't my report, it had been compiled and written by the other reservoir engineer. That caused the girlfriend to look our way, and Pat calmed down a bit.

He wanted me to rewrite the report "to be more useful." I asked him to explain, and maybe give me a couple of examples. Pat said he didn't have any, he just wanted it improved because he "did not understand it." I agreed to rewrite the report and reminded him it would take a few days. He nodded and said the late report would be the first black mark next to his name, and that he was furious *at both of us.*

I rewrote the report, pissed off the entire time for doing another engineer's job on the weekend. Somehow, we all survived submitting a late deliverable. (I hated the word *deliverable* back then, and still do.) From that point forward, the boss would review the other engineer's work, rewrite it, then give it to me. I'd correct the grammar and spelling errors made by both and finalize the reports.

I did receive an attaboy on my next performance review. I have no idea what the consequences were for the other reservoir guy, if any.

Tales From the Spit Cup

I worked for or with a handful of people who enjoyed tobacco in the office. They were constantly spitting the nasty stuff into a smelly cup they carried with them everywhere, and it was impossible to avoid their minty, nauseating crap-breath. All were guys; I've yet to come across a woman who dipped.

One guy left his Styrofoam spit cup in my office so often I assumed he did it on purpose to annoy me. I'd poke a couple of colored pencils I had "borrowed" from a geologist through the cup on opposite sides for handles. Then I gently carried it like unstable nitroglycerin to the break room and toss it in the trash, pencils too. I often considered grabbing a Sharpie, writing on the cup "PLEASE RETURN TO ____" with the dipper's name, and leaving the disgusting thing on the HR lady's desk. I almost always resisted the temptation.

I give one dipper credit for creativity. Selected to represent the Company at a university job fair, he traded his spit cup for a small pill bottle with a lid. He kept it tucked inside his shirt pocket, out of sight. And he wore a brown shirt and tie, just in case.

"From the splatter pattern we believe the perpetrator was sitting here, and only spit once."

The conference room was full for the morning operations meeting. A guy named Pat was sitting near the middle of the table, listening intently to the daily drilling report. Pat leaned forward to spit tobacco juice into his ever-present Styrofoam cup. Somehow, he missed the target, and a stream of brown spittle splashed on his spiral notebook.

I was sitting against the opposite wall facing Pat and saw the entire, horrific spectacle. The reservoir engineer sitting next to Pat looked as though he was trying not to laugh or vomit at the same time.

The entertainment continued. Pat used the side of his hand to squeegee the juice from his notebook, then whipped his hand below the table to fling the nasty stuff to the carpet. The engineer and I locked eyes, both of us in shock. Pat calmly flipped to a new page in his notebook and started scribbling as though nothing had happened. (Perhaps for him, nothing had.)

After the meeting, the engineer and I described what we had witnessed to an engineering manager who also enjoyed smokeless tobacco. The manager couldn't believe it, then said, "I always swallow, I never spit." When I stopped laughing, I suggested he might not want to say that out loud ever again, and definitely not in the office.

Later that afternoon, Pat called a meeting with our team in his office. I had a difficult time focusing on the discussion. Pat's notebook lay open on the table, a large brown stain covering half the page.

A Too-Close Encounter of the Worst Kind

I had some time before my flight began boarding in the Houston airport and found a couple of empty seats in a nearby gate area. One was smeared with what looked like special sauce from a Big Mac, so I sat in the next chair. I was checking my phone when someone sat down next to me in the messy seat. It was my boss Pat from a former company a few years earlier. He had a big dung-eating grin, and I smiled right back, knowing he had just soiled his management slacks with burger juice.

We were both catching the same flight back to Tulsa. Pat had a low number on his pass and boarded the plane several minutes before I did. It occurred to me there was a good chance Pat would invite me to join him and slide over from his aisle seat to make room. I wanted to avoid that for two reasons: Pat would no doubt spend the entire flight spitting tobacco juice into a Styrofoam cup.

Plus, the seat he would vacate for me would be stained with Big Mac butt-sauce.

Fortunately, Pat was in a window seat and someone else had the aisle. The middle seat was open, but Pat wouldn't expect me to sit there when better seats were open in the back. I nodded to Pat and kept walking, feeling lucky.

At the Tulsa airport I passed through baggage claim and managed to catch the parking garage shuttle bus just before it pulled away. The bus was almost full and as you probably guessed, Pat was sitting right in the middle with that same sly smile.

"Here, Steve, we'll make room," Pat said, sliding over and smooshing the woman next to him. Clearly, the Gods were angry with me. I accepted my fate and stepped forward. Sure enough, there was a greasy spot where Pat had been sitting. I muttered a thank you, sat down and stared toward the front of the bus to avoid tobacco breath.

Moments like this made me realize the Circle of Life was actually the tip of Fate's middle finger, pointing directly at me.

The Only Manager Who Yelled at Me

Before the Tech Wizards gifted the People of Earth with cell phones, email, and Internet data transfer, there were facsimile machines. Many companies depended heavily on daily reports faxed to the office early each morning from the field. A technician organized the reports, made dozens of copies, and distributed them to managers and teams. Management met each morning to review the reports and set priorities.

There was quite a range of reactions to missing reports among the various corporate cultures. Some managers shrugged it off, assuming they would see the reports later or the next day. Other managers flipped open the clear plastic cover and pushed the Big Red Button to initiate a Level 5 communication daisy chain. Every engineer, technician and field foreman was tasked with acquiring and delivering the missing information before the first pot of coffee finished brewing upstairs in Mahogany Hall.

It was one of those days when my boss appeared in my door and started listing all the reports he didn't have in his hands. I hadn't had my first cup of caffeine yet. I nodded along and when he finally paused, I told him I was already on it, I knew the drill, and didn't he trust me to get him the reports?

Well, that was stupid. It was a dumb thing to say, and it set him off. He stepped inside and slammed the door behind him. "DON'T YOU TALK TO ME THAT WAY!" he shouted, jabbing a Vienna sausage finger at me. Using impressive volume and energetic enunciation, he went on to explain how vital the information was to his manager and therefore to him, and therefore to me. He had no choice but to thunder down the halls every damn day to scramble the staff to get the missing reports. (Which, more often than not, had been eaten by the copy or fax machine.)

Realizing my big mistake (huge, really), I sat quietly until he ran out of steam three days later. It was my own fault; I forgot who I was talking to and popped off. Still, it was the first and only time a manager literally shouted at me in anger. It kind of left a mark. To my boss's credit, things quickly returned to normal, and the incident was (mostly) forgotten.

We've all heard stories of altercations between and among employees and managers in workplaces of all kinds. I'm grateful to have worked in corporate environments where professionals nearly always treated each other with respect.

He took home the centerpiece decoration, too.

At the company Christmas party, names of employees were drawn from a glass bowl for door prizes. The biggest prize was an extra week of paid vacation. The winner was a Vice President. After hearing grumbling among the crowd and even a few quiet boos, the President stepped forward and told the emcee to draw another name. I was standing close enough to hear to hear one executive say to another, "I told Pat not to put his name in the bowl; the prizes are for the staff, not Management."

Manager's Inhumanity to Man

During a meeting to discuss a potential acquisition, I was asked by the CEO to retrieve a copy of the price forecast used in the economics. I hustled down four flights of stairs, made a copy of the document, then returned to the conference room. Empty. He wasn't in his office either. I asked around, no one knew where the CEO had wandered off to. I knew he needed the price forecast for a conference call with the Board in just a few minutes. I made a lap around the executive floor (*wait…the Managers have Starbucks coffee up here?*), then circled back and found the CEO standing in his office, looking down at something on his desk.

I knocked and handed him the copy. He didn't say a word but stared at the forecast. I waited a long moment, he said nothing. It seemed obvious he wasn't going to thank me. In fact, the CEO was acting as if I was no longer in his office, so I made it so. I assumed he'd break his vow of silence if he needed anything else.

A few months later I held the elevator for a VP and one of his managers. They were having a conversation and didn't toss me a thanks or even a nod. They got out on their floor and never even glanced my way.

I've worked for many supervisors, department managers, and executive leaders at several companies. Most were polite and friendly, and many cheerfully engaged with the staff at all times.

But I found it difficult to remain motivated working for a handful of jerks who wouldn't even acknowledge your existence or exchange common courtesies like "good morning" and "thanks for holding the elevator." How did these personalities rise to the top?

At some intellectual level, I knew the answer to that question. I also knew I could never act as they did to get and stay ahead in the corporate world.

"How About a Maybe-Maybe?"

A super-sharp engineering technician with a newborn baby asked me whether I thought our manager might approve her working longer days Monday through Thursday in exchange for Fridays off. This would be a big help with her child day-care situation. She promised to work on any Friday if something special came up, with a little notice so she could line up a sitter. It was fine with me; everyone only worked a half-day on Friday already and she was an excellent tech. I suggested when she made the request to our department manager to be sure to describe it as a win-win situation: she would never leave the Company short of help if something important came up, she would put in a full 40 hours by the end of Thursday, and it would be a huge help to her family.

She stopped in my office after her meeting with the boss. She looked defeated; he had rejected her proposal. Later, Pat took a seat in my office. He knew the tech had discussed her proposal with me.

"I had to tell her no, we couldn't set that precedent."

I was feeling my oats. "What precedent is that?"

"If I gave her Fridays off, then everyone would want Fridays off."

Well, everyone already wanted Fridays off. Mondays too. I took another stab at it. "What about setting a positive precedent? If every one of 300 employees came to you, each with a genuine win-win, no-lose proposal, where the employee received something they wanted, and the Company didn't give up a single thing—and in fact gained a happier, loyal employee—wouldn't that be a good precedent to have established?"

Pat looked blank for a moment. "Maybe. That's an interesting way to look at it," he admitted and left my office.

The technician took a similar job with another company a few months later.

The 3% Solution

One supervisor shared his method for motivating engineering technicians. Corporate leadership set the across-the-board annual salary increase at 3%.

The boss told one technician he had gone to bat for her because of her quality performance the previous year. After fighting hard, he was able to get her approved for a 3% raise, which was *higher than average.* He encouraged the tech to keep up the good work.

The boss told a second technician she was only receiving a 3% raise, which was *less than average,* and he hoped she would be able to improve her performance over the next year.

I thought this was kind of slimy, disingenuous at best. Worse, he had also told me the techs' detailed salary information, which was bad form and unprofessional. Plus, I could no longer trust whatever he said about my own salary adjustments.

1001 Creative Uses of Barbeque Tools, No. 47

My manager—let's call him Pat—told me he just had an unpleasant phone conversation with a staff engineer at corporate headquarters. Then he said this: "I'd rather ___ with a wire brush than talk to ____ again." He made a point of repeating this jewel to every one of his staff (and twice to some of us).

The next day Pat stopped me in the hallway. Corporate had called again and requested I run additional divestiture economics with something like thirty-eight new price scenarios. *That's absurd!* I thought to myself, but inadvertently laughed out loud.

Pat decided this was a teachable moment, not just for me but also for those working in nearby offices. Less than one day after describing his affection for his favorite tool to everyone in the office, he chewed me out—with volume—for laughing at Corporate's request. He told me to show some respect and act like a professional. I apologized, knowing it was what he wanted me to do within earshot of my coworkers.

But in my head, I flashed on the scene in the movie *Office Space,* when Michael describes someone as a No-Talent Ass Clown.

Vice President? Of his *own company*?

During a team meeting our leader casually said someday he'd like to have his own company. I joked and said he could probably rise to be Vice President. He wasn't listening close and said, "Yeah! That would be great!"

A few months later one of the engineers gave me a business card he found in a work file. The name on the card was Harold W. ____, Vice President of Harold W. ____ Inc. I still have a copy of the card in my Laughs file.

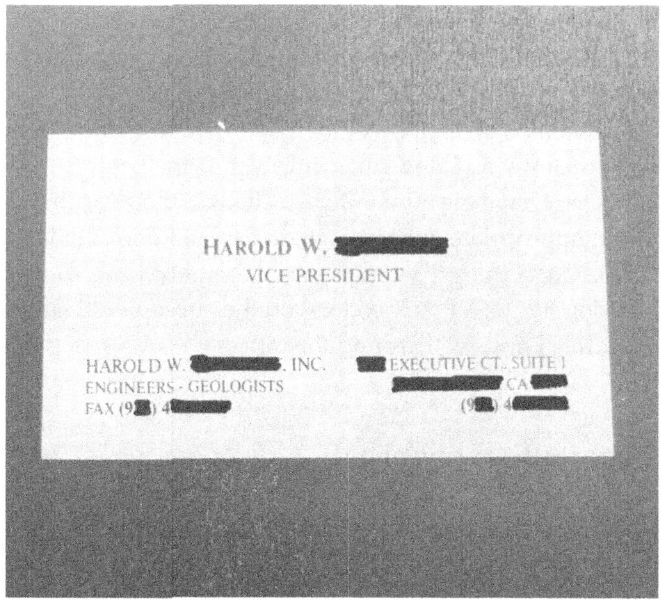

The CEO needs something to do

On a business flight to Houston, I overheard the Vice President of Exploration complain that the CEO wouldn't allow him to carry over two days of vacation into the next calendar year. I shook my head and looked out at the clouds. I felt a tiny bit sorry for the VP, and a whole lot of sorry for the hard-working employees of the company. And for the stockholders, many of whom were also employees, including me.

Why did the Vice President of the Company have to ask the CEO for permission to schedule his vacation? With a compensation rate of roughly $1200 per hour, was this the best use of the CEO's time? What "jolly" did the CEO get from exercising his Board-given right to veto a couple of days of vacation for his right-hand manager?

This seemed symbolic—or, perhaps, symptomatic—of the way the Company was being run at the top. If the Senior Leadership Team didn't have the autonomy to schedule their vacation as they thought appropriate, what else were they not permitted to do?

It's a good thing I wasn't cynical, I might have thought this admission by the VP helped explain the sub-optimal culture and low morale I observed around the office.

A rant worth ranting about

At nearly every company where I worked, senior management had no problem with highly paid engineers and geologists doing low-level data management and administrative tasks. Geology and engineering technicians were on staff, but always shared by several professionals, setting up numerous priority conflicts.

Techs were also frequently monopolized for special projects requested by management.

I understood the goal was to keep G&A costs low. One CEO stated if he had to increase head count, he'd rather hire an engineer or geologist than a technician. I always thought I'd rather have the admins and techs doing the data entry, file searches, and economic case setup so the professionals could focus their time and efforts on generating cash flow and increasing net asset value. I believed if I had the dedicated support of one full-time engineering technician, Management could double or even triple the size of my reservoir engineering assignment. Of course, this never happened, and a significant percentage of my "engineering" time was spent on mundane tasks that killed time and brain cells.

The point was brought home nicely by a production engineer named Pat one afternoon. A large group of engineers and geologists had worked a massive acquisition evaluation and were scheduled to present our work and recommendations the next day. Pat asked one of the techs to punch holes and bind a bunch of documents, and she indicated that as a technician, she should be doing tech support and not clerical or admin work.

She lit the fuse, and Pat fired off like a 4th of July rocket. I'll paraphrase his rant; please try to imagine it delivered at mug-rattling volume with more than a smattering of f-bombs used as adjectives:

"Look, you and I can both make copies. We can both find notebooks and punch holes and copy maps. But only one of us can prepare our slides and notes and presentations for the review tomorrow. Only one of us will be standing before the CEO, justifying and recommending he approve spending hundreds of millions of dollars to purchase assets. Only one of us can answer technical questions about the reservoirs, production, offset wells, and complex economic evaluations. So, it has to be you making copies and punching holes. Or would you like to make the presentation to the Corporate Leadership team, and I'll make the copies for you?"

Harsh, but also spot-on brilliant. Thirty years later, I was still surprised to be doing my own well files research, data entry, formatting and copying, instead of analyzing reservoir performance, solving technical problems, drafting money-making project proposals, and applying my education and experience to achieving the company's goals.

Folding or mutilating, however, is totally acceptable

On the flip side, a few technicians achieved great power, which came with great responsibility—for the engineers.

Shortly after I joined a reserves group, I was informed by the supervisor that when filing reserves documentation, I should never use staples, only binder or paper clips. The admin-tech who made copies at year-end hated the hassle of removing staples before running pages through the copier. Feeling the pain, she owned and solved her problem: she "managed up" and convinced the boss to implement a No Staples policy. Nicely done!

"Would you mind chiseling my assignment into this stone tablet, too?"

After a number of communication issues and confusion over who-was-assigned-what, the next time Pat gave me a work request I asked him to please put it in writing.

"Sure," he said, and picked up his pen. Then he wrote it down. *On his desk calendar.*

I counted to ten, then said, "Uh...thank you? Could you also write it on a piece of paper for me to keep, to make sure I do exactly what you want?" He said no, he'd just keep track of it on his calendar.

I realized (again) that I would never be promoted to first-line supervisor, I wasn't qualified. I did not have the mind-set and skills to duplicate the logic and thought processes of Management.

"Okay, then why ARE you here?"

One of my teammates was discussing a challenging leasing issue with our manager. Apparently, the boss was not in the mood.

"So? I'm not here to ___ your ____ for you."

It was every bit as crude as (some of) you can imagine. People nearby heard the landman attempt to stay calm by taking a slow, deep breath before starting to count backwards out loud.

From one million.

Men's Room Follies, Part 5: Yelling "FIRE!" in a Crowded Restroom Stall

One of the senior engineers—I think his name was Mayo, or Mustard, definitely some kind of condiment—fell asleep in a stall in the men's room. He was snoring so loudly that I and two other guys, laughing quietly so we wouldn't wake him up, had difficulty focusing on our respective tasks. A manager walked in and heard Mayo sawing logs instead of dropping them. He immediately spun and walked back out.

While I was washing up, the manager returned carrying a fire extinguisher. He shoved the nozzle under the stall door, yelled "Fire!" and lit the sucker up. Mayo's final snort morphed into a terrified yelp and he jumped, banging into the walls and rattling the doors. The manager grinned and walked out, his work done. We gave Mayo a round of applause when he stepped out, his face as red as the extinguisher. To this day it's the funniest thing I've ever seen in a men's room.

A rare, delicious moment

We had recently drilled the Company's first horizontal well on a small heavy-oil lease north of Bakersfield. I was assigned to the project since I had experience with thermal steam injection operations from my time in Bakersfield years earlier. Before the well was completed, I advised the production engineer of the importance of installing the rod pump as deep in the well as possible after stimulating with cyclic "huff and puff" steam injection. Setting the pump low would minimize both fluid levels in the wellbore and back pressure on the reservoir.

After completion and steaming, the well was put on production and produced poorly. My production engineer and I were summoned by the production manager.

"So: where's all that hot oil production you predicted, Steve?" My manager looked kind of satisfied, he wasn't a fan of the project from the beginning. However, I knew what I was doing.

"About 200 feet below the pump," I replied. The heavy-oil reservoir was very shallow, especially by mid-continent standards. "We're not in Oklahoma anymore. The reservoir pressure is only about 25 pounds, and it doesn't take much of a fluid level to kill production. Drop the pump to the top of the perforations and we should be fine." The manager didn't want to drop the pump lower to avoid sand issues and I argued with him.

The manager finally gave in. "At this point, I guess we don't have anything to lose." The production engineer called the field and arranged for a pulling unit to lower the pump. Five days later the well was producing oil at decent rates. The production engineer thanked me and admitted his mistake. In his mid-continent experience, setting a rod pump a few hundred feet above the perforations was considered "pumped off."

I never heard anything more from the production manager, but I still enjoyed the win.

PERFORMANCE EVALUATIONS:

_____ Frequently Exceed Expectations
_____ Occasionally Exceed Expectations
_____ Meet Expectations
__X__ Fail to Meet Expectations

I think most people would agree the corporate review process "Needs Improvement." It is a dismal chore unwanted by both management and staff, which of course means it's a sparkly, shiny *precious* to be carefully protected by the trolls of HR. Early in my career I had a lot of anxiety about performance evaluations. The idea of being officially judged by my supervisor was supremely unpleasant. I assumed it would be an adversarial experience, a corporate version of *Mad Max Beyond Thunderdome:* Two men enter, one manager leaves.

I wasn't all wrong. I've already described my first three evaluations in the early 1980s, being placed on Double Secret Probation by a new supervisor, and working hard for a year to recover, only to be terminated a few months later.

Let's play "Spot the Trend"

Five months after bouncing to my second job, I received a terrific review from my supervisor. The appraisal form included some helpful graphics: My overall assessment was indicated by an upward-pointing "stable" arrow drawn through the "Job Requirements - Exceeds Some" box. My boss recommended me for promotion to the next grade, which I received a few weeks later.

I was then reassigned to a new team reporting to a different supervisor. To normalize my evaluation schedule to the calendar year, I received another review just four months after the first. My new boss praised my written communication skills while his hand-written appraisal ironically included several spelling and grammatical errors, such as: "Steve has *beening* working as a reservoir engineer..." and "Steve's objectives are to *access* what must be done to provide..."

My overall rating dropped to a left-pointing "positive trend" arrow through the "Meets All Job Requirements - Medium" box. My goals for the next review period included *"develop confidence in your engineering ability to sell your ideas."*

One year later I received a similar, awkwardly written review from the same manager: "Steve is an excellent communicator of technical facts in writing. Steve's performance *continues to improver* as he gains more experience." My overall performance was only satisfactory; I was dinged for failing to complete a particular pressure falloff analysis report. When I reminded my boss he had assigned that project to the other reservoir engineer on the team (who did, in fact, blow it off), he lined out the negative remark on my evaluation. I requested that he rewrite the appraisal and reconsider my overall rating. He refused.

The other reservoir engineer on the team blissfully meandered along his life path to the erratic beat of a drummer the rest of us could not hear. I frequently revised or completely reworked his projects and reports. I wrote a letter explaining why my performance was more than satisfactory and attached it to my signed appraisal form. This pissed off my boss, but he agreed to write a letter to my file documenting that I had shouldered most of the reservoir work on the team. As far as I know, this never happened.

The following year our team was assigned to yet another supervisor. (I had five different supervisors in four years with the company.) In my next annual review I was praised as a team player, and my overall rating improved to a positive-trend arrow through the "Meets All Job Requirements - High" box. What a difference a year and a new manager made!

Still, once again I received a familiar chestnut: "A secondary objective is for Steve to *work on more effectively selling his engineering interpretations and recommendations to management.*" I was beginning to get a clear perspective on my authentic self.

I received many "be more aggressive" recommendations from managers throughout my career, but I remained reluctant. My attempts to assert myself in my first job resulted in probation, stress, and ultimately, perhaps, termination. I preferred to rely on the quality and thoroughness of my work to demonstrate to management I was a valuable corporate asset. Over time this proved to be a successful strategy for securing and sustaining employment and maintaining my engineering reputation. As a plan for getting promoted, it sucked. I was the reservoir engineer holding the management ladder steady with both hands, hoping the other engineers wouldn't smoosh my fingers as they scampered up the rungs.

"Steve should continue to pay attention to details in general..."

I recognized a recurring theme during my career: I often received praise from management for doing detailed, high-quality work. At other times—sometimes from the same managers—I received criticism for getting bogged down in details and failing to keep in mind a larger perspective. Apparently for me, detailed engineering was a *strengthness*: both a strength and a weakness.

This personality trait also impacted my relationships with significant others, going all the way back to high school. My attention to detail, and commitment to doing all the little things right, initially appealed to the ladies. Later, these attributes became sources of irritation to my companions, until something went wrong or needed to be handled. Then my engineering personality was useful again, at least for a time.

The challenge, of course, was to strike the right balance. During my second performance review, I was criticized for doing too much analysis and not making timely decisions. The boss was right. My work reflected my understanding of the nature and essence of *engineering* work: Scientific, technical, detailed, and thoroughly analytical. It was why I went into engineering in the first place. I loved science and was good at math. I had deep respect for America's space programs and the nerdy engineers who put astronauts in space and brought them home safely. I was confident the Space Shuttle did not achieve orbit because engineers cut their analysis short to make a speedy decision. (Sadly, the Challenger disaster may have showed I was correct.) Perhaps I should have recognized "too much detail" was a hint that reservoir engineering was not a good fit. My response to the guidance I received was to maintain my own standards of detailed engineering and try not to let it be visible to others.

Later in job interviews, I'd be asked to describe my strengths and weaknesses. I declared my dedication to detailed work a positive attribute but admitted at times it had been considered by others to be detrimental. I hoped a reservoir manager would rather hire an engineer who did too much work over an engineer who would do too little.

"And from the pictures of your kids on your desk, I can also tell you're spending too much time with your family."

I started work at my third company just before I became chairman of the local section of the Society of Petroleum Engineers. Coincidentally, the previous chairman I was replacing worked for the same company. I let my boss know I was slated to take over the chairmanship, and he assured me the Company supported their engineers participating in SPE.

Months later, I was surprised to get dinged on my performance review for spending too much time on SPE matters during the workday. This was in the late 1980s, long before the Internet, email, and mobile phone texting. To communicate with others on SPE issues, you generally had to call during business hours. There was also a fair amount of written correspondence required, most of which I composed and typed on my own time. I was doing the same level of SPE work as Pat, my predecessor, who was also a reservoir engineer reporting to my manager. When I pointed this out, my boss said he could tell how I was spending my time by the amount of SPE paperwork on my desk. He pointed out that Pat never had SPE stuff laying around his office.

Pat was a friend, and I knew how active he had been as SPE chairman. He was also a neat freak who stored everything in files and three-ring binders. He kept his desk clutter-free, using it only for current projects. If the boss used the what's-on-your-desk method to gauge Pat's productivity, he would have nailed him for not working on anything.

I explained to my manager that I used my desk to sort and store paperwork, including SPE correspondence. I did my engineering work at the table in the back of my office, facing away from the door. He just shrugged and said since my term as SPE chairman was coming to an end, there should be an increase in my productivity.

From that day on I kept my desk loaded only with materials and maps supporting a current hot project so the boss wouldn't get the wrong idea. It may have helped, as my appraisal and overall rating improved at my next review. Still, the wisdom of evaluating a staff engineer's performance by the type and quantity of paperwork stacked on his desk eludes me to this day.

"Hey boss! How about setting better goals so you'll be a better goal setter?"

An actual goal set by my supervisor and included on my performance appraisal:

"Format deliverables to provide maximum usability."

This was about as useful as telling someone to do good work so they'll be a good worker.

"May I rewrite that for you? Please?"

A nice comment on one of my appraisals, with a touch of ironic irony:

"Steve is a dependable communicator and has *helped our group with communicate more effectively with other departments."*

Solid advice

I enjoy comedy and satire and jokes, and had always used humor as a coping strategy to get through tough days (and years). There were others who always maintained a corporate demeanor of professional seriousness.

During one performance discussion, I asked the reservoir manager to summarize the things I might do to be a top performer in his group. I don't recall specifically what he said, but my evaluation notes one year later indicate he told me, "You have done those things." It was nice to hear, and I received a good review.

The manager then gave me an Important Safety Tip. While he enjoyed my sense of humor and dry wit, he advised me to be careful around Senior Executives, that some of them had "long memories." I learned that all of the managers met each year to rank the employees and allocate salary adjustments. A supervisor in an unrelated department like Accounts Payable could tank the rating of a technical professional with a simple comment like, "I don't know, that guy is kind of a downer."

I appreciated the advice. In my notes from this discussion I wrote: "One man's passion is a crappy attitude to another." Not elegant, but it captured the idea. I had received another solid clue: Working in a corporate environment and being politically careful with my humor was obviously a sound and safe strategy, but it was not a good fit for my personality.

Another company, another boss, another performance review (sigh)

The A&D manager delivered my review in person, reading from the form. Then he signed it and handed it to me. I noticed none of the "Expectations" boxes were checked, but for whatever reason didn't think anything of it. I signed it, and the boss said he'd make a copy for me and submit the original to HR.

Looking at my copy later, I noticed the box "Meets Expectations" had been checked. The previous A&D manager gave me a rating of "Exceeds Expectations" the year before. My overall performance assessment had been downgraded, and my manager not only failed to mention this, *he marked the box after I signed the appraisal form.* What a sleaze ball.

I went to the reservoir engineering supervisor (my functional "second boss") and he manager-splained that HR had decided there were too many "exceeds" in the company. Supervisors had been directed to adjust the company average by downrating many people to "meets." (This also happened at one other company for whom I worked.)

My take was this: The change in performance evaluation standards failed to meet *my* expectation, and communication by HR and Management "needs to improve." Was it really necessary to force rank or otherwise ensure a significant percentage of Company employees were average (or lower)? If managers, recruiters, and HR staff did a great job of hiring high-quality people, wouldn't it be a good thing to have a company 100% staffed by winners? Apparently not. I'm sure there were legal considerations involved, tied to fiduciary responsibilities and the need to avoid litigation from—

Aw, forget it. I'll just sign the damn thing and get back to work.

By 2012 it was clear: I was not a natural Reservoir Engineering leader. An excerpt from my performance review that year: As the Senior Reservoir Engineer, you are expected to be a leader for the team...Be more aggressive in directing staff priorities. Overall Rating: Meets expectations.

Management wanted more assertiveness and leadership from me. I wanted to be a technical expert in solving problems and getting projects done. My goals did not fit the Company's needs. I resigned a few months later.

"Steve needs to develop tolerance for humans during the next review period."

At one company the review process called for employees to submit self-appraisals to their managers, who would then complete their own evaluations. I thought this was a time-saving cop-out by Management. They could just tweak a word or two of the self-appraisal, add a Goal and a Needs to Improve and be done.

I had become frustrated with the "reservoir engineers finish last" attitude that was prevalent at the time. Senior Management had set a high priority goal for the Reservoir Engineering Department: book the maximum reserves for new wells as soon as possible. This priority was not effectively communicated to—or acknowledged by—the district management and staff. I was completely dependent on out-of-state geologists and engineers to provide the necessary technical data and maps. I had to follow up constantly, and often had to plead for cooperation. This inspired me to add this to my list:

Moore's Law of the C's:
Without Communication, Coordination and Cooperation, you get Crap.

On my self-appraisal under "Needs to Improve," I was tempted to write, "Steve needs to develop greater tolerance and patience for professionals who fail to meet their Team responsibilities." Ultimately, I put it this way:

At times I over-communicate, with too much exposition. I should adjust my interest and passion for optimizing workflows and data management to be more in line with the Company culture and corporate environment.

My reservoir engineering supervisor at the time was a good guy who had previously worked the same District and experienced similar frustrations. To his credit, he removed my sarcastic self-improvement goal and praised my contributions to improving communication and the reserves process.

Moore's Law of Data:

The degree of urgency imposed by management is inversely proportionate to the volume of data available to complete the evaluation by the deadline and justify the decision.

As one who was frequently criticized for "getting bogged down in details" while often praised at the same time for doing "detailed, high-quality work," I noticed the same irony could be used to describe Senior Management. During project reviews and acquisition evaluations, engineering executives almost always wanted to see as much data as possible, to support making the best decisions. Many (but not all) of these same managers showed no interest in supporting the systems and staff that acquired, processed, and analyzed the myriad kinds of data needed to make good oil and gas investment decisions.

Water production data is a good example. In many reservoirs, water production is a key component in analyzing and understanding reservoir behavior and forecasting reserves (and, therefore, economics and asset value.) Some companies don't even *pretend* to collect and report produced water volumes. In some cases, water volumes are reported at a gross level and not properly allocated back to the wells. Have you ever tried to forecast production for a water-drive reservoir—or, I don't know, maybe a *waterflood* project?—without half-decent water production data?

"The chance of me winning the argument was zero"

I was told by my boss to remove all zeros from a database for a particular asset so the production graph wouldn't have these dramatic dives to the axis interrupting the trend. The well tests were inconsistent, and I argued that the zeros were not null values but actual data. They reflected the erratic nature of the production such as oil production but no gas, or vice versa. Or they might indicate problems in the data gathering or reporting system.

I pointed out that editing the raw data in the database used to produce the graphs was not reversible (at that time, for that system), and the zeros would be lost forever.

It was not a hill on which I wanted to die. The boss overruled me, and I received Zero brownie points for my attempt to preserve all the data. The new plot looked pretty, the morning meeting went smoothly for my manager, and the sun came up again the next day.

57 Varieties of Production

"Hello, this is Steve."

"I need a graph of MoneyPit District production. Oh, and a tabular table of reserves."

"Yes sir, Mr. Vice President of Northern Hemisphere Production. And when do you need these?"

"For the two o'clock Managers Meeting this afternoon."

Steve checks his watch—1:14pm—and sighs. He untacks a piece of paper from the wall near his phone.

"If I may clarify sir? Gross or Net volumes?

"Uh...both."

"Operated, Non-op, or combined?"

"I'm not sure...what do you usually do?"

"Sir, I just started working here Wednesday."

"Operated. No, wait...both."

"Would you prefer monthly volumes or daily averages?"

"Daily rates are much easier to relate to."

"Yes sir. Would you like to include NGLs, and if so, show them separately or converted to oil volumes? And same question, please, for condensate?"

"Whatever."

"Just a couple more questions, sir. Gas volumes: shrunk or unshrunk? Reserves as of year-end, or rolled forward to the end of the quarter? Proved only, or 3P? Include contingent reserves as well? Do you require any subtotals, by field, zone, operator—"

"NEVERMIND!"

The call ends. Steve tacks the list of reserves and production categories back on the wall and heads to the break room with a tiny, satisfied smile.

(Reserves)

Gas Shrunk / Unshrunk MCF MMCF MCFe MMCFE
Cond BBL MBO MMBO BOE MBOE MMBOE BCF BCFe
NGL (w/ or w/o) " " "
Wtr BWPD BWPM MBWPD MBWPM
Gross / Net

Colors: Red, Green, Blue, Other

By Well — By District — Proved — Producing
By Zone — Region — Prob — Shut In
By Fault Block — Engineer — Poss — Behind Pipe
By Field — Team — Resource — Undeveloped
Operated — Contingent — Other
Non-Operated
By Operator

Cum PROD
REM RESERVES
ULT (EUR)

VOLUMETRIC EUR
ECONOMIC EUR

RESERVES (As of date?)
Potential (Reserves? plus Resource?)
Unassigned potential in FB?

MCFD — Calendar Day Average Prod (ARIES - 30.4167 day average)
MMCFD — Producing Day Average Prod
MCFM
MMCFM — Daily Test Data vs Monthly Vols
BOPD
BOPM
MBOPD — Gross Prod
MBOPM — Gross Sales
NGL YIELD — Net Prod
COND YIELD — Net Sales
GOR
GLR — B/M
MNGLD — B/MM
MNGLM — gal/M

"I don't know about the production data, but *I* need an adjustment"

During one of my brief escapes over the wall that surrounded the Reservoir Engineering Department, I was fortunate to work with my friend Danny and his team of coders designing a unique, powerful data management system that included digital field reporting, a robust data warehouse, and real-time production variance analysis.

My small contribution included development of the Field Adjustment Factor; a somewhat complicated variable used to adjust daily production volumes reported by the field to current, same-day net sales estimates. And no, it wasn't quite as exciting as it sounds.

Danny and I met at McNellie's downtown one evening to celebrate a milestone in the project, and for grins I purchased a custom beer mug engraved with "Field Adjustment Factor." For my convenience, it hung on the wall at McNellie's for several years before I moved it to its final resting place in my Scotch cabinet.

FIELD ADJ
FACTOR

MOORE ON MANAGING PEOPLE

I realize this section will confirm that I was never management material, but what the heck. Here are the highlights of my philosophy regarding Management and the role of Supervisor, developed after years of careful observation and not a little anguish.

"Meet Peter Dilbert, your new supervisor"

The famous Peter Principle holds that people in a hierarchical structure are promoted until they reach the level at which they are no longer competent. And yes, I am aware this is a perfectly good explanation for why I remained a Senior Reservoir engineer for many years.

Scott Adam's Dilbert Principle explains that people are promoted to the level at which they can do the least damage. Anecdotal evidence and personal experience led me to conclude that both Principles are true and coexist.

Invert the Pyramid

The traditional organization chart has the Board of Directors and CEO at the top. Just below is the Executive Leadership Team, which consists of eleventeen Vice Presidents of Something, hovering above an expanding pyramid filled with people who all wish their names appeared higher on the chart.

My idea: one day each month the CEO should pretend the pyramid is inverted and he or she is at the bottom of the chart, supporting the massive human resources above. What can he do during that one day to help his employees do their job better and produce higher quality results?

The possibilities are literally endless: Survey employees up and down the ranks to identify bottlenecks and inefficiencies. Review IT resources for potential economic upgrades. Ensure that adequate training opportunities exist for maximum productivity. Check staff morale: Do people feel good about their jobs or work while constantly aggravated? Investigate the merits and popularity of awarding employees more time off versus modest annual salary increases. Choose three or four employees at random, invite them to lunch and listen closely to them for an hour. Maybe compose and send an encouraging email to all employees with the latest corporate news and thank everyone for making this the Best Company ever.

I don't think it's too much to ask for the Chief Executive Officer to hoist the entire company on his or her shoulders for one day each month. The CEO will probably just delegate it to one of his VPs to handle anyway.

The Role of First-Line Supervisors

I believe that people work best—doing high quality work to achieve a worthy goal—when they are also striving for something personal. It might be a promotion, an increase in salary, peer respect, or a flexible work schedule. Whatever the motivation, it should result in the employee doing more than the minimum necessary to get through the day (or, sometimes, to just make it to lunch).

At one company there was a terrific senior engineering technician who had a great desire to work in a private office instead of a cubicle. The instant management response was "techs work in cubicles, not offices." I suggested the company promote the tech to a new position or title like Staff Specialist that came with an office. Management responded, "If we do that, then all the techs will want to be promoted."

Hello? Anybody home, McFly? News flash: everyone already wants to be promoted. Why not establish a precedent that excellent work results in promotions, raises and private offices? Seems like a great way to motivate techs to strive for excellent performance.

If office incentives aren't practical, how about a special award like an extra week of paid vacation? Maybe send a high-performing technician to a boondoggle training course in Las Vegas or Orlando, somewhere other than an oil town like Houston or Bakersfield?

I have long believed that one responsibility of a supervising manager should be to get the most and best out of each member of their staff. To achieve this, managers have to get to know the personalities of each of their direct reports and figure out what works best in terms of motivation, compensation, perks, and morale.

Joe works best in a team. He loves the feeling of belonging and contributing to something bigger than himself. He's a people pleaser, and actively participates during staff meetings.

Jennifer works best by herself and does not work and play well with teammates. She has no patience for others and generally thinks her ideas are best. She does excellent work on special one-off projects when she has total control of her time and tasks.

Jerry hates being micro-managed and requires nothing from his manager. He works best when given specific objectives and deadlines. Set him up with a project or task and turn him loose.

Jane needs attention and loves feedback. She thrives when her boss spends a few minutes every day visiting and going over her work. She is open to receiving direction, takes it personally and makes a sincere effort to improve and respond positively to the advice she receives. She requires more validation from management than most people but produces above-average results.

Jonah does solid work but is chronologically challenged. He arrives late most mornings but works one to two hours late every night. When reprimanded for tardiness or missing a meeting, his attitude sours and can affect team morale. He frequently works half-days on Saturdays when the office is quiet.

John is an average, steady performer. He is not a risk-taker, and rarely does more than the minimum effort. He is a reliable resource to assign menial work no one else wants.

Steve does high-quality, detailed work. He believes he communicates well and expects others to do the same. He responds well to clearly defined project objectives and will meet every deadline. He is skilled at coordinating complex workflows and projects like reserves reports and capital budgets. He prefers working in a team environment but is easily frustrated when others fail to provide timely information necessary to the project, forcing him to work overtime hours to meet deadlines set by Management. Steve *hates* working overtime because someone else didn't do their job. If only Management would communicate the proper priorities to all the staff and follow up with those who don't take the budget seriously. Badgering engineers and geologists for data really bums him out, they *know* he can't complete the roll-up and compile the summaries until he gets the last bit of information from the last engineer. Why, just the other day, Jonah went to the field for two days and "forgot" to complete his cap-bud cases, and now Steve will have to work over the weekend to—

Sorry, back to my point: A supervisor who understands his employees well and engages each with a customized approach and style will obtain the most and best from his Team. This of course requires time and effort by the supervisor, and in my experience it rarely happened. First-line managers almost always treated everyone the same —perhaps under the guise of treating everyone "fairly"—and expected the staff to be high-performing, self-motivated professionals who "didn't need managing." A great number of us were indeed self-motivated and most of the time metrics and results were good. Still, I wondered: did Leadership ever consider the incremental benefits, including an increase in profits, that might occur if supervisors optimally managed individuals and improved morale among their troops?

How to Train Your Reservoir Monkey

I became frustrated numerous times over the years when using an evaluation tool or reserves process that was clearly out of date and inefficient. (I'm looking at you, 1993 planimetering software still being used in 2014.) I struggled to understand why Management did not insist that engineers work as quickly and efficiently as possible to move projects forward and achieve the Company's goals.

I was successful a handful of times in contributing to the updating of processes and tools, thanks to teaming up with many talented, like-minded individuals. In other cases—including those

I considered "no-brainers"—it was impossible to implement change. People responded with shrugs, head shakes, and "I don't know, we've always done it this way."

During my research I came across a great article explaining why this attitude was so prevalent and persistent. For my fellow reservoir engineers, I have paraphrased the explanation to be more relatable.

1. Take 5 reservoir engineers actively engaged in a reserves cycle and lock them in a tall cage with several large wooden blocks. Gather a bunch of PVT reports, pressure buildup summaries, and an isopach map or two and hang them all in a net at the top of the cage. In a short time, usually no more than a half-hour, the reservoir engineers will start messing around. One of them will figure out how to stack the blocks, climb to the top and grab the sweet, juicy data he so desperately craves.

2. Just as the reservoir engineer reaches for the data, use a water cannon set to Absolute Open Flow and blast him from the stack of blocks. Soak the rest of the group too.

3. Soon the first RE or another will try again, and just before reaching the prize, blast the entire group again with the water cannon. Eventually all 5 reservoir engineers will give up and go back to work without the data they need. This is called "learned helplessness."

I learned a variation of this concept from a way-too-calm IT specialist. He never became agitated or annoyed, no matter the problem or how screwed up things were. When asked how he stayed so cool, he said he was like the mouse trapped in a maze with a chunk of cheese at one end. The mouse solves the puzzle, but the cheese is yanked away before he can eat. Repeat this several times and the mouse eventually won't move at all, even when the cheese is placed tantalizingly close. The mouse has learned to accept his helplessness, just like the experienced IT guy.

4. Back to the reservoir engineers, who have all learned it is a bad idea to try to obtain data for reserves. Transfer one of the engineers out (to another cage, of course) and replace him with a new RE, number 6. Eventually RE6 spies the data at the top of the cage and starts stacking blocks to make his move. Before he can climb onto the first block, the other four engineers will beat the crap out of him to avoid being blasted with water. RE6 quickly learns he should not go for the data to avoid a beating, and gives up.

5. Now replace RE2 with another newbie, RE7. As soon as RE7 starts to climb, the rest of the group will attack him immediately. He has been completely dissuaded from going after the data, but knows nothing of the water cannon. Eventually you can replace all 5 of the original engineers with 5 new engineers who understand they should not attempt to get the data they need, but none know the real reason why: the nasty water cannon fired long ago at the first reservoir monkey.

This little parable helped me understand Corporate Inertia: a policy, department, or culture at rest tends to remain at rest. Stephen Covey (of *7 Habits* fame) encouraged people to evaluate a current practice or policy as if it did not exist: if you were starting fresh with a blank slate, would you do it the same way? If the answer is no, you've just labeled the original practice "unacceptable." Why spend one more day continuing unacceptable policies or practices? I thought it was an outstanding recommendation.

MY FAILURE TO ACHIEVE SELF-ACTUALIZATION

Brett Farve's 500th Touchdown Pass

Monday, October 11, 2010, 10:15pm. I'm in my favorite chair reading *Tuesdays with Morrie* by Mitch Albom with the Jets-Vikings game on television with the sound muted. I'm near the end of the book, engrossed in (spoiler alert!) Morrie's funeral service.

I turn a page and glance at the game as Bret Favre throws a long pass to Randy Moss for the Viking's first touchdown. Favre sprints down the field to the end zone, pumping his fist in the air. ESPN flashes a banner: Favre just completed his 500th career touchdown pass. The camera stays on him as he celebrates, chest bumping teammates and coaches. He's obviously a very happy guy. I grab my notebook and move to the kitchen table to capture some thoughts.

Does Bret Favre know how fortunate he is? To have a career with opportunities to experience moments of frabjous joy and celebration? The game was his two-hundred eighty-somethingth consecutive start. No doubt he's had many fun moments like this one during his long career.

I consider my life in Moore World. What is the equivalent in my career of passing for 500 touchdowns? What accomplishment at the office would cause me to burst into jubilant celebration, high-fiving and chest-bumping my coworkers? Forget 500, what's the reservoir engineering version of scoring one touchdown? No one ever hoisted me up in the air at one end of the conference room for "crushing it" with my capital budget presentation. No one displayed a banner announcing I just completed my 27th consecutive year-end reserves cycle. I never teamed up with a fellow engineer to pour a bucket of ice-cold Gatorade on the Reserves Manager after our Team finalized the SEC report just ahead of the deadline.

Obviously, it's not valid to compare my reservoir engineering career to that of an NFL quarterback. I'm 100% certain that Aaron Rodgers has never fit a hyperbolic trend to monthly oil production on a semi-log plot. Still, I can't recall any deeply satisfying, *joyful* moments that occurred because of my engineering work. I was involved with—and, occasionally, directly responsible for—several successful projects; none made me feel or act as happy as Brett Favre. My professional energies were consumed by completing thousands of uninteresting tasks, working to please managers and coworkers, and fighting boredom much of the time.

I finish writing my notes just in time to see Favre throw touchdown pass 501 on the Viking's next drive. He runs down the field again, celebrating with the same energy he displayed just minutes before. It's amazing watching a guy who still enjoys his job like that after working for so many years.

Self-Actualization: The Best of All Actualizations

I could write hundreds of pages filled with stories of tremendous individuals, outstanding teamwork, and the super-creative problem solving I was privileged to observe and to which I occasionally contributed. But that's not why you're reading this book, is it?

The full title for this semi-professional memoir is:

Plugged & Abandoned: My Epic Failure to Achieve Self-Actualization after 40 Years of Reservoir Engineering in the Oil and Gas Industry.

What is self-actualization? A cartoon by Scott Adams I have pinned to the wall of my writing studio shows the famous engineer Dilbert complaining. Despite working every day he doesn't feel completely self-actualized. When the pointy-haired boss asks him what that means, Dilbert replies: "I don't know, it's something I heard."

I like the simple definition often attributed to Abraham Maslow: fulfillment of one's potential. After fifteen years or so I realized this was not happening, and I blamed only myself. I didn't exactly drive my career into a ditch and crawl away from the smoldering wreckage of Failed Reservoir Dreams. It was more like I forgot to fill up and ran out of fuel. After coasting as long as possible, I finally drifted off the Path to stop on the cold shoulder. I continued plodding ahead, on foot and without enthusiasm.

You know you've reached a dismal point in life when you browse the self-help section of the bookstore and you don't care who might see you there. I felt exactly like the expression on Paul Giamatti's face in every movie in which he appeared. My journey to transcend the ordinary life of a staff reservoir engineer was not going well.

Da DUH duh DA duh. I had the reservoir engineering blues.

My Blue Quest

It became clear that not only was I not going to rise to manager level, I wasn't management material to begin with. I was firmly entrenched in Group B. Okay, fine. I still wanted to achieve...*something.* Without realizing it, I was already engaged in a Quest: for fulfillment, actualization, or an occasional warm, fuzzy feeling. Unfortunately, even though Aesop, Dr. Seuss and Joseph Campbell all tried to warn me, I was searching for the Wrong Thing and had pointed myself in the wrong direction.

I've already described much of my story, and the following pages will put even more *me* in this *memoir*. I'll summarize my existential odyssey, including how I (sort of) figured it out, what I did to (unsuccessfully) escape, and how it all (probably) ended. (Hint: you're soaking in it now.)

In real time, of course, my life was a jumbled-up mix of experiences, lessons learned, and personal growth from the study of human and corporate nature. A chronological presentation would be a dog's breakfast to write and to read, so I've simplified my strange, long head trip into a handful of topics for clarity.

I'll keep it pithy so you can finish reading this one-sided therapy session within the customary 50 minutes.

"There's Never a Grail Temple Knight Around When You Need One"

Remember how I became a reservoir engineer after I used the word "reservoir" first answering a what-do-you-want-to-do question during a campus interview? I don't think the reservoir guy from Tenneco even heard the "or production" part of my answer.

After seeing *Indiana Jones and the Last Crusade* in 1989, every time I think of my choice of words during that interview or my decision to accept that first reservoir engineering job offer, I remember what has become my all-time favorite movie line, delivered by the knight guarding the Holy Grail:

"He chose...poorly."

Early Failures

Majoring in petroleum engineering was not a bad decision after high school. It was logical given my math skills and ongoing interest in science and technology. It was also intriguing, as I knew very little about the energy industry.

Throughout my career I was competent enough in my reservoir work to stay employed, enjoy a terrific paycheck, and receive annual bonuses and stock incentives (once they became a "thing" and were awarded to staff engineers.) I am happy with my overall work ethic and productivity over the years, and proud I was able to continuously support my family.

My early career struggles resulted from my ignorance and lack of experience. I assumed my job would be about 80% actual engineering work and the rest of the time would be meetings, paperwork, and preparing for presentations. I was surprised to learn it was the other way around: 20% engineering during a good week and 80% other stuff (spelled s-t-u-f-f, but pronounced "bull crap"). If I had known how little time I would spend doing true engineering work, I might have considered a different profession.

Plus, I did not know how to thrive in a corporate environment, my instincts were mostly wrong. I had the engineering degree but no mentor. No one in my family had worked for a large company. I did not understand office politics and the importance of building key relationships. I hoped to succeed in business while really trying to be a good engineer, but I was in way over my head.

I've already described some early misadventures, including my attempt to be assertive with my new supervisor. Risk-taking did not come naturally and being placed on Double-Secret Probation drop-kicked me into feed-the-family survival mode. I have remained somewhat stuck in that mindset ever since.

Still, by year five I had learned much from my mistakes and watching others succeed. I went into engineering to work on technical problems. I was not interested in finance, accounting, politics, or the business side of oil and gas. I was not cut out for management. I held the logical but somewhat misguided belief that oil and gas companies needed solid, competent technical staff to evaluate, design and implement successful projects. I assumed high-quality reservoir engineering work would ultimately be recognized—and rewarded—by Management.

I was attempting to master reservoir engineering to achieve success *as an engineer*, but soon discovered the technical career ladder only existed on paper. Engineers and geologists were treated well and paid nice salaries, and the benefit packages were excellent. But the corner offices, cool corporate perks, and largest financial rewards went to those who became part of the Management Team. I failed to recognize the order-of-magnitude difference in potential upside between those who pursued a technical career and those who climbed the management ladder.

If I had understood the opportunity cost earlier, perhaps I would have considered a "whatever it takes" strategy. Be more assertive in proposing projects. Wear a mask of fake confidence.

Maybe even try that "obsequious sycophant" thing. Or maybe, after getting laid off in 1986, I might have abandoned the good ship *Reservoir* and switched to another career.

Of course, then you wouldn't be reading this book.

Actively Engaged in Self-Directed Personal Development

My studies of personal and professional development began when I read the hottest business book of the early 1980s, *In Search of Excellence* by Tom Peters and Robert Waterman, Jr. After studying 43 successful American companies, the authors presented 8 principles of excellence, including two that resonated with me: *productivity through people,* and *autonomy and entrepreneurship.* The book made sense to me, and I wondered why managers weren't reading the book and implementing the recommended "best practices."

I subscribed to *Forbes* magazine and read *The Wall Street Journal* to learn and monitor business trends, but my interest dropped with the downturn and layoff in 1986. I focused my energies on my new job, staying employed, and feeding my family. And to make things even more challenging, I registered to take the PE exam in 1988, then took a job with another company in 1990.

Maslow and Three Critical Items

Sometime during those busy years my friend Buddy introduced me to Abraham Maslow's Hierarchy of Needs theory: people must meet basic, lower-level needs first (air, food and water, shelter) before they can strive to meet higher-level needs like self-esteem and self-actualization.

Buddy also told me about a principle discussed in one of his MBA classes. There are three critical items that must be in place for one to have an optimal, satisfying job experience: adequate financial compensation, meaningful work, and recognition of your efforts.

At that time, as Maslow predicted I was mostly concerned with basic needs and my paycheck, and thought I was doing okay. I hadn't (yet) considered the meaning and value of my work, and while I certainly would have enjoyed a little recognition, it was pretty much nonexistent for everyone at that time.

The 1990s

My studies of excellence and personal development picked up again in the mid-1990s after I moved back to Oklahoma to work for a growing independent company. I read *The Seven Habits of Highly Effective People* by Stephen Covey. It was terrific and inspired me to complete two Seven Habits courses during the next two years. I was impressed with Covey's common-sense approach to managing priorities, time, work-life balance, and getting the most and best out of people. I also attended other conferences with dynamic speakers like Malcolm Gladwell, Tom Peters, and Jack Welch.

Tom Peters

One lesson from Tom Peters really stuck with me. Consider the character and personality attributes of people included in a 10th grade history book for achieving great things. The list would include passionate, creative, risk-takers, quirky, persistent, peculiar, irreverent, even obnoxious. They were improvisers who thrived on chaos. Peters urged the audience to hire folks who "colored outside the lines." They not only got things done, they were also sources of company-making innovations.

At the time, I could think of at least one coworker in each of my previous companies who fit this description. They didn't always conform to the culture or standard business hours, but they were known as fire-fighters and rat-killers, frequently tapped by Management to "get it done" or lead special projects.

Driving from the Left Side of My Brain to the Right

I read *A Whole New Mind: Why Right-Brainers Will Rule the Future* by Daniel Pink (2005) twice in two years. I was intrigued with his exploration of right-brain creative thinking and his predictions of a future in which content would become increasingly important.

Pink's 2009 book, *Drive: The Surprising Truth About What Motivates Us* had an even greater impact. After describing how 20th-century carrot-and-stick motivation methods are no longer effective for 21st-century information-age professionals, Pink describes the value of intrinsic motivation and three critical elements:

Autonomy: self-control of task, time, team and technique
Mastery: achieving competency and experiencing "flow"
Purpose: the work must have meaning and value, and serve a cause greater than oneself.

Drive seemed like it was specifically written to address my life questions and career issues. I shared the book with coworkers and over a series of pizza lunches we discussed Pink's recommendations and how they might be implemented in our company and in our industry.

At some point I realized I had likely read more management books and business articles than all of my first-line supervisors combined. I believed I was more interested in improving Company culture and striving for excellence than Management. How could this be?

A friend suggested an answer: Technical people are generally not good at supervising and motivating other technical people but can still be useful to Senior Leadership as *managers* in achieving corporate goals. It is possible to improve bottom-line results even if communication is poor and morale sucks.

To make a small contribution to the cause I purchased several copies of *Drive* and gave one to every manager for whom I worked the rest of my career. I shifted my focus to personal topics like self-actualization and writing. My friend Buddy and I continued our series of email and phone conversations discussing the philosophy of Joseph Campbell and books like *The Writer's Journey* by Christopher Vogler and *The Artist's Way* by Julia Cameron.

I'll head to the Morning Meeting as soon as I finish my Morning Pages

A couple of years later, I saw this article in *E&P* magazine:

GET THOSE CREATIVE JUICES FLOWING!
By Rhonda Duey, Exploration Editor (April, 2010)
It's hard to find oil in the minds of men when those minds are tired, pessimistic, and overworked.

The article summarized a presentation by two geologists titled "Creativity in Exploration." The left- and right-brain functions of the creative process were described along with examples of "eureka!" moments in exploration.

To spark creativity, exploration professionals were encouraged to try informal drawing and writing. I was stunned that one of the presenting geologists cited author Julia Cameron and her Morning Pages exercise from *The Artist's Way*. Each morning you fill three pages with longhand, stream-of-consciousness writing to clear your brain, overcome pessimism, and spur your creativity.

I knew from personal experience that this daily writing practice worked and wondered how many engineers and geologists who saw the presentation or the article gave it a try.

Kudos to Doug Strickland and Ted Beaumont for encouraging more creativity in the industry, and to Ms. Duey for writing the article.

No Country for Old Creatives

In addition to frequent attempts to be clever and creative around the office, I also urged others to give it a try. It wasn't always successful.

I was helping a young engineer named Alex solve an evaluation workflow problem. I suggested a brainstorming technique using mind maps, where you start with a central idea or topic and add related ideas using various shapes, colors, and connectors to visualize multiple flows and solutions. Alex was interested, so we pulled up some examples from the globe-spanning Web and off he went to make his own.

When I saw him later, he looked defeated. Alex had created a cool workflow map but made the mistake of showing it to Pat, his manager. Pat told him, "That doesn't look like something an engineer would make."

I shook my head and listened for the faint whooshing sound as the last bit of inspiration leaked out of Alex.

The Protagonist in My Own Story

I had studied Joseph Campbell's work and already concluded I was on my own version of the Hero's Journey. (Audacious, I know, but there are some people—mostly geologists—who think reservoir engineers are heroes for doing reserves work no one else wants to do.) I slipped around numerous Threshold Guardians along the way and encountered Shapeshifting Supervisors at every turn. But alas (no one says 'alas' anymore, 'tis a bleedin' sorrow), where was the wise Mentor who would guide me on my career trek?

I was an Engineer with a *Thousand Faces,* seeking *Autonomy, Mastery,* and *Purpose, Driving* myself forward on a *Hero's Journey, Searching for Excellence* and knowledge of the *Seven Habits* of people who were *Highly Effective* in *Following their Bliss.*

I burned to complete my Quest, slay the Reservoir Dragon, and snatch the leather purse containing the Twelve Jewel-Stones of Creativity. Only then could I return to my ordinary world and pursue some other, you know, *cool stuff.*

Reality Check

An engineer I worked with in California once asked me: If you could be doing anything you wanted right this minute, what would it be?

I was caught off guard. (I'd be much better prepared if he asked me today.) I said something inconsequential, like "I'd be on the beach, soaking up rays and reading a novel."

"Okay," he said, "You can actually make that happen, if that's what you really want." It was a great perspective check. Yes, I could walk off the job and head to the coast. But I had to feed my family, pay the mortgage, and prepare for the future. I concluded what I really wanted was to read on the beach only after acting like an adult and meeting my responsibilities, most of which were natural consequences from my past decisions.

Words of Wisdom from Winget

I enjoyed reading motivational author Larry Winget, whose books include titles like *Grow a Pair* and *Shut Up, Stop Whining, and Get a Life.* My favorite two lessons, combined and paraphrased:

Your life is how you want it to be. If you wanted it to be different, it would be different. If you want to be happy, you must give up everything that makes you unhappy.

From Maslow to Mooreslow: My Personal Hierarchy of Needs

In 1943 Abraham Maslow published his paper, *A Theory of Human Motivation.* His theory postulated that as humans met their basic needs, they then sought to satisfy higher needs in a generally structured hierarchy:

Self-Actualization: fulfillment of one's potential
Esteem: respect from others, confidence, achievement
Love/Belonging: family, friendship
Safety: security, resources, employment, health
Physiological: air, food, water, shelter, clothing

Doing some personal development work and introspection in 2015, I conducted an internal performance review to evaluate my progress scrambling up the pyramid. I created "Mooreslow's Hierarchy of Needs," a chart that was actually more of an action plan:

MOORESLOW'S HIERARCHY OF NEEDS

O WIN!!
O Be Satisfied
O $$ from Creativity
O ID Creative Outlet
O Improve H & F
O Need to Exit O & G
O Need to Exit Company
✓ Family, Wealth, Routine
✓ Security, Community, Social
✓ Food Clothing Shelter

After more than 30 years of working to insure the basic lower-tier needs were met, I was ready to level up.

My Self-Actualization Dream Team Cocktail Party

Welcome, come in! We've got some time before dinner, let me show you around and introduce you.

That's Tom Peters standing next to the bookcase with a glass of Excellent bourbon. Tom's trying to talk that quirky-looking guy wearing the propeller beanie into working for him.

Steve Covey is the guy on the couch, the one listening intently to those two women. Nice guy, he'll talk your arm off but always insists you speak first to make sure he understands you. Steve's already asked me what is planned after dinner ends so he can be prepared.

Whoa! Did you see that old gentleman stumble over the Threshold into the kitchen? That's Joe Campbell. He's probably getting a refill of Elixir, but he'll Return to the living room soon. Be careful around him, he gets unbelievably high on Bliss.

Speaking of the kitchen, Abe Maslow's working back there. He'll come out and socialize later, after he's satisfied there's enough food and drink for everyone.

See that tall, shiny bald guy that looks like he's preaching to that young couple? Last name's McGraw, but we just call him Dr. Phil. He's probably warning them not to drive their marriage into the ditch or talking about dogs that don't hunt or—whoops, there he goes out the patio door. He'll be right back.

Dan Pink will join us for dinner too. Man, that guy is Driven, always wants to be in Control and fix his own dinner like he's some kind of Master chef with a Mission. He was getting into it with Abe in the kitchen, so I told him to wait in the car until the proper Time or he'd Regret it.

That's Julia Cameron siting in the corner scribbling in her notebook. The guy standing nearby and talking to himself is Larry Winget. Most motivated guy you'll ever meet, but no one likes him because he keeps telling people stuff they don't want to hear. Not sure who invited him tonight, it wasn't me. Last time he told me my parties suck, and if I wanted them to be better, they would be.

Okay, get yourself a glass of liquid courage and dive right in. Maybe you'll learn something!

And then frustration set in...

"We judge ourselves by what we feel capable of doing, while others judge us by what we have already done."
- Henry Wadsworth Longfellow

Engineers are hatched with a strong, natural trait to solve problems. We crave order in the universe and think we can make it happen. While the rest of humanity creates problems, engineers step forward with solutions.

After studying business and motivational self-development literature for several years, I recognized the potential for improvements in each of the companies for which I worked. I believed I could help make things better, but few people around or above me shared my enthusiasm. Okay, fine. My pain, my problem.

As Stephen Covey put it so well, my Circle of Concern was larger than my Circle of Influence. I followed his advice and worked to achieve small, positive improvements but I was preoccupied, wondering why Management had so little interest in applying new strategies and tactics that apparently worked well in other companies. It was frustrating, like being confined to a round room and being told I could only sit in the corner.

Several times during my career I tried to apply the knowledge I gained from books and business gurus. I wrote at least a half-dozen mini-manifestos, complete with executive summaries and detailed discussions of problems, the benefits of improvements, and how to best implement solutions. I don't recall any serious consideration or even a positive response by Management to any of my proposals. (I realize, again, this probably says more about me than my managers.) Here's an example.

The Year-End Reserves Post-Mortem: "It's dead, Jim."

Reserves cycles were always a challenge: deadlines, missing or late-breaking data, complex workflows and the need for cooperation from people in other departments. In fact, Moore's Law of the C's was formulated during a particularly chaotic fourth-quarter crap-storm. Year-end reserves never failed to Grinch up the holidays, turning mildly depressed Charlie Browngineers into snarling reservoir dogs demanding updated isopach maps right freaking now or Drilling was going to have to fish a stuck Yule log from the annulus of a certain geologist.

One year-end cycle was particularly tough. After a poor presentation of District reserves to corporate staff, the Company Reserves Manager wrote a blunt, scathing email to our reservoir engineering manager. The boss immediately forwarded the highly critical message to all of his staff, even though the Reserves Manager had specifically requested the email not be shared with the engineers "given the sensitive nature of some of my comments." Fortunately, the email had no effect on the morale of the reservoir engineering group; we had achieved absolute zero weeks earlier.

I wanted to solve some of the problems, and initiated discussions with the reservoir engineers and technicians. Over the next three days we met several times, analyzed what went wrong, designed new workflows, and composed thoughtful recommendations to ensure the next cycle went better. I drafted the memo for the rest of the group to review and revise, then emailed the final version to our department manager and copied the reservoir staff.

Chirpy crickets would have been preferable to the silence. Our reservoir engineering manager refused to acknowledge our proposal. We had made a serious effort to address mistakes and offer solutions and were completely ignored.

I was *demoorealized and* started looking for ways to extend my morning commute to the office. Instead of zipping around a city bus picking up passengers, I waited patiently behind for seven straight stops, enjoying the thick, sweet tailpipe exhaust.

I'd drive by the parking lot entrance and go around the block to hear the end of a song on the radio I didn't even like. I circled the parking lot six times, pretending to look for a close or shady spot, then park as far from the building as possible to get in some slow, extra steps.

I'd wave off the person stepping into the elevator to take the next one. Then I'd forget to push the UP button and stare at my phone until someone else arrived and summoned the 'vator.

These were not the signs of a normally-gruntled employee. The silent rejection of our team's recommendations and other disappointments spurred my decision to leave the company six months later. I gave copies of the book *Drive* to two of my managers on the way out, including the District Vice President, who sent me a nice thank-you note a few weeks later.

Managing Up Using the Golden Rule

My friends and coworkers (I admit there is *some* overlap in these two groups) know that I love to twist words and reverse situations for laughs. One brainstormy afternoon I recommended staff professionals lead by example and take action to reassure and motivate our managers.

An entire department should drop in unannounced on a Senior Manager in his office to communicate how much they appreciate his efforts. Perhaps they could cite specific examples of outstanding decisions or expert delegation of tasks and projects.

A large group of employees should coordinate an impromptu meeting with the CEO and greet him as he steps off the elevator at 9:45am, or surprise him in the Executive Lounge pouring himself a non-Styrofoam mug of Super Premium BigBucks coffee.

The staff should tell the CEO that during these uncertain times, they will do their very best to not quit the company. While they can't promise there won't be mass resignations in the future, they will do everything possible to avoid or minimize them. The employees should specifically state how proud they are of the CEO, that everyone knows who does the real work inside the Company, and they all recognize that the Senior Leadership Team is the company's greatest asset.

Then we'll inform the CEO there's no need to come back after lunch. The staff is giving him a well-earned afternoon off, to get in 18 holes or polish his boat or whatever.

On a scale from 1 to 10, I'm a C

My friend Wayne shared this knowledge nugget after attending a seminar:

If weaknesses and strengths are listed and numbered 1 (weak) through 10 (strong), most people instinctively believe they should work to improve a weakness, perhaps turn a 2 into a 3, or raise a 4 to a 6.

Wayne suggested people would benefit more by raising a 7 to an 8 or 9 instead of improving a 2 to a 3. The incremental value gained by increasing a strength would likely far exceed the marginal value of improving a weakness to a slightly better weakness. This adaptation of playing to your strengths made a lot of sense to me, although I worried that my 8s, 9s, and 10s were mostly not valued by my managers.

I ran across a somewhat similar concept described by Kyle Maynard in *Tribe of Mentors,* by Tim Ferriss. When attempting to determine the relative value of tasks or activities by ranking them between 1 and 10, never use a 7. If someone asks you to do something and it feels like a 7, you will almost always decide it is worth doing. Forcing yourself to choose 6 or 8 makes it easier to decide whether to consider the request.

In 2001 the Company held a leadership training course. Engineers, geologists, and their managers attended. Surveys were completed and personality profiles were established using the DISC categorization system: Dominance, Influence, Steadiness and Competence. Information on styles D and C are summarized below from the course manual and my notes. (For brevity and relevance I've omitted personalities I and S.)

D (Dominance) personality traits and styles include high ego strength, self-confidence, results oriented, and do-it-now impatience. D's fear loss of control and being taken advantage of, and need to rely more often on their teams. D personalities prefer people who are direct and open to their need for results.

C (Competence) personality traits include perfectionistic, analytical, and detail oriented. C's fear criticism of their work and need to be less dependent on knowing all details before making decisions. C personalities prefer people who value accuracy, minimize socializing, and provide details.

It's C's versus D's in a Winner-Take-All Battle Royale Cage Match!

As you might expect, all engineers were C's, and all managers were D's. (Geologists were a mix, mostly S or I with one or two C's.)

The instructor called for a volunteer C to stand up. He predicted the engineer would have several bills of cash in his wallet. The engineer confirmed he did. The instructor then predicted that the engineer not only kept his cash sorted by denomination, but that the presidential heads of the bills would all be facing the same direction. The engineer sheepishly admitted it was true and sat down quick.

The personality descriptions perfectly matched my anecdotal experience, but here's the kicker: In terms of compatibility, C's (engineers) and D's (managers) *don't play or work well together.*

The rest of the course included role-playing, group exercises, and recommendations for effectively communicating to and working with various personality styles.

To work effectively with a D, you should let them initiate, communicate briefly and to-the-point, and *respect their need for autonomy.* (Emphasis added. Apparently, Daniel Pink was right.)

To work effectively with a C, you should provide clear expectations and deadlines, indicate your dependability, and value high standards. (There was no mention of a C's need for autonomy, clearly an oversight.)

A day or two later the HR manager delivered small plastic picture frames to everyone who attended the seminar. Mine was bright yellow and identified me as a "C and proud of it!"

I thought the course provided some useful insight and was disappointed when nothing really changed. Engineers who got bogged down in details (ahem!) and managers who vaguely requested quick results continued doing what they did best.

"Lemme tell ya, reservoir engineers don't get no respect, no respect at all."

I started my career in California thermal enhanced oil recovery operations, in which reservoir engineers had a prominent role in technical analysis, decision making, and adding value. After relocating to Oklahoma this was still the case with my new company. In just a few years, however, technical reservoir engineering work, such as optimizing performance or designing secondary recovery projects, was significantly reduced in favor of reserves reporting, acquisition and divestiture projects, and preparing capital and operating budgets.

I preferred the technical work to budget and reserves, but I recognized the Company needs and priorities were shifting. Still, I was often frustrated by reservoir-engineers-go-last workflows. REs were responsible for reserves and economics, which first required information from our production, drilling, land, and geology teammates before we could complete our part of the project. Late-breaking updates, such as new geologic maps or revised drilling cost estimates, meant restarting much of the reservoir engineering work and scrambling to meet deadlines. I recall frequently receiving new information the afternoon before a scheduled project review with Management the next morning. I'd work late into the night or early morning running seventy-eleven economic sensitivities and updating summaries for the 9am meeting. Meanwhile my teammates were getting a good night's sleep ahead of their presentation.

I realize that sounds whiny. That's what the job called for, so I did it. My point is my teammates rarely had to wait on something from me to get their work done. And this simple comment from a manager could easily result in six hours of last-minute overtime: "Oh yeah, Corporate just released their new price deck so make sure your economics are up to date for the meeting." I mostly accepted The Way Things Were, but it wore on me.

If you were forced to cast Rodney Dangerfield as a petroleum professional in a prime-time oil-and-gas TV sitcom, would he be a happy-go-lucky geologist? A confident production engineer or a rough-and-tumble drilling engineer? Of course not. Rodney would be a reservoir engineer. In the holiday episode, Rodney would not be skiing with his family in Tahoe between Christmas and New Year's Day. He would be in his office, mumbling to himself and tediously tweaking the forecasts of 1400 marginal wells for the reserves summary the CFO expects to find on his desk first thing in the morning on January 2nd.

"Reservoir? We don't need no stinking reservoir guys at the meeting!"

I don't mean to imply my entire reservoir engineering life was Dickens-level dismal. I had several satisfying moments and occasionally frank discussions with senior management. After evaluating and documenting reserves for a new high-profile horizontal well, the Exploration Vice President praised my work. I took advantage of the conversation and made some recommendations to improve communication and make better use of reservoir engineers to add value. He admitted the Company historically had been driven by Land and Geology, and that Management really didn't know how to use reservoir engineers beyond project economics and reserves reporting. It was a nice admission on his part, but I left his office understanding there was little chance anything would change. This was confirmed several months later.

For an acquisition evaluation, the Production Manager gave me a list of several hundred well locations and a drilling schedule from which I was to construct individual economic cases. Using a complex workflow I developed during a previous evaluation, I worked all afternoon and had constructed most of the cases when the Production Manager returned. He told me to ignore what he gave me that morning and handed me a revised list of locations and a new schedule. I had to scrap the cases and start over.

I learned there had been a meeting right after lunch to further discuss the development drilling plans for the acquisition assets. The meeting included the Production Manager and department heads and staff from Land, Geology, and Drilling. Everyone except the reservoir engineer who would be constructing the hundreds of economic cases critical to determining the value of the acquisition. This was not an oversight; it was The Way Things Were.

I was furious. Not only had I wasted four hours of time, it was clear no one recognized the value of reservoir engineering input. I flashed on a twisted mental image of a "demotivational" poster displayed on the wall in the break room:

There is no "Reservoir Engineer" in T-E-A-M.

That's me in the corner, calculating volumetrics

Gradually, over several years, I started losing my religion. I questioned whether my work had meaning and significance beyond earning a paycheck and subsidized health care. I was aware that much of my reservoir engineering work served the purpose of reducing risk and providing some estimate of value. But the calculations and numbers themselves started to lose their meaning, like a child who repeats a word out loud until it becomes a nonsense sound.

Volumetric calculations are a good example. Estimates of porosity, water saturation, and reservoir pressure are combined with the mystical log analysis results provided by geo-wizards or magic software. Toss in some WAGs (Wild-Ass Guesses) for drainage areas and recovery factors. A single number is calculated, representing the volume of hydrocarbons that might be produced from a well or reservoir.

Let's ignore for a moment that the source data for this calculation are from a well (or wells) penetrating a minuscule fraction of the reservoir being evaluated. I learned from Dr. Hawley in physics lab at TU that the uncertainties of calculation parameters do not cancel each other out, they are multiplicative. When the plus-or-minus percentages are carried through the entire calculation, the resulting volume is encircled by a whoppingly significant cloud of potential error.

If the reservoir engineer is lucky, the geologist who provided many of the volumetric parameters won't be replaced. The new geologist will review the logs and maps and revise one or all of the parameters with as much confidence as the previous geologist, and the reservoir guy will have to update the calculations. Managers will focus on The Number and expect the production forecast to recover the calculated volumes (or more).

Sometimes, it actually works. Even a powerless reservoir engineering clock has a greater than 90% probability of expressing the correct time twice a day (+/- 22.34%). Right?

One might expect that the application of petroleum science and technology and careful calculations would yield predictable, positive results. After the geologic and reservoir evaluations have been completed, voluminous volumes of economics have been run out of each and every wazoo in the office, and multiple managers have approved the projects, wells are finally drilled and completed.

And every time, without exception, the entire team of highly-trained, highly-paid professionals eagerly await the morning report, *hoping* that Rock gave up Fluid. The right kind of fluid, that is, in paying quantities.

Today's forecast calls for Moore forecasts.

At the beginning of my career, I used one or two triangles and a pencil to create reasonable-looking forecasts on 11x17" manual production plots. Years later, computer software applied mathematics to create forecasts that fit production trends of official state-reported production volumes. (Which reminds me: does anyone know why the State water volumes are exactly identical to the gas volumes? Anyone? Buellar?) These "best fit" forecasts looked terrific, and if you tweaked the b-factors a bit you could easily add eleventy-gazillion units of reserves and ensure second-boat bonuses for Management and a two-pizza per month raise for you and your family.

Somewhere around 2010 (+/- two years), I completed training on probabilistic reserves evaluation. The process accounts for the uncertainties of critical parameters and results in a range of outcomes. I really liked this approach and appreciated that Management embraced this methodology.

At my next company, I encouraged probabilistic reserves evaluations with some initial success, even receiving an attaboy email from the VP of production. However, executive enthusiasm declined exponentially (see what I did there?) and soon the reservoir group was back to using canned volumetric spreadsheets and raising oil and gas projections to dizzying heights.

Monkey Shifting: Who's got Bobo?

In the second year of my career, the Company hosted a handful of short seminars on useful topics, such as effective presentations and time management. The instructor of the Relationship Skills class introduced back-clinging, scat-flinging monkeys as a metaphor for problems, and drove home this point: It's your monkey, get it under control.

Moore's Law of Problems:
The person who *feels* the pain, *owns* the problem.

The rest of the course discussed various techniques of managing monkeys, mostly applicable to managers who had staffs: Delegation, empowerment, coordination, team building. All were clever variations of launching manic monkeys into the air to land on the backs of others.

It turned out I had awesome monkey-catching skills but couldn't get rid of them. It never felt right tossing one of my monkeys at someone else to deal with.

The simple concept of "your pain, your problem" eventually confirmed the obvious: optimizing my career was up to me. If I wanted to stop doing tedious, boring work I would have to develop effective simian disposal strategies or eventually perish under a massive pile of smelly monkey flesh.

Drop the Cookies! Do it Now!

Another engineer introduced me to the clever design of a Monkey Trap. Put some tasty cookies inside a wire cage with a narrow opening. The monkey snakes his paw through the opening to get the cookies, but with a fist full of treats he can't pull his paw back through the opening. To escape, the monkey must let go of the goodies, if he is smart enough to figure this out.

Ouch. That one hit close to home. It reminded me of a line from the movie *The Big Kahuna,* that sometimes you have to chew your own leg off to get out of life's traps.

Rainy days and Mondays and never-ending reserves cycles always get me down.

Annual year-end reserves cycles (with a mid-year update) eventually turned into quarterly reserves reports, each requiring most of the quarter to complete. It was like riding a perpetual low-speed roller coaster that passed through numerous Tunnels of Despair but had no hills or thrills to break up the monotony.

A friend accurately described my job as "administrative engineering." I began to think of myself as a square peg working with a bunch of holes. Later, it occurred to me I might be the round one trying to accommodate multiple square pegs. Either way, the experience was less than optimum and starting to feel *unconthrable.*

Like Michael Palin of Monty Python who longed to become a lumberjack (cue the song), I too yearned for another vocation. I continued studying the craft of writing and storytelling and collecting funny ideas and anecdotes from my office life that would eventually become this memoir.

Still, my monkey paw was holding tight to those dollar-sign sugar cookies, and I was unable to extricate myself from the cage.

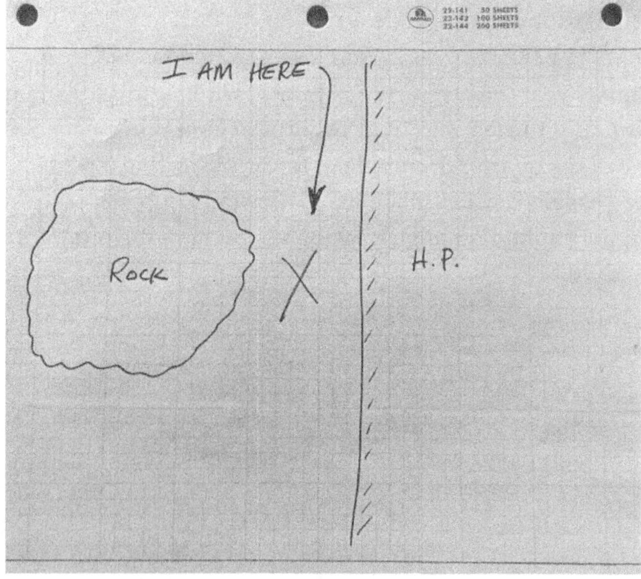

Scrambling Over the Wall While Chained to the Desk

I made several attempts to improve my situation and ascend to a higher level on Mooreslow's Hierarchy of Needs. After a couple of years as reserves process coordinator, I became Budget Guy for a few cycles. This transitioned into serving as a liaison between IT and the engineering community and tackling special projects. Working with an outstanding team of information tech and software development specialists, we completed several cool, company-enhancing projects. It was the most satisfying work of my career.

Then the company started hemorrhaging reservoir engineers, losing about one per month to competitor companies. The new engineering manager panicked like Punxsutawney Phil seeing his shadow. He popped out of his office, spotted me, and yelled "there's one, get him!" I was yanked from Special Projects and dragged back to Ordinary Reservoir World.

A quick side note: Soon after being recalled to Reservoir Engineering to work California assets after 6 years as Budget Coordinator and Special Projects Guy, my supervisor included this guidance on my annual performance review: "Needs to revitalize and update engineering skills and knowledge." No shinola, Sherlock. I silently asked him what part of "escape from Reservoir" was confusing, and wrote this response on the review form:

"I am now in my 17th year of working on oil and gas properties in the San Joaquin Valley of California. I would appreciate the chance to gain engineering experience in areas other than California as opportunities occur and circumstances allow."

My positive experience with special projects prompted me to accept an engineering Product Manager position with IHS, working on development and training projects for PowerTools and PETRA software. Product management had some unexpected perks, such as attending training courses in cities other than Houston, like Chicago and Tampa. I met people who worked in companies like AT&T, Sears, and Proctor and Gamble. Who knew there was a whole World to experience beyond oil and gas?

My IHS experience was going well until 2008, when the foul smell of economic effluent impacting on the oscillating artificial wind device put me in a panic. I voluntarily jumped back into Energy, this time in Business Development. I liked acquisitions and divestitures work until history repeated itself two years later. A Reservoir Manager running low on engineers stood on top of the conference table and looked around, one hand shielding his eyes from the glow of his own brilliance. I hollered "Don't look, Ethel!" but it was too late. Once again, I was assigned to an asset team as a staff reservoir engineer.

Occasionally, I indulged myself with an Escape Fantasy: Late one afternoon I would slip down the stairwell to the first floor and bolt through the back door. I'd strip off all my clothes and race across the parking lot into the woods, shrieking with glee. The Regional Vice President would casually glance out his top-floor office window and see one of his reservoir engineers streaking off into the sunset.

"Is that Moore? Must be Wednesday."

My Favorite Cookie Fortunes

My all-time favorite Chinese cookie fortune is one I wrote myself: ***You are about to eat a stale cookie.*** Here are a few cookie-based fortunes I received during my career and stored in the Moorchives:

Your principles mean more to you than money or success.
This explains my current lack of both money and success.

Risk may cause failure, but success cannot come without it.
This pairs nicely with my favorite quote from Joseph Campbell, well known for encouraging bliss-chasing:
"The Cave You Fear to Enter Holds the Treasure You Seek."

Your love life will be happy and harmonious.
This fortune included not one but two smiley faces.

Doing what you like is freedom. Liking what you do is happiness.
This made me wonder if the person writing cookie fortunes all day was happy with their job.

Minimize expectations to avoid disappointment.
I was disappointed that I did not receive a more optimistic fortune. Still, I got this one twice a few years apart, so I enlarged it on the copier, stuck it on my office wall, and incorporated this guidance into my daily operating philosophy.

Finally, I take these last two very seriously:
You are capable of tremendous creativity.
You are a lover of words, someday you should write a book.

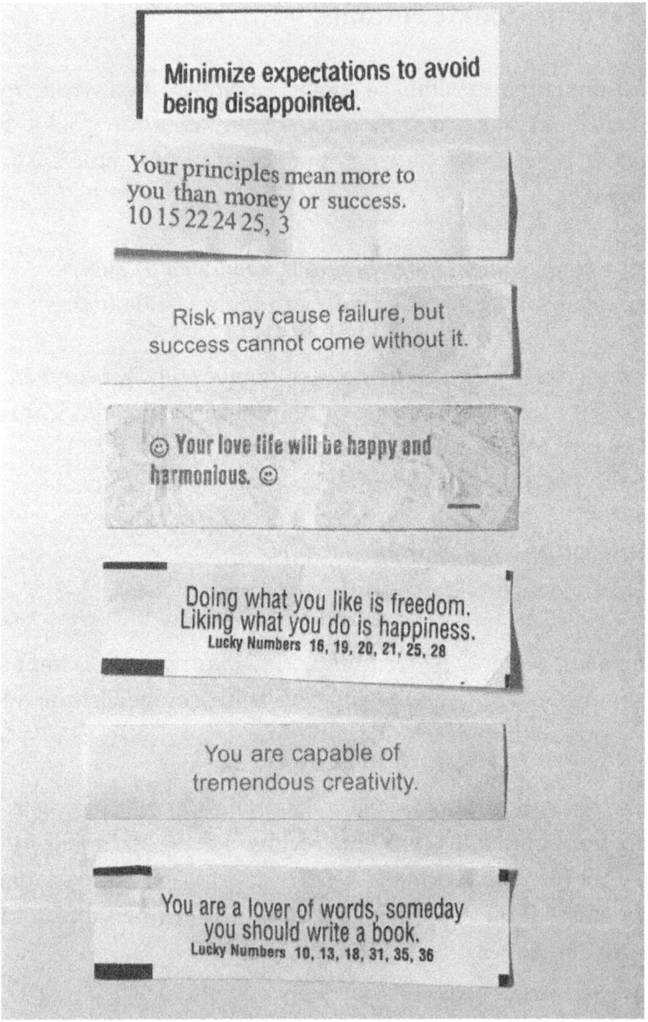

Minimize expectations to avoid
being disappointed.

Your principles mean more to
you than money or success.
10 15 22 24 25, 3

Risk may cause failure, but
success cannot come without it.

☺ Your love life will be happy and
harmonious. ☺

Doing what you like is freedom.
Liking what you do is happiness.
Lucky Numbers 16, 19, 20, 21, 25, 28

You are capable of
tremendous creativity.

You are a lover of words, someday
you should write a book.
Lucky Numbers 10, 13, 18, 31, 35, 36

"We walked barefoot in the snow to the keypunch room every night and made our own Hollerith cards out of empty cereal boxes."

Many years ago, I attended a Nodal Analysis training course in Houston taught by a colorful expert from Schlumberger whose last name was Granger. He was from Louisiana and insisted we pronounce his name "Gron-zhay" so we just called him Carl. He was a bit of a comedian, and after name-dropping Marshall Standing (known for his famous 1947 Correlation, among other things), Carl described him as "so old, he was a roughneck on Drake's well." We all cracked up, and I wrote that nugget down in my training manual to use in this memoir 39 years later.

I'm not as old now as Muz Standing was back then, but I've been around long enough to note quite a few changes. When our neighbor Mr. Taliaferro (whose yard I used to mow) heard I was going into engineering, he gave me a slide rule as a graduation present. I was grateful but didn't have the heart to tell him my senior high school class was the first to be allowed to use calculators in math and science classes.

Everyone seemed to start out with Texas Instruments calculators, but in college many of us switched to more expensive HP models and the more intuitive RPN format. (If you want to have some fun, give an RPN calculator to someone only familiar with traditional math notation. Without fail they will each swear something is wrong with the device. And if this is your idea of fun, you may be an engineer.)

In college in the late 1970s I learned Fortran and spent many long nights in the computer lab keypunching Hollerith cards.

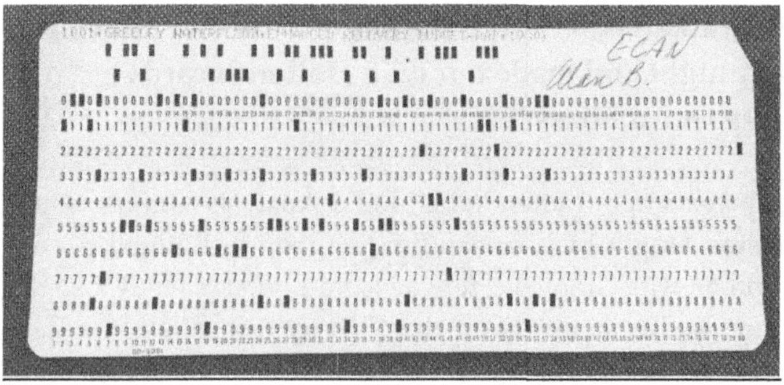

As a senior in 1980, I took the first class ever offered on solving petroleum engineering problems using Personal Computers. We called them *percomps* for short. (No, we didn't.)

When I started work in 1981 there were no PCs in the office yet. We connected to a mainframe system to run economics and compile budgets. The program was called Tenneco Oil Economic System (TOES), and when the system went down, we called it TOE Jam. All other work was done manually with the aid of calculators.

In college I learned to estimate the annual decline rate on a semi-log graph of monthly oil or gas volumes by matching the straight edge of a triangle through the data, then sliding a second triangle along the first until it lined up in the grid corner formed by the volume and time scales. It was a simple and elegant technique used often by engineers and managers.

Flash forward to 2010. I felt like going back to the basics for some reason and plotted some production volumes manually on semi-log graph paper. I was drawing the trend line through the data when Pat, a young reservoir engineer, stopped in my door and asked me what the hell was I doing?

I explained I was using a French curve to draw a trend through the data. Pat had never seen one before and just grinned at the old Pleistocene fossil sitting behind the desk. I showed him my collection of plastic curves and admitted I didn't use them much anymore. Then I showed him the two-triangle exponential decline trick and Pat seemed impressed.

Forward again to 2021: New senior management had been installed at the Company, and the CEO and COO were kicking it old school. In conference room meetings they always required hard-copy production plots, and eyeballed decline rates using straight edges from notebooks or pieces of paper. Eventually the business development manager purchased a set of "executive" triangles that were stored permanently in the conference room.

I wasn't sure how I felt about that. As a senior engineer, I could appreciate the CEO and COO's methods, but wondered why they thought it necessary to do their own analysis while a large staff of perfectly competent engineers sat nearby watching the Chiefs check their work. Didn't they have better things to do, like grow the company or add stockholder value?

I really like that when I started my career, engineering time on the computer was very close to zero, and by the end of my career 100% of my work was done on a PC located on or under my desk (with TWO monitors!). When I am summoned to the Great Conference Room in the Sky for my Final Performance Review, I'm sure my collection of triangles and curves will end up in a dumpster, and I'm okay with that.

Falling on Death Ears

Occasionally I let my inner comedian out to play and didn't always get the desired results. Sometimes this was because the joke wasn't funny, most of the time it was because I was using material far too old for my audience.

Two reservoir engineering coworkers and I arrived early to an SPE lunch meeting so I could say hello to my old friend and college roommate, Earl Logan. Earl was SPE program chairman and busy setting up dual projection screens in each corner of a hotel ballroom for the large crowd expected.

After greeting each other and catching up a bit, Earl gave us some advice. One of the projectors was giving him some trouble. Earl used his right hand to point to his left, and suggested we not sit on that side. Then he used his left hand to point to his right and said we would be able to see better over there.

It came to me in a flash, and I let it rip. "Okay, thanks Lo-gon. Important safety tip: Don't cross the *screens*."

I cracked myself up. It may have been the most perfect movie-line callback setup in the history of the planet. But Earl didn't get the reference, and neither did the two engineers. Sometimes the Universe just toys with you.

Several years later I was discussing an ARIES issue with Bill, my manager. (ARIES stands for A Really Irritating Economic System.) Bill and I agreed to set up a database parameter in a particular format to avoid a complication. I said, "Okay, important safety tip." Without missing a beat, Bill responded perfectly with "Don't cross the streams." It made my day and sparked a glimmer of hope for my professional future.

One Moore favorite, from my ever-cheerful friend David Wysocki. Referring to another ARIES challenge we were facing,

David broke the tension by quipping, "We've got a better chance of playing pick-up sticks with our butt cheeks than getting the upgrade installed this afternoon." It was a perfect application of therapeutic pop-culture humor.

A Reservoir Fossil

I turned down the music when a 30-something reservoir engineer walked into my office. He asked who I was listening to, and I told him it was The Alan Parson's Project.

"Never heard of them. Are they new?"

Ouch.

During a staff meeting in early 2021, we heard a coworker had broken his leg on a ski trip and discussed who would fill in for him during the reserves cycle. I made an obvious reference to *The Six Million-Dollar Man* television show.

"Gentlemen, we can rebuild him. We have the technology."

Other than quizzical expressions, no one reacted at all. None of them had been alive when that show aired in 1973. I had worked beyond my use-by date, passed through Dad level, and was now telling Granddad jokes.

I was a dinosaur, mired in a pop-culture tar pit and flailing wildly. I would die, decompose, and eventually morph into a tiny deposit of previously-owned hydrocarbons (gaseous, no doubt), perhaps to be included in a reserves calculation made by a Reservoir Bot in the far distant future.

Men's Room Follies, Part 6: Dazed and Really, Really Confused

Another sign I was getting old and burned out:

After several hours of caffeine-fueled production forecasting, I needed a break. I pushed through the door to the men's room and stopped. There was a woman standing at the urinal. Realizing I'd made a god-awful mistake and walked into the ladies' room, I back-skedaddled out and checked the sign on the door: MEN. Still, there was a woman at the urinal. I was confused and my brain hurt. Maybe I'd had a stroke?

I aborted the entire mission and returned to my office, worried I had fritzed out. A *woman* was *standing* at the urinal. That didn't seem right...

I snapped my fingers and relaxed, relieved to have figured it out. It wasn't a woman, it was Pat, a young geologist who wore his hair in a man-bun. I was tired. My brain identified a woman, instantly announced BIG MISTAKE YOU MOORON and activated GTFO mode.

Every time I saw Pat around the office I not-so-fondly remembered the afternoon when I walked into the Ladies' Men's Room and blew my own mind.

"That's the Fact, Jack!"

I was fortunate to work one-on-one with Jack Vogel (famous for his Inflow Performance Relationship equation) on a low-quality steam simulation study while we both worked at Tenneco in the early 1980s. Jack was old school in many ways (and smoked like a train) but he was up to date on thermal EOR modeling. The company also hired outstanding experts and more than a few industry legends to lead in-house technical training courses.

I attended a week of pressure-transient analysis training in Palo Alto in 1982. (I remember the year well as I went to see the fantastic new movie *Blade Runner* one evening by myself.) The course was taught by Hank Ramey of Stanford, and one afternoon he turned the class over to guest instructor Marshall "Muz" Standing (previously described as ancient by Carl Granger). Standing was semi-retired and taught the session wearing a loud, embossed purple shirt. He was heading to the bowling alley for League Night after class.

I remember a myth told by a professor at TU and Standing confirmed it was true: he initially completed his famous compressibility z-factor chart by using a French curve to fill in a mathematically inconsistent portion of the correlation. Subsequent research confirmed his assumption was valid.

I recall only one thing from a facility design course I attended in Bakersfield. Bill Rieken, the highly experienced instructor, described obsessing over tiny details: "That's like picking fly shit out of pepper." Suggests quite a mental image, doesn't it?

I attended a two-day seminar in Los Angeles taught by two Texaco engineers. The first day ended around 3pm, sooner than expected. The two instructors had to drive back to Bakersfield that evening and wanted to get a jump on traffic. Texaco, known for being cheap, had a strict travel policy and would not pay for a hotel room that was less than 150 miles from the office. While the rest of the engineers from Bakersfield were enjoying cocktails and expense-account steak dinners, the instructors drove two hours back to Bakersfield, then got up extra early the next morning to return to LA for the second day of class. (My favorite Texaco joke from those years: Why are all Texaco company cars 2-door models? Because no one makes a 1-door car.)

During a week of training in Houston (the same trip in which I tried and immediately gave up handball), some enterprising young man in a spider man costume scaled the office building across the street using suction devices. It caused quite a sensation and a huge traffic jam. We watched from our 20th floor training room as police removed a couple of windows above spider man to convince him to abandon his stunt. Instead, he pushed off, opened a parachute, and tried to sail to a getaway car a couple of blocks away. He came up short and was apprehended but entertained us with a cool diversion from class.

After the industry updated standards, and probabilistic reserves became trendy enough for geeky TikTok videos (had TikTok existed at the time), the Company hired an Industry Expert to teach us the latest Rules and Regulations. It was tedious and I became bored. I texted my friend across the room: WHERE'S A RIP IN THE SPACE-TIME CONTINUUM WHEN YOU NEED ONE? He texted back RIPPED HIM? DAMN NEAR KILLED HIM! I admit this is you-had-to-be-there humor, but I'm including this anecdote anyway as it still makes me smile.

From Cave Drawings to SEC Regulations

Near the end of a very long day attending a reserves seminar in Houston, the final presentation topic was "An Update on the Interpretation of SEC Regulations and Industry Comment Letters." The speaker was an oil and gas attorney, and it was every bit as riveting and thrilling as you would expect. I scribbled this note on the scratchpad thoughtfully provided by the hotel hosting the conference:

How did humanity get to this point? We went from scrawling selfies with burnt sticks on cave walls to dozing in uncomfortable banquet room chairs while lawyers recite arcane regulations and attempt to interpret incomprehensible government language so corporations can pay millions of dollars to thousands of professionals to produce year-end reports that start out wrong and inaccurate and become hopelessly obsolete no later than the end of the next fiscal quarter? We did this to ourselves…why?

Okay, my actual note was "Cave paintings => SEC regs?" but my point remains the same. Like little Cindy-Lou Who, I ask one more time: Why?

The Knights Who Say N-E-P !

In 2015 I noticed a popular and recurring strategy employed by many technical professionals and more than a few managers: Partially completing a project or task to meet a deadline and leaving the unfinished work to be handled later by somebody else. I named the strategy N-E-P: Next Engineer's Problem.

Still burdened by getting the details right after 30 years, I made every effort to avoid doing this to my successors. The term N-E-P became somewhat popular with the reservoir engineers mired in endless reserves cycles. A variant was also spawned: N-M-P: Next Manager's Problem.

Five years later I returned to the company as a contractor and heard an engineer say, "That's NEP." It was satisfying to learn I had left a legacy, however small.

CORPORATE WEALTH & HELLNESS FAIR
Wednesday Morning - Training Room H

Agenda:

9:00 - Noel Brownstein, Technical Services
"Don't Call IT! Becoming Self-Reliant in the Digital Age"

9:15 - Lloyd Wapner, Life Coach
"Friday's Coming! Maintaining the Appearance of Motivation Between Paydays"

9:30 - Shawna Flippman, Office Services
"Avoiding the Pepsi Syndrome: Tips for Lunching at Your Desk"

9:45 - Shelly Whipple, Human Resources (Corporate)
"H is for Human: Staying Cool Dealing with the HR Fool"

10:00 - Felicity Smith, Nutritionist
"Yesterday's Donuts - They're Not Just for Breakfast Anymore: Scavenging Strategies for Your Unplanned Overtime Dinner"

10:15 - Jonah Maximus, Director of Personnel Development
"Mega-Multi-Tasking Your Way to Middle Management"

10:30 - Phil Merriweather, Reserves Manager
"Door Slamma-Jamma: Isolating Your Office or Cubicle from Noisy Colleagues"

"Avoid strenuous forecasting when using *Reservoir*, as abnormal behaviors have been reported."

I believe humans are not built to sit in a box mesmerized by pretty colors on a digital screen. I wish I had realized long ago that sitting at a desk in a bad chair staring at a monitor for 8-10 hours every weekday was seriously unhealthy. When I finally did figure it out, I didn't have the will or fortitude to compensate with good nutrition and exercise. I put in tens of thousands of hours on the wrong kind of treadmill, and at the end of my 35-year workout there was much more of me than there should have been.

Living or working incongruently is stressful, and it took a huge toll on my health and fitness. At some point I figured out there was a finite number of Time-Energy-Life units for me to spend. I started making better decisions to avoid early depletion of my TEL reserves. Kudos to the professionals who spend long days in the office and respond with healthy lifestyle choices. From what I've seen, the younger folks have a much better handle on this than I did at their age.

Perhaps when I was first considering *Reservoir* as a petroleum engineering career option, I should have read the disclaimer:

Exercise caution when using Reservoir during engineering activities. Don't evaluate complex economics or attempt to speak during morning operations meetings until you feel fully awake. Lingering in the break room, excessive snacking, and sarcastic interruption of coworkers have been reported by those under the influence of Reservoir. Other annoying but common side effects include snarkiness, negativity, and a predilection for telling others better ways to complete their tasks.

In despondent engineers, Reservoir may intensify feelings of ennui. Depression may worsen from using Reservoir; alcohol may increase this effect. It may also help; you'll just have to try it and see. Allergic reactions such as loosening of the tongue and forgetting just who you think you are talking to can occur and may cause an extinction-level career event. Ask your life coach or mental health professional if Reservoir is right for you.

"Now that I think about it, no. I've never had a bad day at work."

In July 1993, a Pennsylvania man working to clear land was trapped when a tree fell on him. After yelling for help for an hour, he saved himself by cutting off his own leg—*with his pocketknife!*

After tying off the stump with a chainsaw cord, he crawled 30 yards uphill to a bulldozer, then drove a quarter mile to his pickup truck. He managed to drive the truck—*with a manual transmission*—to a farmer's house a mile away. He not only survived the ordeal, after receiving an artificial leg *he eventually returned to work.* Incredible!

A couple of months later, in October 1993, I read a newspaper article about another guy in Colorado who did the same thing. A physician's assistant was fishing alone and became trapped when a large boulder fell on him. He tied off his leg with a tourniquet, amputated his leg at the knee—also with a pocketknife—then crawled to his truck and drove for help.

I pinned these two stories to my office wall as terrific reminders to maintain a healthy perspective and realize every day was a good day.

Symptoms of Burnout, No. 14: Spending hours at work reading articles on Burnout

Over the last 40 years, I created oil and gas forecasts for over 42 million wells. Or maybe it was one well that I forecast 42 million times, I can't be sure at this point. My engineering brain is fried.

Several years ago, after reading an article on burnout, I took a quiz and learned I had 13 of the top 12 symptoms. (I had twice the qualifying level of "cynicism, sarcasm, and irritability.") I had become a nattering Moore-bob of negativity. My wife told me I looked gray each night when I arrived home from the office.

A character in an excellent novel published in 2010 perfectly described my mental state:

"Sometimes when I'm brushing my teeth, I'll look in the mirror and I swear my reflection seems kind of disappointed. I realized a couple of years ago that not only am I not super-skilled at anything, I'm not even particularly good at being myself."

\- Charles Yu, *How to Live Safely in a Science Fictional Universe* (Used with permission.)

Steve Moore

A Typical Day at the Office

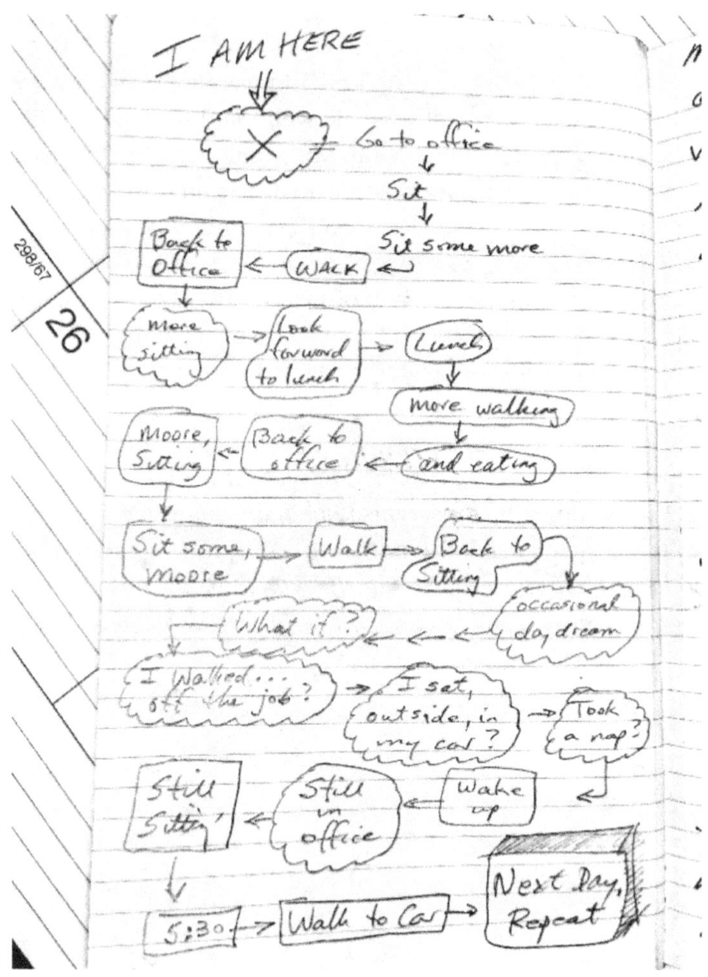

I had been trying to tell myself something for years, and finally started listening. I read somewhere when you find yourself in a negative situation, you can change it, accept it, or leave it.

I expended great energy and time trying to make positive changes to my reservoir world, sometimes succeeding but often falling short. I made more than a few attempts to escape routine reservoir work and engage in special projects. Each time supply-and-demand forces pulled me back into an asset team doing the same old reservoir work with very little growth. I made use of various coping strategies which got me through each day but had little impact on my long-term situation.

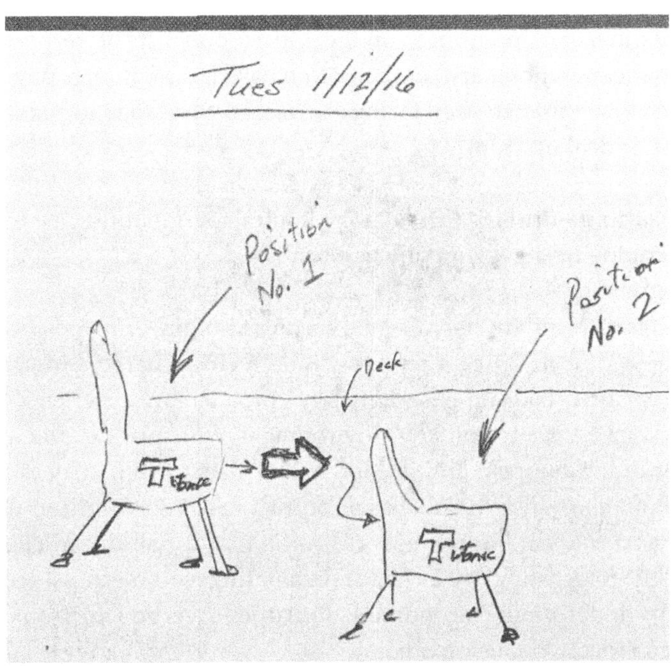

To be happier, I was going to have to stop doing things that made me unhappy. It was time to bust a move. Time to step across the Threshold and transcend my role as staff reservoir engineer. Time to release the cookies and slip the monkey trap. Time to step inside the scary-looking cave and claim my long-sought treasure.

Like George Costanza double-dipping his chip, I needed to "just end it" and finish my corporate reservoir engineering career.

It was time for me to become…a *contractor*.

Contractor: One who provides any service to or completes any task for a Company without receiving insurance benefits, long term financial incentives, or the tiniest pretense of respect, in exchange for monetary compensation based on an hourly pay rate much lower than desired by the contractor, who failed to negotiate a better deal up front.

Consultant: Professional gender contractor identifies as when describing his new temp job to his mother.

I resigned from my last full-time corporate engineering position at the end of June 2016. After a few months to recharge, I hoped to join a start-up oil and gas company to broaden my experience and work in a small-company environment with upside potential. That didn't happen, and in March 2017 I set up Blue Quest LLC and made myself available as a contract reservoir engineer. Over the next four and a half years I worked for a half-dozen clients, mostly forecasting wells (sigh), evaluating volumetrics (deeper sigh), and running economics until they overflowed from my wazoo (deep, cleansing breath).

Things That Suck Working as a Contract Reservoir Engineer

1. Doing very little actual engineering.

Most of my "consulting" time was spent on data: searching, gathering, processing, and database construction and maintenance. All of which, frankly, I do pretty well. There was a bit of analysis too, such as developing production type curves from data sets filtered for various completion and reservoir parameters. (Yeah, me too. I yawned as I wrote that sentence.) Still, 90% of my contract work could have (and probably should have) been completed by engineering techs.

2. Completing numerous numbers of "warm body" tasks.

One of my contract assignments was to complete a massive data entry task after the TU summer hire who started the project went back to school. That's right, I was no longer contract reservoir guy, I was **Assistant <u>to</u> the Regional Intern**. I was so bored I started wondering: instead of getting paid a modest fee each hour to enter tons of data, how much would I be willing to pay to hire a sub to enter it for me?

3. Getting paid by the hour.

Every minute I worked in the office was a billable minute. Unlike full-time salaried employees, if I took a long lunch I hurt myself financially. Going to the dentist in the middle of the day was two billable hours lost (or I could make up the time working precious hours in the evening or on the weekend). At the end of the workday the urge to work for 15 minutes more, then another 15 after that, was too strong to ignore. I hated that my freelance work turned me into a clock-watcher, which had another negative side effect. I started thinking of every personal expense or purchase in terms of how many hours I had to work to pay for it. This was unsettling and didn't feel healthy. It was also a great reason to initially negotiate the highest possible contract pay rate.

4. Not getting paid in a timely manner.

I'm not referring to your-check-is-in-the-mail delay. Mostly it was "your invoice has not yet been approved; It's on the boss's desk under that greasy Quizno's wrapper." It took 7 months of badgering my first client before I received payment of $800 for a small one-time project. Contractors don't have any leverage trying to hurry payment from a company they don't work for as a full-time employee. It reminded me of the Seinfeld episode when Kramer is fired from his fake job.

Kramer: "But I don't even really work here."

Manager: "That's what makes this so difficult."

5. Not being part of the Team.

As a contractor, I was rarely invited to participate in value-adding decisions, acquisition reviews, or development planning sessions. There were many days when, other than a coffee bar greeting, I had no conversation with any employee at all. My contractor experience confirmed that I thrived much better in a social environment and working with a team.

6. Cubicle life.

Some companies don't have enough office space to play Hide the Contractor. For several months I was parked near the middle of a maze of cubicles, trying to run acquisition economics while the woman on the other side of the fabric-covered wall was telling someone on the phone that she accidentally selected a sausage burrito instead of the bacon burrito she really wanted from the big bag of breakfast in the break room that was dropped off by a service company ten minutes ago and if you hurry you can probably come down and get one before they're gone and maybe I'll go back and see if there are any bacon burritos left but I don't know getting two seems kind of wrong besides the sausage one tastes okay but maybe the bacon burrito is a just a tiny bit healthier don't you think where do you want to go to lunch today maybe we can try yada blah yada blah yada blah…

(Contractor prays silently for the sweet, sweet release of termination.)

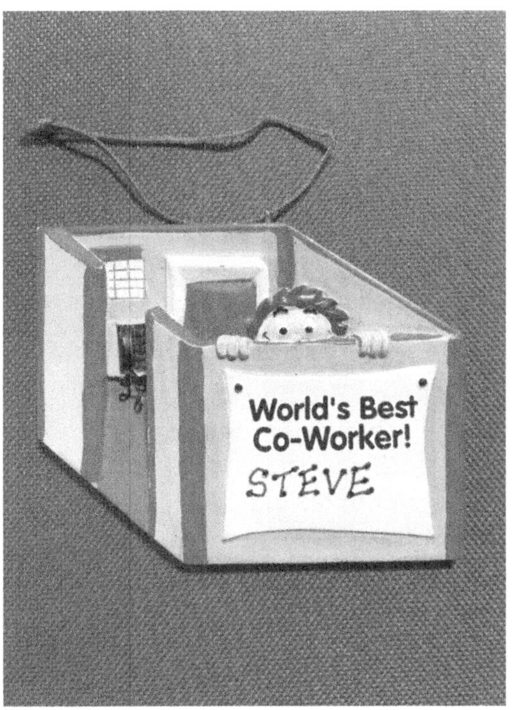

"Maybe a Geologist can talk him out of it?"

An actual text message exchange between me and my wife in 2018:

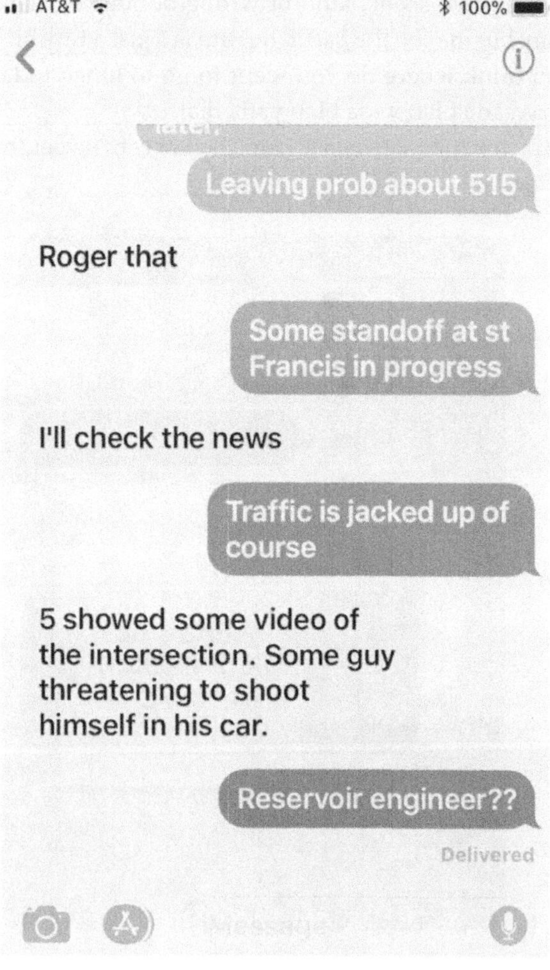

"What's that flushing sound?"

In March 2020 the Company terminated my contract engineering work as crude oil prices swirled to the bottom of the bowl and the Virus introduced itself to the world and shut down supply chains. Since I had a copy of the 1,500-page Bradley Petroleum Engineering Handbook, I wasn't worried about a shortage of TP.

Technical Papers. What were <u>you</u> thinking?

I had the house to myself and tons of free time. I really liked the idea of answering, "What did you do when everything shut down?" with "I wrote a novel." I finished the book I had worked on for years and published ***A Fortune of Reversal*** in November. (Available wherever books sold online by Amazon are sold.) It seemed like my time as a reservoir engineer might be over, and I started looking forward to my Second Act as a writer.

"Sorry, sir. There will be short delay before your Flight of Fancy can take off."

In a stunning reversal of my free-time fortune, in January 2021 a former manager offered me a cage full of cookies and I instinctively stuck my arm in up to my shoulder. I worked the rest of the year as Contract Reservoir Guy, grateful for the opportunity to generate cash flow in uncertain times. Writing would remain a sideline hobby for a while longer.

Hard to get, easy to let go

By June it felt like my career was winding down. I decided not to renew my professional engineering registration with the state of California. It had been a nice kicker on my resume, but in 28 years I did not use my Professional Engineering license one time for anything official. Unlike the five attempts it took to get, I only had to fail to pay the renewal fee once for my license to expire.

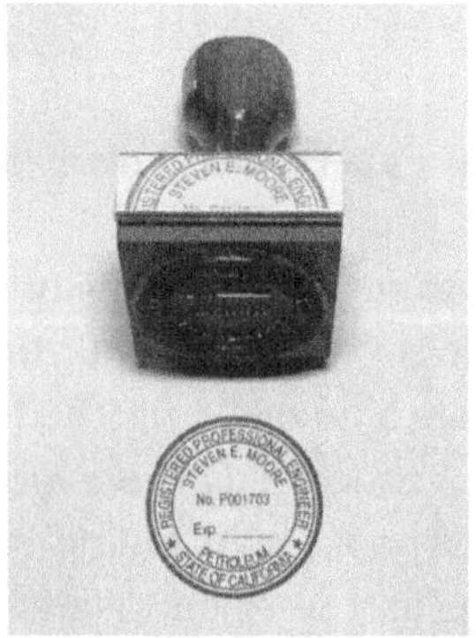

Finally, a use for this very expensive stamp.

The Way My Mind Works

Late in 2021, I needed to update production for a handful of key wells for a review the next day. Instead of executing an export/import process, I decided it would take about the same time to copy the public data from an industry website displayed on one monitor by manually typing them into the production table displayed on my second monitor. It was a perfect task for 1) listening to a favorite podcast, and 2) logging another billable hour.

The production volumes were all three-digit numbers, and I established an easy click-click-click rhythm with my keyboard. For some bizarre reason my mind flashed on a scene in *National Lampoon's Christmas Vacation,* when Clark Griswold greets a line of executives filing into a conference room. The cadence of Clark's words synced perfectly in my head with the 3-click input pattern: "Merry Christmas. Merry Christmas. Merry Christmas. Kiss my ass. Kiss his ass. Kiss your ass. Happy Hanukkah."

Yes, I agree with you: this probably wasn't the behavior of a normal engineering mind.

Clash of Cultures

After a helpful yet irritating prompt from IT that it was time to change my network login, I continued my habit of using Bill Murray movie titles and changed my password to *Zombieland2021*. Two weeks later, Management announced the Company was for sale. Maybe my forecasting skills were better than I thought.

Morale, already low, remained mostly unchanged. While some people naturally worried about the future and their families, others perked up ever so slightly at the prospect of Something New and perhaps better.

Around the same time the sale was announced, a large, energetic positive-vibe church moved into the top three floors of the building, which they had purchased from the Company a few months earlier. It was a distinct clash of climates and cultures. While the oil and gas folks were going through the motions of organizing files and compiling asset sale packages, we could feel and hear tremendous thumping bass notes from the "everybody dance" music breaks that happened several times a week on the upper floors.

One morning I stepped into the elevator and noticed new labels had been posted next to the upper floor buttons, cheerful names like *Good Faith* and *Joyful Relationships*. The buttons for the lower floors where the Ogres of Energy toiled remained plain and simply numbered. I immediately imagined potential descriptions the church leaders could assign to our floors, like *The Dark Abyss,* or *Here Be Dragons.* I sipped my coffee and punched the button for Floor 2:

The Soul-Sucking Pit of Despair Where Reservoir Dreams Go to Die.

"Please, ma'am...Could I have some more?"

The church folks were unfailingly friendly and depressingly cheerful. They frequently delivered cookies to our break rooms and invited us to barbeque lunches. One morning around Thanksgiving I found a Starbucks gift card on my desk, a gift from the Church (after receiving permission from the Company VP of Human Resources, of course.) The following week we were given

Chick-Fil-A gift cards, and the week after that a gift card for Target.

It occurred to me the Church was acting as if they had oil money; they were buying buildings, spreading cheer, and providing goodies and refreshments to their employees and neighbors. Our Company was acting like a small, impoverished church: The employees were praying to keep their jobs while Management was organizing asset bake sales to raise money. "Just set that platter of Wilcox producers on the card table next to those extra-long Granite Wash horizontals."

Meanwhile, the Land staff and Reservoir Engineers had escaped from the nursery, wandered over to the highway overpass, and were busy building a blanket fort out of oversized stratigraphic cross-sections tucked up in the corner under the bridge.

Not to be outdone, the Company distributed corporate holiday cheer too. A few days before Christmas I returned to my cubicle and a lady from HR was talking to a coworker nearby. She asked my name, checked her list, and handed me a Reasor's grocery store gift card. "We're giving these to everyone, *even contractors.*" Emphasis added—by the HR rep. It was a perfectly nice way to remind me I was not one of Them.

She might as well have added, "And if you go to Reasor's on Thursdays, you can score three-day-old meat for half price."

"Sorry, Folks! The Oil and Gas Industry in Tulsa is closed. The moose out front shoulda told ya."

My contract reservoir engineering gig ended late December 2021, when the work ran out and the Company no longer needed my services. As I mentioned earlier, it sure *feels* like I am retired from the oil and gas industry. After this memoir is published it will likely become official. I can't imagine anyone will be interested in hiring me as a reservoir engineer after reading this book.

If I had a time machine...

How cool would that be? I'd go back in time and tell my young self not to worry about the future. "Everybody has access to a time machine and you can just slip back a few years and fix stuff. Party on, dude!

"Still, after you put in a few years in reservoir you should move on to something with more tangible results, like production engineering or facility design. Reserves reporting and economics get kind of fuzzy and nebulous after a while and sort of lose their meaning. It's like riding an unconthrable wooden horse on a perpetual merry-go-round with that brass ring always just out of reach. Don't get me wrong, you'll be half-decent as a reservoir guy, but it's going to turn you gray. Not just your hair, *all of you*. Don't be afraid to make a change, either. *If the career don't fit, you must quit!*

"Oh, one more thing. Dad was right: If you save a dime from every dollar you make starting now, everything will turn out sweet and you'll have tons of options later when you need them.

"Okay, see me later—or maybe sooner!" (Poof!)

Old Reservoir Engineers Never Die...

They just become marginally productive and leak gas until depleted. They become shut-ins and eventually are plugged and abandoned.

I have great respect and appreciation for the energy and products provided by the oil and gas industry. I am grateful to have worked alongside many brilliant, high-quality professionals, and for the terrific friendships made over the years.

I plan to use my remaining reserves (ha!) of Time-Energy-Life units to continue writing humorous science fiction novels. I'm also considering embarking on a comedy tour called *Farewell to Forecasts,* complete with a PowerPoint presentation of my greatest-hits budget slides.

Which would you like to see first: the dog or the pony?

If You've Read This Far, You Might As Well Finish

EPILOGUE

"Meetings are Thursdays at 7pm in the basement of the Petroleum Club."

"Hello, everyone. My name is Steve, and I'm a reservoir engineer."

Group (morosely): "Hi Steve."

"It's been more than three years since my last forecast and…well, I know I'll always have this problem, and I have to give myself up to a higher power-law decline curve equation and carry on somehow."

Moderator, nodding encouragement: "Please continue."

"Okay, thanks. I'm, uh, working on Step 8 of our 14.3-Step Program, "Documentation." I know it must be completed and submitted two weeks after the calendar year-end per regulations. It kind of puts a damper on the holidays, but of course we reservoir engineers know all about that, don't we? Anyway, I'm looking forward to completing the project and moving on to Step 9, "Making Amendments and Revisions." And I just want to say to all of you that I really appreciate your support. This is a great group, and—"

Steve stops and wipes his eyes. "Sorry guys, experiencing some premature water breakthrough here."

Steve returns to his seat and the group politely golf claps. The moderator squeezes his shoulder. "Thank you for sharing, Steve. Now, who's the next reservoir engineer courageous enough to disclose his parameters to the group?"

A Future Podcast Interview

"Welcome to episode number 943 of *Stuff You Might Enjoy*. I'm Mike Rowe, and today we are joined by author and former petroleum engineer Steve Moore, whose new book, *No Hard Hats in Hell* is the latest in a string of best-selling energy industry thrillers. Steve, welcome to the podcast."

"Thanks, Mike. I'm a longtime fan, pleasure to be with you and your audience."

"Steve, your novels are stories of devious businesspeople committing unique crimes, along with an inside look at the oil industry that can't be found anywhere else. Talk about how you came up with those disturbing stories and crazy characters. It's all fiction, right?"

(Steve laughs) "Yes, Mike, everyone should *assume* that all of my novels are fiction."

(Mike clears throat) "From that answer, one might infer otherwise. Did you draw on real life experience to create such deliciously demented characters?"

"Sure, as many authors do. Most of my characters are composites derived from several individuals, but a few villains were based on real-life coworkers or supervisors to whom I reported. All I had to do was describe their actual behaviors and give them a fictitious name. Some of them turned out to be quite frightening."

"Boy, I'll say! I was particularly struck by the scene in which the CEO orders his assistant to arrange for the reservoir engineer to be kidnapped, taken to a drilling site, and dumped into a mud mixer, whatever that is."

(Steve chuckles) "That was in my fourth book, *Death by Drill Bit*. It was inspired by an actual incident where the Vice President of Engineering suggested one of my fellow reservoir engineers would be more useful if he was processed into lost-circulation material. I changed the murder weapon to a mud-mixer for technical reasons, but I plan to use the lost-circulation idea in a future book."

"The novels are great, Steve, really great. I understand one of your books has been optioned for a movie?"

"Yes! I'm very excited about that project. A screenplay is under development for my seventh book, *Blood Cores*. I understand Tommy Lee Jones has been approached to play the role of North American exploration manager. Tom Hanks is also rumored to be interested."

"Wow! We'll all be looking forward to that. What's up next?"

"I'm working on the next book in the series, *The Perils of Perforating*. Then I'm taking a break to set up a non-profit organization to provide support and counseling to former engineers and technicians recovering from the effects of long-term Reservoir abuse. We are also developing training courses and educational literature for energy industry executives, to teach them 21st-century management theory and best practices for motivating technical professionals."

"Well, Steve, it sounds like both you and the oil and gas industry are much better off since you left and started your writing career. Best of luck on your next book, and thank you for visiting with me and our audience on *Stuff You Might Enjoy*."

A Sunny Afternoon in the Park

The man strolled along the sidewalk as though conserving energy and taking in every moment. He scanned his surroundings: college kids tossing frisbees, a golden retriever chasing a tennis ball, kids on the playground laughing and chasing each other.

Glancing ahead, the man froze for a micro-instant, then continued walking. A sharp observer might have noticed a slight increase in his speed, but there was no sign of panic. A half-minute later he politely stopped twelve feet behind a woman pushing a baby carriage.

"Excuse me, Miss?"

The woman spun around, eyes narrowed. "What?"

"I'll explain in a moment, but please hurry forward several yards. Now!" The tone of his voice imparted serious urgency without conveying any hint of a personal threat.

The woman responded, pushing the carriage ahead quickly while instinctively looking up. "Oh my!"

She was five feet ahead when two young squirrels plopped to the sidewalk in a noisy, furry mess where the baby carriage had been seconds before. The squirrels untangled themselves and ran off.

"Thank you!" the woman gushed. "How did you know that was going to happen?"

The man shrugged. "I observed the squirrels chasing each other onto that narrow tree branch," he said, pointing upward. "The branch started to bend, so I analyzed the rate of decline, applied a forecast to the trend, and calculated the time when the branch would no longer produce adequate support for the weight and motion of the squirrels." The man stuck his hands in his pockets and looked down at his shoes. "I, uh, used to be a reservoir engineer."

A small crowd had gathered. "Hey! I know you!" said a middle-aged bald man. "You're that engineer that tried to book those oil-equivalent nitrogen gas reserves at 12-to-1 instead of the usual 6-to-1 ratio to account for the lower BTU value. Man, that was some fine work!"

The man shook his head. "Sorry, that wasn't me."

"No," said a woman with a hybrid British-Okie accent. "I recognize him! He's that engineer who convinced his boss to lower the rod pump to the bottom of the perforated zone in that heavy-oil well in California. Production nearly quintupled! Brilliant!"

The man shook his head again. "Nope, that was someone else."

A bent-over old man pushed his way through and studied the face of the reluctant hero. "Tell you what, this feller reminds me of that boy who knocked the spigot off the Moa-Moa punch dispenser back in '75. That was some show, quite hi-larious!" The man laughed himself into a coughing fit.

The reservoir engineer waited politely for the old man to recover. "Naw, that wasn't me," he said, turning his head to stare off into the distance.

"That was Phillip."

The Engineer Calculates, and having Solved, Moves on...

The audio-amplification device is held stationary at a height of five feet nine-and-three-quarter inches, then released. It descends with an acceleration rate of 32 feet per second squared and impacts on the surface of the raised platform. Boom!

Self-actualization achieved.

The Writer laughs audibly at a decibel level suitable for aural reception by others and walks away.

STEVE MOORE
STEVE MOORE
STEVE MOORE
Steve Moore
STEVE MOORE
S.E. MOORE
Steve Moore
STEV MOORE
STEVE MOORE
Steve Moore
Contractor
Steve Moore

Appendix 1: MOORE'S LAWS

1. Moore's Law of the C's

Without Communication, Coordination, and Cooperation, you get Crap.

2. Moore's Law of Fruit Salad

It's okay to count apples and oranges together, as long as you are only concerned about the total fruit inventory.
Otherwise, don't do it.

3. Moore's Law of Communication

You must first have communication, before you can have a communication problem.
Manager hears no problems; manager doesn't have to deal with any problems. Even though information has been transmitted, communication has not occurred until the receiver "gets" the message.

4. Moore's Law of Leadership

In the absence of direction, the staff will choose their own.
The manager will then be displeased with the choice made.

5. Moore's Law of Leverage

The person who cares the <u>least</u> controls the relationship.
And the person who cares the most is screwed.

6. Moore's Law of Problems

The person who feels the pain, owns the problem.

Monkey-shifting is often employed to transfer pain and problem to someone else.

7. Moore's Law of Corporate Lubrication

(Don't worry, it's not what you think)

The squeaky wheel in the Corporate machine does not get the grease, it gets replaced. At the first downsizing opportunity.

Empty boxes can be found stacked in the hall outside the break room.

8. Moore's Law of Pessimistic Optimism

I don't know if the glass is half full or half empty, but when someone knocks it over, I'm the guy who will have to clean it up.

9. Moore's Law of Getting Things Done

Never put off procrastination.

10. Moore's Law of Intelligence Distribution

There are some really smart, clever people in the world. Most people are not them.

11. Moore's Law of Data

The degree of urgency imposed by management is inversely proportional to the volume of data available to complete the evaluation by the deadline and justify the decision.

12. Moore's Law of Laws

The minimum number of Laws in a list is 12.

This allows the publication of a wall calendar for display in a cubicle or office.

Appendix 2: RAULS OF THUMB - MASTER LIST

(Contains both written and verbal flubs)

Steve Moore:
"That will get you out of here faster than nothing."
"The different areas are different."
"We can do the first ones first."
"Let's do a semi-dry run."
"We are trying to do what we are trying to do."
"That's a plus in its favor."
"That was earth-to-ground lightning."
"Those are just snagments."

Vice Presidents:
"Truth is stranger than friction."
"You'll be writing your own grave."
"We'll just frac the pee-waddy out of the zone."
(Yeah, I had to look this one up too.)
"I encourage you not to limit yourself to what you're responsible for and what you're not."

Engineering Managers:
"It's far from final, but damn close."
Enthisize *(emphasize)*
"The stock price will fall through the roof."
Conthrable *(comfortable)*
"As a worst case, you get a better deal by paying for them all up front…"
Voluminous volumes

Tabulate the data in tabular form
"It's six of one and six dozen of the other."
Please be adviced... *(be advised)*
"I talked to Bill about that at length for a little while."
Remaining remnants
Just a vacation *(justification)*
"He listens with one ear and thinks with the other. His mind is in the ghetto."
Rehashing the hash
"We've sang the song before, and we know the answers."
Lacks a lot to be desired
"We went to the Capitol and had to go through the radar detector."
Least path of resistance
Per diem per day
Physical year *(fiscal year)*
Pressure sink hole
Gram density *(grain density)*
PTA, PTL *(PTS - Petroleum Testing Service)*
Beam up a well *(bean)*
Matalock *(Matlock TV Show)*
"Check the volumetric calculation of the volumes"
"Copy it verbose. You know, word for word." *(Verbatim)*
Substatiate *(substantiate)*
Access what must be done *(assess)*
PF *(abbreviation for Petrophysics on meeting agenda)*
"Be sure to include cave outs" *(caveats)*
Billet *(bullet)*
Food for taught *(thought)*
"That left a lot of ill taste in a lot of people's mouths."
Satistics *(statistics)*
"And one more thing as a follow-on aside..."

Critic the report *(critique)*
"That's the brunt of the development, the cruxt of the situation."
Improvement tone *(improved)*
"Talk to the gate guard at the guard gate."
Occurred *(accrued)*
"All you have left over is the residual residue…"
Ross *(Russ)*
Tabulize *(tabulate)*
Tabularize *(tabulate)*
Preconceived assumption
"That's just sematics" *(semantics)*
"You don't know what's going on behind the screens" *(scenes)*
"That doesn't amount to hell or beans" *(hill of beans)*
"That will give the owners another sword to sword at us"
"First we will figure out which road we will take, then we will figure out how to climb it."
"I called this meeting to make sure all of our pulses are beating in the same direction."
"The kit and whole caboose"
Refutiate *(refute)*
"It's a lesson in futility, but it can be done."
Postulation *(postulate)*
"I'm surprised Linn is taking it up the annulus."
Orientate *(orient)*
GOR contact *(GOC)*
WOR *(WOC)*
WOC *(WOR)*
"Then you can add or delete to it"
"It can be semi-ruled out"
"I have served as a roll model…" *(Dinner roll? Sausage roll?)*
"It looks like tumestone to me." *(tombstone)*
"It fell on death ears." *(deaf ears)*

"Steve's performance continues to improver" *(improve)*
"Be varify with me" *(be sure to verify)*
"Use be ware" *(User beware)*
"From PhD down to the best professional..."
"Steve has beening working as a reservoir engineer..."
"Steve's objectives are to access what must be done to provide..."
"Evaluate observations from a cause and affect point of view."

"The 191th joint..."
(Note: sometime around 1990, the "Only in L.A." newspaper column by Steve Harvey reported the city of Los Angeles was changing a sign near LAX from 111st *Street to 111th Street. Progress!)*

<u>Reservoir and Production Engineers:</u>
"Be flexible, except for change."
"That project is on very back hold right now."
"Point in case..."
"This data is fixed in time, it is not time-dependent."
"I have a roundabout answer that may be more direct."
"He got raped over the coals!"
"Minimize it more."
"It's state of the cutting edge"
"Writeage"
"It was really realistic."
"It's not all peachy-cream."
"That sticks in the back of my craw."
"Mother, pie and applehood."
"It's reported in the report"
"It gassed out quickly due to gas."

3rd-Party Reservoir Engineer, pointing to erratic production data on a graph during audit:
"Were those little who-knows-whats?"
Me: "Yes."

<u>Geologists</u>
"The central core in the middle"
"Like shooting ducks in a barrel."
"It is important to ensure quality control is ensured with particular emphasis on…"
"The declining decline…"
"A number of numbers…"

<u>Others</u>
"It became self-aware of itself…"
- *Speaker at SPE Computer Conference*

"I don't want to mislead you into what I'm about to say…"
- *Unocal Pipeline Representative*

"The doctor reached in with his biceps and pulled the tubes out of her ear."
- *Engineering Technician*

"We have these add-ons that we add on."
- *Simulation Training Instructor*

"Daily well production information reflects 24-hr strapolation"
- *Field production report*

"We want to ensure that everyone has the ability to do their work and access all necessary information; however, if need be we will consider limiting the individuals that can work in the backside.
- Email (and good common sense) from Corporate Reserves Coordinator, after voluminous volumes of tabular tables were deleted from the master database

"Many companie—and Bechtel is one of them—are embracing an approach often called 'Quality Management.'"
- Management Memo to all employees from Steve Bechtel Jr., November 15, 1989. (I think the Quality Program needed greater enthisis.)

<u>Everyone</u>
"Remaining Reserves"
As a writer, this repetitive redundancy has always bugged, annoyed and irritated me.

Acknowledgments

If you search the Internet for "stuff made from oil and natural gas," you'll need an hour or two to read through the massive list of products. The journey that a drop of oil or a whiff of natural gas takes to ultimately become fuel for your automobile or those little plastic tips that keep your shoelaces from unraveling is truly remarkable. I have nothing but respect for the talented people of the energy industry who make the magic happen.

A huge thank you to my talented daughter and artist **Indi Martin** for another outstanding cover. Please visit her website and enjoy her art at Indimartin.com

To my long-time friend **Buddy Bothwell**, with whom I experienced voluminous volumes of *unconthrable* corporate craziness early in my career: Thank you for your ongoing friendship and support. Our "buddy" trips during the last 16 years are the source of many favorite memories.

To **Deb FitzSimons**, friend and fellow writer: thank you for leading by example and encouraging me to keep working on this book to the end. May the best of our writing adventures lie ahead.

To **Vana**: I'm so lucky and proud to have you. If you had been only half as supportive as you were while I struggled through first my career and then this book, I couldn't have asked for more. You have all my love.

Steve Moore is a most-likely retired petroleum engineer and the author of the humorous science fiction novel ***A Fortune of Reversal***.

Please visit his sporadically-published blog at **TunnelWriter.com**

Made in the USA
Coppell, TX
14 December 2024

42487006R00215